GREENBERG'S GUIDE TO

LIONEL HO
Volume I • 1957-1966

George J. Horan
Vincent Rosa

Revision edited by George J. Horan
Collection Courtesy of Richard and Linda Kughn

Greenberg Publishing Company, Inc.
Sykesville, Maryland

Copyright © 1993
by Greenberg Publishing Company, Inc.

Greenberg Publishing Company, Inc.
7566 Main Street
Sykesville, Maryland 21784
(410) 795-7447

Second Edition

Manufactured in the United States of America

Greenberg Publishing Company, Inc. publishes the world's largest selection of Lionel, American Flyer, LGB, Marx, Ives, and other toy train publications as well as a selection of books on model and prototype railroading, dollhouse building, and collectible toys. For a complete listing of current Greenberg publications, please call 1-800-533-6644 or write to Kalmbach Publishing, 21027 Crossroads Circle, Waukesha, Wisconsin 53187.

Greenberg Shows, Inc. sponsors *Greenberg's Great Train, Dollhouse and Toy Shows*, the world's largest of its kind. The shows feature extravagant operating train layouts, and a display of magnificent dollhouses. The shows also present a huge marketplace of model and toy trains, for HO, N, and Z Scales; Lionel O and Standard Gauges; and S and 1 Gauges; plus layout accessories and railroadiana. They also offer a large selection of dollhouse miniatures and building materials, and collectible toys. Shows are scheduled along the East Coast each year from Massachusetts to Florida. For a list of our current shows please call (410) 795-7447 or write to Greenberg Shows, Inc., 7566 Main Street, Sykesville, Maryland 21784 and request a show brochure.

Greenberg Auctions, a division of Greenberg Shows, Inc., offers nationally advertised auctions of toy trains and toys. Please contact our auction manager at (410) 795-7447 for further information.

ISBN 0-89778-359-X

Library of Congress Cataloging-in-Publication Data

Horan, George J.
    Greenberg's guide to Lionel HO / George J. Horan, Vincent Rosa.
        p.   cm.
    Rev. ed. of : Greenberg's guide to Lionel HO trains / by Vincent
Rosa and George J. Horan. c1986.
    Includes index.
    Contents: Vol. 1.   1957-1966.
    ISBN 0-89778-359-X (v. 1) : $35.95
    1. Railroads--Models.   2. Lionel Corporation.   I. Rosa, Vincent.
II. Rosa, Vincent.   Greenberg's guide to Lionel HO trains.
III. Title.
TF197.R67   1993
625.1'9--dc20
                                                        92-38714
                                                        CIP

CONTENTS

PREFACE

This book is a revision and expansion of a book I coauthored with Vincent Rosa, entitled *Greenberg's Guide to Lionel HO Trains,* published in 1986. In its new form it is the first volume in a new series of Greenberg books on Lionel HO. This one covers the early production, 1957–1966; a second volume, written by me and appearing shortly in its first edition, covers the MPC (Model Products Corporation) line, 1974–1977.

It should be noted that since Vincent Rosa was unable, due to personal commitments, to contribute to this new book, any use of "I" in this volume should be understood to mean George Horan.

As I prepared in the late 1970s and in the 1980s for publication of the first book on Lionel HO, my sole purpose for getting involved was to inform the new collector and enthusiast about the line marketed from 1957 to 1966. I knew this area of HO would provide a challenge to both the novice and the seasoned collector of Lionel models.

Many O Gauge collectors are unaware that the loads used on HO-scale cars were often the same ones used on the larger cars. They may even be surprised to find that many of the popular O Gauge operating cars, as well as popular road names on the more traditional items, were duplicated in the smaller line. Lionel HO is an exciting field of study — one that contains a number of challenges. As we shall see, Lionel's trains were manufactured by several producers, who did not always use the Lionel catalogue numbers on the models they produced for Lionel. Thus, collecting these trains can present some interesting problems. While the familiar Lionel logo, an L within a circle, appears on many of the items, its absence on others provokes some questions. This book will address some of these questions and present others.

I have spent over a dozen years compiling information. To aid the new collector in identification of pieces, I have attempted to describe the smallest details. It has been my hope that this approach will stimulate interest and help those who have the interest but not the experience in collecting.

Now I wonder if I have instead done a disservice to my fellow collectors. I refer to the new chapter in this book, Chapter VIII, that covers the forgeries that have surfaced in four different states in the last few years. Has increased appreciation of Lionel HO encouraged imitators? It was terribly difficult for me to admit that this practice by some brought a need for such a chapter. Please notice: I use the word "some," and not "some collectors." That is because I consider this type of individual an "anything-for-a-buck" guy — not a collector of anything but dollars. I am at least thankful that this chapter does not need to take up too much room in this book, even if it is necessary. I hope it will serve the same purpose as the small notice about the "unmarked" reproduction boxes I had seen and recognized, which appeared on page 67 of *Greenberg's Guide to Lionel HO Trains.* That notice seemed to cause the repro boxes to suddenly disappear from the market. It also prompted some letters from LCCA and TCA officials inquiring as to the name of the seller — which I have not disclosed since the boxes have not been seen since late 1986.

It is my hope that the rubber stamps being used to reproduce the Athearn-made Lionel cars will also disappear quietly. I would not hesitate one minute to move on this situation if I had a name of a manufacturer of these remade stamps (which are poor to say the least). The bottom line is that the Athearn-made cars only held the two sizes of rubber-stamped Lionel logos in the sizes stated in the previous book, and they had fairly sharp clear edges, although the circle was not always complete on every car's side. The letter "L" within the circle never appeared with straight legs on any Lionel product this author has ever seen. And the point is, let's all pay more attention to what we're paying for and help keep things clean.

The prices on more than half of the collectible pre-1966 Lionel have risen dramatically from 1986 to date, but we still have the never-satisfied type out there we must watch for. (More about values will be found in the Introduction.) I can assure my fellow collectors that also in writing the book on Lionel's 1974–1977 HO items, I have done my utmost to give the most detailed identification information possible and keep the "buck" guys out of our hobby.

G.J.H.

ACKNOWLEDGMENTS

Many collectors, train dealers, businessmen, and other individuals have contributed greatly to the compilation of this book and the earlier *Greenberg's Guide to Lionel HO Trains*.

Thanks go first to **Richard** and **Linda Kughn**, for permission to photograph their collection for this volume. And a special thank you to Richard Kughn, "Mr. Lionel," who very graciously agreed to have Bruce Greenberg, the book's editor Elsa van Bergen, the Greenberg photographer Al Fiterman, and me visit his Madison Hardware operation in Michigan for four wonderful day in August of 1992. Thanks to the Kughn collection curator at Carail in Detroit, **Sue Childers**, for invaluable assistance, and to **Don Watkins** and his staff at Madison Hardware, **Bill Button, April Goff, Jim Hoff, Jim Malzone, Eugene Nuytten**, and **Woody Woo**, all of whom bent over backwards to help and make us feel welcome. I realized immediately that Don, Sue, and Bill, who were directly involved, held a wealth of knowledge of Lionel models and were eager to provide help. It was an eye opener to see the effort put out in completing mail orders for Lionel trains. I found myself in the middle of not only a grand assortment of trains but among people who knew and understood what magic these trains hold for all of us. Standing in the Madison warehouse is what it must be like in heaven. The assistance of my good friend collector **Ken Fairchild**, who supplied further details and models to be photographed, is much appreciated. All objects are from the Kughn collection unless otherwise noted.

A thank you is in order to many collector friends across these United States, who provided assistance since the publishing of *Greenberg's Guide to Lionel HO Trains* in 1986. I would like to thank those who have helped in the many hours spent in researching and developing the information presented in this book and the previous volume, and those who helped in acquiring the items needed for the photographic illustrations, namely, **Kent** and **Tom Armenti, Paul** and **Kevin Besser, Geoffrey Bunza, Richard Coleman, Fred Coppola, Ed Devincentis, Ken Fairchild, Jack Fulton, Joe Jerome, G. Buckley Juhasz, Richard MacNary, Bill Mitchell, Mike Nechapor, Joe Otterbin, Matt Padgett, Chris Potter, Gerald Potts, Bob Robbins, Joe Robinson, Ed Schols, I. D. Smith, Ed Timlin**, and **William Tucker**. Special thanks to **Ron Mapps**, TCA #729, an old friend, a Trenton, New Jersey, firefighter, and father of five who somehow still found time to run a Lionel Service Station for the last twenty years. Ron has a wealth of knowledge on the subject of Lionel trains and provided instruction and repair sheets. My good friend Mst. Sgt. **James McKinney**, U.S. Army, retired, of Como, Italy, lent a great deal of first-hand knowledge of the Rivarossi production and spent many hours with me, identifying the models, as he had worked for Rivarossi after the end of World War II.

When accurate identification could not be made from a picture or by letter or description alone, many models were sent without any type of charge. I was surprised many times when an unexpected piece would show up via UPS with a letter to the effect that it should be held onto as long as needed. Special acknowledgments apply to Chapter VIII, Oddballs and Forgeries: this chapter could not have been written without the help of the fellow collectors who recognized a problem could be starting in the hobby we all love and want to keep honest. Thanks go to Fred Coppola, Ken Fairchild, Joe Otterbin, Matt Padgett, Gerald Potts, Bob Robbins, and Bill Tucker.

To **Christine Powers** goes thanks for the many hours of typing my original notes. And to **Ann Polito**, thanks for the many hours of typing, inserting corrections, and following through of all the details of preparation of this edition. I would also like to offer much love and thanks to my two children, **Mark** and **Stacy,** for putting up with my moods while working on this book.

In regard to his work on the original version of this book, Vincent Rosa would like to thank **Bruce** and **Linda Greenberg** for giving him the chance to write the book and to act as production assistant for the project. He adds special thanks to **George Horan** for sharing his extensive knowledge of and writings on HO, which helped greatly to expedite the work; to his wife, **Bonnie**, who helped edit and type much of the manuscript, as well as data sheets and letters sent to collectors; to his good friends, **Paul Summers, Joe Sadorf**, and **Carl Sclafani** for their support; to **Dennis Cimino** and **Thom Shepler** whose early listings indicated the breadth of the Lionel HO production; to **Allessandro Rossi**, president of **Rivarossi**, who kindly answered all correspondence and provided viewpoints and recollections essential to the story of his company's relationship with Lionel; to **Lenny Dean** and **Sam Belser**, two Lionel Corporation executives who shared their recollections for our historical narratives. In addition to those named above by George Horan, Vincent Rosa thanks the following individuals who helped by completing data sheets and providing comments and suggestions used in the production of the original book: **Norman E. Anderson, Larry Backus, Lou Bohn, Frank Brua, Harold Carstens, Lester Case, Fred Heimann, James Kimenhour, T. C. Lasky, Tom McComas Michael J. Ocilka, Robert C. Royer, Douglas Ruhl, Jim Stabley, Bernard Stekoll, Joe Tucker, Howard Twilley,** and **Gary P. Vitolo.** Nat Polk of Polk's Model Craft Hobbies kindly provided material from his company's *Blue Book of Hobbies*. Additional thanks to **Bowser Manufacturing Co.** and *Railroad Model Craftsman* magazine.

Thanks also to the staff at Greenberg Publishing Company for their efforts in producing this book. **Elsa van Bergen** supervised the revision process, edited this volume for clarity of text and presentation, and coordinated communication among readers. **Donna Price** proofread for accuracy, style and completeness and prepared the index; **Al Fiterman** photographed the Kughn and the Fairchild Collections; and **Bill Wantz** developed all the black and white prints and prepared the stats used in this book. **Norm Myers** and **Maureen Crum** designed the cover and **Wendy Burgio** and Maureen Crum designed and executed the interior. **Bruce C. Greenberg** and Managing Editors **Samuel Baum** and **Allan Miller** provided support and guidance throughout the production of this volume. **Dallas J. Mallerich III, Linda Greenberg,** and **Cindy Lee Floyd** edited the earlier volume, for which Dallas also provided information from his book, *Greenberg's Guide to Athearn Trains*, for the historical narrative in Chapter I.

INTRODUCTION

COLLECTING HO

The Lionel name has always been synonymous with Standard Gauge, O Gauge, and O27 Gauge trains — the "big trains" that people remember from bygone Christmas gardens and childhood train sets. In a telephone interview on June 12, 1984, former Lionel Corporation service manager Lenny Dean suggested that "Joshua Lionel Cowen's baby was the O Gauge line — Lionel HO was his stepchild." For a while it seemed that a sizeable portion of Lionel collectors had adopted this feeling.

Back in 1976, Howard Godel wrote a book called *Antique Toy Trains, The Hobby of Collecting Old Toy Trains.* In Chapter 12, he took a deep breath and projected his thoughts to the future. Under the heading of "sleepers" (items that have not yet become popular and tend to bring currently low prices), he states, "a series that is just beginning to be appreciated and is presently a sleeper are the small trains produced by Lionel and American Flyer in comparatively small quantities compared to their O and S Gauge production."[1]

Of the prediction written back in 1976 we can now safely say that the HO series has become a Lionel collectible. Many of the early Lionel HO items have appreciated as much as or beyond the value of similar O Gauge items. This statement may surprise some, but those of us who have been collecting Lionel HO steadily for several years are not surprised at all. Furthermore, many Lionel HO pieces are difficult to collect because they are not around — for any price. Just try and locate a mint Matchbox bulldozer (Lionel 0807) or tractor on a flatcar (0808), a 0610 Lionel/Rivarossi Consolidation Steamer from 1957, or the "Valise Pack" train set 5767 from 1961. These items are all scarce if not rare.

Today, the HO train buff has several possible approaches from which to choose if he desires to collect HO trains. He or she can specialize by collecting and concentrating on one specific manufacturer, such as Lionel (postwar 1957–1966 or MPC 1974–1977), Gilbert (American Flyer HO), Athearn, Hobbyline, Mantua, Marx (yes, Marx made HO too), Penn Line, Revell, Rivarossi, Roundhouse, Varney, and many other domestic and foreign producers. Other choices open to the collector are catalogued and uncatalogued sets, custom-painted models, cabooses, passenger trains, or coal hoppers by the yard. Others may prefer to collect models carrying the name of a specific prototype railroad, such as Atlantic Coast Line, New York Central, Canadian Pacific, or Virginian. Those who prefer the finest in HO scale can purchase some of the brass models currently available or those that have been discontinued for several years. Brass is beautiful — and costly. Many collectors consider brass to be the champagne-and-caviar of HO collecting. Regardless of the choice, the collector can go as far as time, money, and imagination allow.

Mass-market HO trains, like Lionel produced after 1958, may have been subjected to collectors' sneers and scoffs when they were first released, but they are not being criticized today. Regardless of your reasons, Lionel HO trains provide a fascinating field for the collector. The trains are not only attractive, but they are quality products, ingeniously designed and manufactured, which operate very well when properly maintained. One collector proudly told me that he displays his HO Gauge locomotives in front of their O Gauge equivalents, on the same shelf. "It makes a great display," he said, "They're cute, real cute. They look like scaled-down versions of my O Gauge."

Lionel's postwar HO items are part of HO's tinplate heritage as well as a part of the larger history of the Lionel Corporation itself. By 1962 more than 50 percent of all home train sets and layouts were in HO scale, and almost all of these used compatible equipment produced by a variety of manufacturers.[2] It was inevitable that many of these "ready-to-run" items would become collectors' items. Lionel HO was a sleeper whose awakening has come. Collecting Lionel HO does present a great challenge, especially to those who want to pursue all phases and variations of production. Remember, though, challenges make collecting what it should be for all of us — fun!

PURPOSE AND ORGANIZATION OF THIS BOOK

The main purpose of this book is to provide a comprehensive listing with current prices for Lionel HO-scale locomotives, rolling stock, and trackside accessories produced from 1957 through 1966. Because another objective has been to aid in identifying which of three manufacturers — Rivarossi, Athearn, or Lionel — produced a specific item, this volume is organized somewhat differently from other Greenberg Guides. That is, after Chapter I — an overview of the history of Lionel HO — and Chapter II — a close look at the ways you can detect the origin of manufacture by examining pieces — this book is structured according to the various manufacturers, with separate coverage of the locomotives and cars within each section.

A reader familiar with the previous edition will see that besides additional listings and corrections, new photographs, and a new chapter, the order of contents of this volume has been revised: we here present all the comparisons of Rivarossi, Athearn, and Lionel productions before getting into the detailed listings of each manufacturer's line. The listings are entered by catalogue number. Sometimes this is the same as that found on the side of the car. When this is not the case, the catalogue number heading a listing will be found in parentheses, and the description will indicate any differing side-of-car number. The car numbers will be listed in number sequence but the reader is then referred to the full listing, under catalogue number.

The three chapters of listings are followed by an expanded chapter (VI) on sets, both catalogued and uncatalogued; Chapter VII on paper items; a new chapter (VIII) on oddballs and forgeries; and three kinds of reference sections: a pictorial "glossary" of trucks, mechanisms, and frames (Chapter IX); a glossary of terms; and reproductions of selected pages from the HO Service Manual. The book concludes with a complete index of all Rivarossi, Athearn, and Lionel HO by both catalogue and car numbers.

We include those variations which have been authenticated. In a few cases, where information is missing or doubtful, we ask our readers for further information. We do invite collectors to participate in the reporting of *any* additional data regarding Lionel HO trains. If you have a variation which is not listed in this book, or a question regarding the details of an item described herein, please write to George Horan in care of Greenberg Publishing Company, Inc., 7566 Main Street, Sykesville,

Maryland 21784. We welcome all comments and suggestions. Happy hunting!

DETERMINING VALUES

Values are reported for each item where there have been reported sales. Since late 1987, I have kept a constant watch on the asking prices at the meets in all six states within four hours driving time of my home. Also, there was a constant flow of Sales Lists from across the U.S. The information gathered reflects the asking price only, as most dealers will not reveal the actual selling price.

Toy train values vary for a number of reasons. First, consider the **relative knowledge** of the buyer and seller. A seller may be unaware that he has a rare variation and sell it for the price of a common piece. Another source of price variation is **short-term fluctuation** that depends on what is being offered at a given train meet on a given day. If four 0635LTs are for sale at a small meet, we would expect that supply would outpace demand and lead to a reduction in price. A related source of variation is the **season of the year**. The train market is slower in the summer and sellers may at this time be more inclined to reduce prices if they really want to move an item. There is also the matter of **regional differences**; certain gauges and/or road names are more popular in some areas of the country than others, and thus the relative value of HO items can vary from one region to another. Another important source of price variation is the relative strength of the seller's **desire to sell** and the buyer's **eagerness to buy.** Clearly a seller in economic distress will be more eager to strike a bargain. A final source of variation is **the personalities** of the seller and buyer. Some sellers like to quickly turn over items and, therefore, price their items to move; others seek a higher price and will bring an item to meet after meet until they find a willing buyer.

I was present at the TCA show in York, Pennsylvania, in April 1988 and witnessed the sale of the #5711 set that included the Athearn-made six cars, headed by the Virginian Rectifier. The set was in mint condition and brought a whopping $750. A few other sets were also purchased by this same collector, also in mint-to-excellent condition, with the same level of pricing. When I questioned him and agreed not to use his name, he revealed he was from an area that has very few train meets, so that a collector must rely on mail-order purchases, and these are not always satsifactory to a buyer.

Overall, the last five years have in most cases shown a steady increase in prices, with the Rivarossi items of 1957 leading. But the Athearn-made models in many cases are just as sought after. The Lionel-made models demand the comparatively lowest prices and seem to be more plentiful at the meets. Researching the 1974–1977 Lionel HO, I found the same trend in pricing, with the non–Lionel-made items having the higher asking prices.

CONDITION

For each item, we provide three categories: **Good, Excellent,** and **Mint.** The Train Collectors Association (TCA) defines conditions as:

Good: Scratches, small dents, dirty
Excellent: Minute scratches or nicks, no dents or rust
Mint: Brand new, absolutely unmarred, all original and unused, in original box.

In the toy train field there is a great deal of concern with exterior appearance and less concern with operation. If operation is important to you, then ask the seller whether the train runs. If the seller indicates that he does not know whether the equipment operates, you should test it. Most train meets have test tracks provided for that purpose.

We include "Mint" in this edition because of the important trade in Lionel HO items. However there is substantial confusion in the minds of both sellers and buyers as to what constitutes mint condition. How do we define mint? Among very experienced train enthusiasts, a mint piece means that it is brand new, in its original box, never run, and extremely bright and clean (and the box is, too). An item may have been removed from the box and replaced in it but it should show no evidence of handling. A piece is not mint if it shows any scratches, fingerprints, or evidence of discoloration. It is the nature of a market for the seller to see his item in a very positive light and to seek to obtain a mint price for an excellent piece. In contrast, a buyer will see the same item in a less favorable light and will attempt to buy a mint piece for the price of one in excellent condition. It is our responsibility to point out this difference in perspective *and* the difference in value implicit in each perspective, and to then let the buyer and seller settle or negotiate their different perspectives.

We receive many inquiries as to whether or not a particular piece is a "good value." This book will help answer that question; but, there is NO substitute for experience in the marketplace. WE STRONGLY RECOMMEND THAT NOVICES DO NOT MAKE MAJOR PURCHASES WITHOUT THE ASSISTANCE OF FRIENDS WHO HAVE EXPERIENCE IN BUYING AND SELLING TRAINS. If you are buying a train and do not know whom to ask about its value, look for the people running the meet or show and discuss with them your need for assistance. Usually they can refer you to an experienced collector who will be willing to examine the piece and offer his opinion.

No Reported Sales: In the few cases where there is insufficient information upon which to determine the value of a given item, we show NRS in the price column. Here again we recommend that you rely on your experience, or on the assistance of an experienced collector to determine what price you should pay for any of these items.

NOTES
1. Godel, Howard, *Antique Toy Trains*. Hicksville, New York: Exposition Press, Inc., 1976, p. 207.
2. Revell 1962 HO catalogue, advance issue.

CHAPTER I
The Early History of Lionel HO

Lionel anticipated the need for smaller gauge trains when they presented their OO (double O) Gauge line in 1938. "HO, although not quite as popular as OO, was introduced to the model railroad consumer by Bing, a German manufacturer, in 1924."[1] The difference between the scales is slight — HO is 3.5 mm to the foot and OO is 4.0 mm to the foot. Regardless of these two small sizes, the king of the model rails in the Lionel catalogues of the late 1930s, 1940s, and early 1950s was still their 1¼ inches between the rails, was first considered by Lionel in 1915, not only because Ives, its direct competitor then, had had its own O Gauge line since 1910 (according to Ron Hollander), but because they "took up less room and were cheaper to produce" than the wide, hefty Standard Gauge models.[2]

Even though the OO Gauge line sold well, Lionel did not revive this well-running small gauge line after the war. OO was primarily a modeler's gauge directed at the true model railroader and serious prototype buff. Since Lionel's O Gauge sales still represented the company's main income in 1946, Lionel decided to maintain its toy train image where exact scale proportions were not top priority and they could "play" with the lengths and widths of trains. What mattered to Lionel were the looks, sounds, and feel of a railroad, not necessarily the lengths, widths, and add-on details. Also, Lionel had to consider American Flyer, its direct competitor at this time, which was adding smoke, knuckle couplers, and chug-chug sounds to its new, small S Gauge trains (⅞ inches between the rails). American Flyer, we should note, had produced HO trains as early as 1938.

In retrospect, we can see that the trend in America followed the pattern set in Europe, where the favorite modeling scale shifted from Standard Gauge to O Gauge and then from O Gauge to HO. But the executives at Lionel must have felt HO was certainly not the scale with which to compete against Flyer, because it was too small to mirror the things Flyer was doing in S at the time — smoke, knuckle couplers, and action cars were at least a decade into the future of HO and certainly not the reason why the modeler used HO. The modeler was looking for the detail and exact reproduction of the scene rather than the action and toy-like play value of the train set itself.

HO MAKES INROADS

Lionel did well with their O Gauge line, and in 1953 the corporation sold more than $32 million worth of trains, toys, and electrical-related manufacturing.[3] This was the highest sales report in their history — the decision to stay out of the modelers' gauges, like OO and HO, seemed a correct one. But in the early 1950s the marketplace started to change. American train consumers began to buy and demand more HO than O Gauge trains. Tom McComas states in his book *Lionel: A Collector's Guide and History, Vol. III* that "Lionel at first did not notice the inroads HO was making because in those postwar boom years, there seemed to be enough business for everyone." According to McComas, the combined sales of HO manufacturers, which included Mantua, Tyco, Athearn, Varney, Penn Line, etc., had exceeded Lionel's O Gauge sales by the mid-1950s. The reasons for this change during the late postwar years may reflect considerations of space, cost, and sophistication on the part of the postwar baby boom generation. Most likely, the new generation of baby boomers and their dads who were weaned on tin trains wanted models that looked like real railroads going through mountains and farmlands all with the same proportions. Lionel's O Gauge, with its arbitrary measurements, looked antiquated compared with the newer HO that was being created.

It is only conjecture to state, as both McComas and Hollander did in their books, that had Lionel stayed in OO, it might have deflected the advance of HO into the toy train consumer market. Yes, Lionel's OO was a small gauge train, but it was incompatible with what most small gauge manufacturers were making at the time. The HO industry was striving for compatibility so that different manufacturers' trains could be used together, and it was aided by the National Model Railroad Association (NMRA), which provided the standard "horn hook" coupler design. Thus, OO trains could not be offered in a field dominated by HO producers. The small HO-scale models, which were constructed primarily of molded plastic and simply formed metal parts (or die-cast pieces, in some cases), were much cheaper to manufacture than OO would have been. By 1957 HO manufacturers were producing standardized, ready-to-run train sets. This posed a direct threat to Lionel's business because highly detailed HO train sets were now directly competing with the less detailed, mass-produced Lionel train sets that sold for $20 or more. You could buy a complete HO train set with track and power pack for as little as $10. So, price was definitely a consideration when making the move to ready-to-run HO.

Sam Belser, Lionel Corporation's sales manager in the late 1950s, explains that "Lionel wanted to get more of the mass market. People by the mid-1950s were becoming more aware of HO and the smaller gauges. Many people were living in apartments and smaller homes with limited space; the need for Lionel to supply products to meet this need was there." While the popular notion held that only a smaller scale such as HO could serve these requirements, Lionel's advertising offered a contradictory message. "In the late 1950s, we were advertising that you could have an O Gauge layout on a card table," states Belser.[4]

Ron Hollander supports Mr. Belser's statements in his book, *All Aboard*. Discussing the inconsistencies of the Lionel Corporation's policy towards HO, he states, "The regular Lionel consumer catalogue undercut its own HO sales by warning parents of the complicated wiring and extra gadgets two-rail HO required. Why buy HO, the catalogue implied, when even a bridge-table top is enough to accommodate a Lionel O27 layout."[5]

In an exclusive October 1957 interview with *Railroad Model Craftsman* magazine, Alan Ginsberg, vice president in charge of sales, disagreed with the idea that Lionel was prompted to move into HO by the trend towards smaller homes with limited space. When asked "Has the trend toward smaller homes affected your entry into HO any?" he replied, "No, O Gauge need not take any more room than HO." Certainly, then, Lionel did not intend for its own brand of HO models to sell better than the traditional O Gauge line. Ginsberg stated that Lionel entered the HO marketplace for two reasons:

1. Objective evidence of increasing consumer interest.
2. It is an entirely different market than the "boy market."

Lionel's first HO scale catalogue, released in 1957. Note: the 4-4-2 Atlantic steamer shown was never offered as a Lionel model. Reproduced with permission of Lionel Trains, Inc., Chesterfield, Michigan

Mr. Ginsberg explained that HO, as Lionel saw it in 1957, was for the permanent hobbyist. "As for the boy market (mass consumer toy train market), HO cannot be as dominant as O for play value. HO is for older, more skillful boys and the mature hobbyist." Indeed, Lionel maintained its position: both the Italian-made Rivarossi models sold in 1957 and the American-made Athearn models of 1958 satisfied preferences of the mature hobbyist.

However, 1960 saw a reversal in this policy. In the catalogue for that year, Lionel emphasized "toy quality" with fanfare: "A first in HO — Brand new action-packed operating cars." In this manner, Lionel introduced its operating cars patterned after successful O Gauge counterparts, an idea later to be imitated — even exploited — by Tyco. That year saw the 0319 Operating Helicopter Launching Car, 0847 Exploding Target Car, 0850 Missile Launching Car, 0301 Pennsylvania Operating (coal) Dump Car, and 0300 Operating Lumber Car introduced. This ushered in a new marketing emphasis and direction to their HO line.

This definitely was not what Vice President Alan Ginsberg and Lionel had planned in 1957, when the emphasis was realism, the catch word was detailing, the main concern was dependability, and, above all, the HO line had to reflect Lionel craftsmanship. Somewhere between April and October of 1957, a decision that was four years in the making saw Lionel plunge into the HO train market, even though by late 1956 "Lionel's overall train business was starting to sink with sales down to $22 million.... It was time, but, unfortunately, in retrospect, the decision came too late. It is interesting to note that by the Toy Fair of March 1957, Lionel still had not exhibited any HO. It seemed that another year would pass before a new HO line could be introduced."[6]

A question remained unanswered among both trade and consumer circles: "Why hasn't Lionel introduced a smaller gauge companion to its O Gauge line?" The authors believe that some of the old guard executives — including Joshua Cowen himself — were reluctant. Tooling for a completely new, unproven line meant a sizable investment. Also, Joshua Lionel Cowen was eighty years old and chairman of the board, and, according to Lenny Dean, his first love was O Gauge. According to Sam Belser, Cowen's son, Lawrence, who was president of Lionel in 1957, "was more enthused about HO and the company's other diversifications than his father was. The old guard executives felt HO would just divert energies."[7] According to Lenny Dean, "The top brass at Lionel felt that they hadn't done all they could do in O Gauge yet and O Gauge was top priority. But with HO, Lionel felt it could capture at least part of the new market."[8]

According to Alan Ginsberg, Lionel's entry into HO would represent substantial total increases in HO sales through the attraction of new customers. He believed that HO was plus business. This he felt would attract more plus business for the industry. He also said that "If Lionel couldn't have come up with enough elements of superiority in HO, we'd have been foolish to enter the field."[9]

SEEKING A SUPPLIER ABROAD

It was Alan Ginsberg who made a trip to Italy sometime between March and October of 1957 to contact Rivarossi, an Italian firm known for making high-quality, detailed HO-scale models. The agreement was that Rivarossi would make the trains and Lionel would distribute them under Lionel's name and pay a percentage to Rivarossi.[10] This would save Lionel the cost of creating their own dies and tools. According to Ginsberg, Lionel had been studying the HO field since before 1953 and found that they could enter the field in a dozen different ways. They chose Rivarossi because of its high-quality products. Ginsburg stated that the Lionel engineering department had conducted amazing tests with it.[11] But the writer from *Railroad Model Craftsman* suspected that Joshua Lionel Cowen's thoughts during those decision-making days of 1957 must have dwelt on the fact that Lionel HO was a far cry from the early, massive Standard and O Gauge trains produced fifty years earlier.

Lionel heralded their entrance into HO with a four-page separate folder that they distributed with their 1957 O/O27 catalogue. Ron Hollander states in *All Aboard* that Lionel HO went into production too late to be included in the regular catalogue, but Sam Belser has another interpretation:

> I was a supporter of a separate HO catalogue. I felt we had to create enthusiasm and show that HO was a vital, viable line on its own. When, in 1958, they included HO into the regular O catalogue, I felt this neutralized the merchandising effect. From the very beginning, our problems in merchandising the HO line came from our limitations in our advertising budget.[12]

1957 was the only year in which Lionel acknowledged that someone else was making their HO-scale models. According to Alan Ginsberg, Lionel's entry into HO was not just a trial balloon: "Lionel's engineering department was into HO with both feet and our 1958 development work was in full swing."[13] At the time he may not have realized that the relationship between Rivarossi and Lionel would be short-lived — one year only — and that Athearn of Los Angeles would assume the complete production of the 1958 HO line.

Rivarossi, then, was instrumental in supplying Lionel Corp. of New York with its first mass-produced, ready-to-run HO trains in 1957. These highly detailed and well-made model trains are among the most desirable and collectible Lionel HO trains today and are top quality, exact-scale replicas of real trains in their day.

The Lionel management indicated that the quality of the new line — produced in cooperation with the world-famous manufacturing firm of Rivarossi and bearing the Lionel trademark (L within a circle) — would insure both firms an extensive share of the HO-scale market. Lionel had won the confidence of the consumer over a period of fifty-seven years and voiced its determination to keep the company's name synonymous with the finest in model railroading.

The new HO line produced by Rivarossi was composed of five ready-to-run diesel and steam freight outfits. There were also separate three-unit diesels in popular and familiar Lionel train names such as Wabash, Illinois Central, Southern Pacific, Chicago & Northwestern, Western Pacific, and Texas & Pacific. They also produced two steam locomotive models, the 0610LT Consolidation, and a cute 0600 two-axle shunting locomotive — along with twenty pieces of freight-type rolling stock with authentic markings, some of which had never been seen previously in HO. It is interesting to note that Rivarossi's line for Lionel did not include any passenger rolling stock. What a beautiful set a Canadian Pacific passenger consist would have made in HO! Nevertheless, all the Rivarossi items were well made, handsome, and highly detailed, particularly the boxcars which had such familiar markings as NYC Pacemaker, Seaboard, Rutland, Minneapolis & St. Louis, New Haven, Timken, and B & O Sentinel.

The Lionel four-page HO catalogue flyer also mentioned that the Lionel-Rivarossi motors were the only motors in the HO field equipped with two sets of miniature steel thrust bearings, thus guaranteeing efficient performance and low friction. The catalogue proceeded to say that Lionel-Rivarossi motors were so precisely engineered and were so expertly designed electrically and mechanically that they would always run coolly while maintaining top efficiency with lower power drain. With sprung trucks, steel wheels, motors articulated and hinge-mounted to follow the motion of the power truck, hand-applied details — such as roofwalks, brakewheels, ladders, and handrails, excellent paint application and graphics — and a one-year guarantee, authorized and backed

Lionel President Lawrence Cowen inspects the new HO line aimed at the hobby market. Courtesy Railroad Model Craftsman.

by Lionel's extensive service station network, it seemed that Lionel was headed for success in HO.

They had done almost everything right — even the package was a selling display in itself. Every component in every outfit, as well as the outfit itself, peered from its own clear plastic window. Separate catalogues and promotional ads were sent to all dealers and vendors. It seemed that truly no efforts had been spared to make Lionel's entry into the HO hobbyist market a successful one. As the *Railroad Model Craftsman* article, "Clear the Tracks for HO," stated in conclusion, "All of the above efforts by Lionel can only result in Lionel enhancing its position as the leader in American Model Railroading."

Everything sounded so promising. The largest train manufacturer in America finally had entered the discriminating hobbyists' domain: here would be "HO railroading at its very best!"[14] As the 1957 and 1958 Polk's *Hobby Blue Books* announced in a mock Western Union telegram, "Lionel announces HO Gauge trains for 1957. HO Gauge definitely has arrived with Lionel's recognition of this important adult hobbyist market."

It is interesting to note that it took Lionel's recognition to prove that HO had finally "arrived." That was the kind of position Lionel held. In the model railroad industry, Lionel was number one, although 1957 was the last year in which the company showed a profit in electric trains.[15]

By 1958 something happened that caused an end to the honeymoon with Rivarossi, even though the excellent Rivarossi line sold well. According to Tom McComas' and Ron Hollander's research, Lionel discontinued its relationship with Rivarossi because the Italian company allegedly could not keep pace with the demand of Lionel and the American public for more trains.[16] That is certainly not the reason given by Rivarossi. In his letter of March 7, 1984, Il Presidente de Rivarossi states:

> We supplied Lionel Corporation of N.Y. for the whole course of 1957 with our product, and the reason why our mutual business-trade suddenly ended was simply due to troubles arisen for payment questions. The first year, Messrs. Lionel opened a letter of credit as foreseen by our payment terms, but when, in 1958, they expected to affect payments by remittance, without any sort of bond or security, we have been compelled to state our refusal as we really couldn't accept such a condition. Messrs. Lionel Corp. did not find our sale-terms any longer suitable for their possibilities and therefore our trade inevitably broke off. That's all that we can say about our short business-ship with Messrs. Lionel, as, due to time elapsed, no further correspondence or letters concerning this matter have been kept apart.[17]

The Rivarossi response sounds historically correct, because Lionel was beset with internal corporate problems by 1958. Joshua Lionel Cowen was semi-retired and living half the year in Palm Beach, Florida.

Lionel seemed to have lost its direction and focus. Remember that the now-famous O Gauge Girls' Train was also being marketed in 1957 and unloaded in 1958. There is speculation that a girls' train was contemplated in HO as well (one author has acquired a Rivarossi boxcar "paint sample" collection and a similar robin's egg blue boxcar with yellow door was found in HO; it matches the O Gauge counterpart), but the conjecture is that the HO-scale set could not be justified because of the miserable failure of the O Gauge project.

ATHEARN ENTERS THE PICTURE

On December 18, 1958, Joshua Lionel Cowen retired, and in September 1959 he sold his shares of Lionel stock. Sales in electric trains dropped from $18.7 million in 1957 to $14.4 million by the end of 1958.[18] The company showed a loss of $469,000, its first losing year since the Depression. By October of 1959, Lawrence Cowen too was bought out by the Roy Cohn group (Cowen's great nephew).[19]

In the midst of all this confusion, Lionel decided to expand their HO line for 1958 and turned to Athearn, an American company which they felt already had an established domestic following. Furthermore, the Athearn line was cheaper to sell. For example, an 0864-50 Rivarossi boxcar in State of Maine livery was $3.75 in 1957. The same boxcar by Athearn sold for $2.50. Athearn produced an excellent quality train, but its motor drive system (with rubber belt transmission) could not compare with Rivarossi's gear drive and steel bearings. The Athearn rolling stock, switchers, and rectifiers looked like miniature Lionels, but it may have been a major mistake to introduce the lower quality, unreliable belt-driven locomotives and diesels to the quality-conscious HO hobbyists that Lionel so desperately wanted to reach back in 1957. One of the beautiful aspects of HO is that the locomotives can creep at prototypical speeds. This was hard to achieve with the Athearn locomotives. Nevertheless, a deal was made with Irv Athearn which, we suspect, included Lionel's terms for down payment and remittance.

Athearn, Incorporated, one of the oldest manufacturers of HO equipment, is also one of the most respected names in HO model railroading. The company produces an extensive line of models sold under its own name and supplies smaller firms with locomotives and rolling stock for various custom-painting projects, such as fund raisers for clubs and limited editions featuring less common road names.

If we assume that Lionel wished to engage a competent subcontractor for the production of its HO-scale line, then we should not be surprised that they chose Athearn. Only a few years prior to Lionel's entry into the HO market, Athearn had begun to produce injection-molded plastic models. With the rapid acceptance and economies of scale associated with the production of plastic kits, Athearn grew quickly. At the same time Lionel was terminating its relationship with Rivarossi, Athearn was expanding into six facilities and enlarging its staff to approximately three hundred. In 1956 Athearn designated certain of its production facilities for the assembly of kits; by Christmas Athearn had begun to produce ready-to-run train sets. Athearn shocked the market with its very low prices. Whether Lionel officials searched widely or not, they certainly would have found this: Athearn produced good-quality HO models very efficiently.

President Irvin Athearn recalls that Lionel officials invited him to New York to discuss the feasibility of a contractual relationship.[20] However, no agreement was made during Athearn's trip. In fact, Athearn claims that he went back to Los Angeles and "forgot about it" before Lionel made its response. In considering the terms set forth by Athearn, Lionel had to evaluate many considerations. First, it had to decide whether its entry into the HO market should be a permanent or a temporary commitment. Had Lionel decided to make it a permanent commitment at the outset or immediately after the Rivarossi relationship, the company might have made a greater effort to manufacture the line within its own facilities. However, if it preferred to take a more conservative, wait-and-see approach it would have been justified in seeking a subcontractor.

Before reaching any conclusions, let us evaluate a few more factors. First, a company the size of Lionel benefits greatly through vertical integration of those production processes that it can handle efficiently. To state this more simply, we can say that Lionel would not be effective at refining oil to produce plastics, nor would it be effective at processing wood pulp to manufacture cardboard for its boxes. Yet, Lionel could aggregate a great deal of diverse functions into its corporate functions. Lionel's structure supported a research and development team to engineer products, a tool-making department to produce dies and specialized fixtures, a marketing department to produce catalogues and advertising, as well as general sales programs, and a variety of production departments, where its products were molded, assembled, painted, and lettered. Its vertical integration eliminated the profit margins that subcontractors would require and thus improved Lionel's own pricing.

Analysis of a Business Decision

Why, then, would Lionel prefer to have Athearn produce HO trains? There are many possible answers. If Lionel officials believed that the company could not afford the time to design and tool for its own line, then they would have chosen a subcontractor for the purpose of making products in an interim period. The interim would have been that between termination of Rivarossi and establishment of in-house facilities (if Lionel had made the permanent commitment) or between termination of Rivarossi and review of the profitability of HO (had the commitment been short-term). Additional issues relate to labor costs, overhead costs and capital requirements.

Of these issues, most likely labor costs and capital requirements are the more significant. In the late 1950s tooling for a single HO boxcar cost approximately $2,500. Amortizing the costs of the die work for a boxcar over its lengthy useful life (as much as ten to twenty years for accounting purposes, longer in actual service for firms such as Athearn), we find a fairly low annual capital expense, which is apportioned over thousands of units of annual output from the die. According to Irvin Athearn, the workers employed in his assembly plants could construct an HO car from kit components in approximately three to five minutes.[21] Information available from the U.S. Bureau of Census indicates that the average wage for workers in light manufacturing fell between $1.65 and $1.95, thus Athearn's unit cost of assembly then might be estimated between $0.08 and $0.16, somewhat greater than the probable capital cost. Note that additional costs, such as social security and unemployment taxes, are incurred by employers. Relative to the labor, capital, and overhead costs, molding and packaging materials contributed only slightly to total cost.

Today, the costs of tooling to produce a locomotive body and mechanism usually amount to ten times the expense of a single piece of rolling stock. Given Athearn's cost of tooling a boxcar at $2500, we might estimate the cost of a locomotive at $25,000. In 1958 Lionel offered a range of HO models which included Athearn F-7, GP-9, and Husky-type locomotives (the Athearn term was Hustler), four different passenger cars, and six different principal bodies in the freight car line. The capital investment that Lionel would have made had it tooled for its own line in 1958 might be estimated as follows. The larger locomotives have a number of common parts in their mechanisms, thus reducing the marginal cost of adding a second body type to the line. Allowing $25,000 for completion of the first unit, we would add approximately $2,500 for the body of the second unit and another $2,500 for the new chassis. The smaller, simpler Husky locomotive may have required a smaller investment, along the lines of $10,000. Summing these amounts, we calculate $40,000 for the locomotives alone. We have excluded the Pacific and the Docksider which appeared in the 1958 catalogue. The Pacific had not been made at this time, while the Docksider was a carry-over from the Rivarossi agreement.

With passenger cars we find more economies, because trucks, weights, and some parts of the dies (roofs and ends between some cars) may be interchangeable. Allowing $2,500 for the first car and $1,500 for each additional type, we calculate the passenger car tooling investment at $7,000. Freight cars, too, use common trucks and weights;

however, the bodies are more distinctly different. Eight types at $2,500 would cost $20,000.

Note that some of the types can be sold in a variety of guises: the flatcar we find with a boat, an airplane, automobiles, bulkheads, or components for a maintenance-of-way caboose. All pieces of rolling stock can be sold also with a variety of paint schemes, thus increasing the utility of the capital investment. The total investment for tooling alone is the sum of locomotive tooling $30,000 plus passenger tooling $7,000 and freight car tooling $20,000, or $57,000. Additional costs would include jigs for painting or lettering the models.

Next on our list is perhaps the greatest concern of assembly plants: labor. Almost concurrent with the introduction of HO, the work force of Lionel made the move toward unionization. While unionization might provide actual improvements in the welfare of individual workers, it tends to discourage the employer from hiring additional employees. As we have seen in this country, a unionized work force also makes the employer more aware of the benefits of mechanization, which quickly becomes a substitute for labor when labor costs increase. Where Athearn employed three hundred workers to produce its entire line, Lionel might have needed seventy-five to manufacture just the HO line. If we assume that labor is in fact the principal or determinant cost, we must ask: why did Lionel prefer to pay Athearn for the cost plus a profit margin for the output of seventy-five workers, when Lionel could have added seventy-five workers in its plant? The most likely answer is the cost differential between unionized and nonunionized labor. Athearn employed the latter, and, in fact, the company split its facilities so that each group of workers would remain in personal contact with management and thereby thwart any incipient tendencies toward unionization.

Now, let us work with several hypotheses to continue our analysis. First, Lionel found that Athearn could produce good-quality models and sell them at a very reasonable price. As preparation for their decision, they invited Athearn to visit New York and to outline a possible contractual relationship. Having made the investment in die work, Athearn could produce additional units from these dies at an extremely low cost. Die work for injection molding wears very slowly, and the cost of plastic for a body shell is minimal. Athearn, then, would bear little or no capital expense in preparing equipment for Lionel; Athearn's principal costs would be labor and overhead. Given the fairly long time spans necessary to prepare die work from original designs and Lionel's introduction of its own models as early as 1960, it might appear that the company's involvement with Athearn arose as a deliberate bridge between termination of the relationship with Rivarossi and the introduction of Lionel HO. However, if one accepts the conclusions regarding Athearn's higher cost efficiency, one must ask why Lionel did not engage a subcontractor throughout its HO production. The answer may have more to do with pride than costs. Any Lionel enthusiast feels this pride. The orange and blue package proclaims it; the ubiquitous logo embodies it. Furthermore, Lionel's pride, which arose from domination of the O Gauge toy train market, may have suggested that Lionel could achieve the same mass-market success with the hobbyists' HO train.

We are not certain of the causal relationships. In the case of Athearn, records are not kept longer than necessary for contemporary operation of the business. Irvin Athearn, who made himself available for interview by Dallas Mallerich, has provided only an outline of these events. With a business career of forty years and a twenty-year professional career preceding that, Irvin Athearn has had a great many business dealings. Since our perspective differs from his, and from those at Lionel, we find that his memories might not include some "pertinent" aspects, and yet he runs a topnotch firm. Executives at Lionel have not achieved quite the tenure of Athearn, and thus we find that primary sources are deceased or retired.

Athearn was an "accepted, good line," stated Lenny Dean, former Lionel service manager. Dean added, "After careful investigation, Lionel went with the people who gave them the best deal — that was Athearn."[22]

Lionel's Marketing of HO

In the transitional year of 1958, Lionel offered both the newly introduced Athearn models and a few Rivarossi carry-overs (excess inventory, probably), including the 0600 tank locomotive and some freight cars. The year brought a banner change in the marketing strategy that would last throughout the production of HO models. This strategy entailed the duplication of Lionel O Gauge models in the smaller scale. According to former Lionel sales manager Sam Belser, "duplicating the O line made sense. Lionel O/O27 was a success, so we all thought why couldn't or shouldn't Lionel HO be?"

In his comment, Mr. Belser lends a great deal of support to emphasis on Lionel's pride. He continued to say that "one of the problems we had with HO from the very beginning was limitation of our advertising budget. That is why the HO line was incorporated into the regular O/O27 catalogue in 1958. That was okay, but I always felt there should be a separate catalogue as well. We had to create more enthusiasm and to show that HO was a vital, viable line on its own. I don't think Lionel ever achieved that important advertising goal."[23]

Lionel's 1958 HO advance catalogue — quite rare in its own right — gave the retailer some surprises. In many respects it had the effect of "being the first kid on the block" with "never-before-seen" HO items. Pages 2 and 3 of the catalogue state: "Now for the first time! The sales excitement of the new-to-HO locos, cars, accessories at prices that make HO scale big-sized business. Never before such accuracy, dependability and power in HO equipment — all backed by the world famous reputation of Lionel!" Nothing was said about the line being produced by Athearn. Lionel certainly produced enthusiastic ad copy; however, the accuracy of those statements leaves something to be desired.

Many of Lionel's principal retailers, such as electrical stores and hardware stores, did not purchase or were reluctant to purchase the new HO line because they did not know much about HO in general. 1958 became the year of dealer orientation. As the line developed and more retailers saw the familiar Lionel road names, engines, and rolling stock, more retailers did buy HO trains.

Unfortunately, 1958 was the lowest point of post–World War II train sales. Bernie Paul and Nat Polk have both commented at length at how bad conditions were in the toy and model train industry due to the coincidence of the slot car road-racing craze and the severe recession. Nat Polk pioneered the model railroad retail industry when, in 1935, he opened a hobby shop in New York City. In addition to providing an accessible outlet for local hobbyists, Polk published an extensive catalogue of hobby merchandise and later extended his business to provide wholesale services to other retailers. Bernie Paul, founder of AHM, has a great deal of experience with importing, wholesaling, and retailing model trains. In fact, AHM began to import Rivarossi products shortly after Lionel discontinued its relationship with that firm. Since the first edition of this book was published in 1986, Nat Polk, who provided much of the information used in the first writings on the Lionel HO line, has closed his New York store. Bernie Paul has also made a move and now heads up IHC (International Hobby Corporation), which still imports Rivarossi models.

"We sold Lionel HO on its own merit," stated Sam Belser. "It was a competitive line that by 1958 was gradually getting public and retail acceptance. With the right promotion, it could have been one of the greatest lines Lionel ever had."[24] Lionel's name in trains was still magic, so a certain amount of HO business went to Lionel in 1958. Belser indicated that the marketing strategy for the time being was to get more mass consumer and retailer appeal. By the time the regular consumer catalogue was ready in the fall of 1958, exact-scale references and quality slogans were being dropped and mass-appeal concepts were being substituted. Lionel's advance catalogue states: "For the discriminating hobbyist. This is HO railroading at its very best." 1958 was the first year in which one could find a 0197 Rotating Radar Antenna in HO and a similar 197 in O Gauge. Likewise, it was the year of the 0590 Virginian Rectifier with pantograph and headlight — an exact miniature of the new 2329 Virginian Rectifier electric produced in O Gauge.

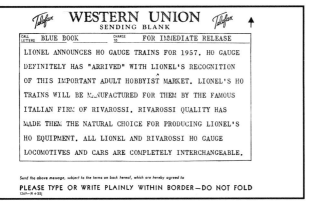

Announcement of Lionel HO line from Polk's Hobby Blue Book

As we have suggested, most of the models made for Lionel came directly from the line that Athearn sold under its own name. Usually, Lionel's models differed from standard Athearn products in minor aspects, such as subtle differences in decoration and one or two structural changes. In many cases, only the Lionel logo differentiated one from the other.

On the other hand, Lionel did lend some creativity to Athearn's production. The Auto-Loader, for instance, duplicated Lionel's O Gauge model. To offer this piece, Lionel requested that Athearn produce a two-tier superstructure to place atop his standard flatcar. Subsequently, Athearn produced the Auto-Loader, equipped with miniature Cadillacs, for both labels. Lionel also suggested and assisted in creating the 0590 Virginian Rectifier. In fact, this model may be the only joint effort between the two firms. Lionel created the die work for the body shell, which Athearn mounted on its own mechanism. Both firms sold the models, although Athearn soon discontinued its version after the conclusion of its relationship with Lionel.

Athearn's production of HO for Lionel continued into 1959–1960, although Athearn no longer served as principal supplier of the line. In these years, Lionel/Athearn products were in almost every case the same as kits sold in the Athearn line, although Lionel sold these models only in ready-to-run form. Until the mid-1960s Athearn's advertisements clearly show the Lionel logo on some of its cars. This probably occurred for two reasons. First, Athearn accidentally photographed models with Lionel logos. Second, Athearn recycled advertisements as much as possible. Thus Athearn continued to illustrate Lionel/Athearn models although it no longer produced them.

Some confusion arises from Lionel's 1958 catalogue, because both Athearn and Rivarossi models are illustrated. The black New Haven boxcar, carried forward from the Lionel/Rivarossi line of 1957, appears in the catalogue. The Lionel/Athearn New Haven boxcar, not illustrated, is orange. In the 1959 catalogue two Athearn boxcars — Timken and State of Maine — appear alongside the Lionel boxcars introduced that year. Athearn provided caboose shells into the 1960s, but, with the exception of these two boxcars and a few passenger cars, the Athearn items had disappeared from the catalogue by 1961.

LIONEL'S OWN HO

The connection with Athearn gave Lionel an interim period for development of its own style of HO. By 1960 Lionel was producing the HO line in its factory in Hillside, New Jersey. Almost all of the freight, rolling stock, and power units from the old Hobbyline or the new Lionel die work carry a line on their sides showing that they were built by Lionel. It can be found with the word "Built" spelled out or as the abbreviation "BLT". In a few cases there is no built date included in the shell decoration.

Sometime in 1958 Lionel approached John English, proprietor of Hobbyline, based in Morrisville, Pennsylvania, and purchased the tooling from his company for $150,000.[25] By 1959 Lionel had reworked and put into service Hobbyline HO-scale model dies. In fact, Lionel purchased all of Hobbyline's dies, except for its passenger cars, which were acquired by Penn Line. In the mid-1950s, Hobbyline had catalogued a Fairbanks-Morse locomotive, but Lionel never produced this item — perhaps they too went elsewhere.

The 1959 catalogue shows a mixture of Lionel's new models and those made for Lionel by Athearn. The word "new" appears next to the catalogue entries for the Lionel items, and thus they can be distinguished from the remaining Athearn models. The catalogue introduced nine Alco diesels in three road names, two GP-9s, an electric, two steam locomotives, a diesel yard switcher, a snowplow, and a motorized gang car. In addition to the many new locomotives, Lionel introduced sixteen pieces of rolling stock using old Hobbyline dies but added the same type metal sprung truck used by Athearn, Varney, and other manufacturers of that period. Two of the flatcars carried metal Matchbox models as loads. Track and transformers were also added, as were accessories, including a light tower, gateman, crossing gate (of Athearn manufacture but never offered as a Lionel item), and five plastic buildings. The buildings were actually Plasticville products packaged in Lionel boxes and were produced by Bachmann Brothers of Philadelphia. Little did the Lionel people know at the time that they would once again turn to Bachmann Brothers in the middle 1970s for help in expanding their HO line for the second time. This time, however, Bachmann would produce the actual train models. (Note: Plasticville items are covered in Chapter V.) The new Lionel drives were much like the band-driven units of 1958 and, in the authors' opinion, less dependable. A worm gear was added to the drive, but rubber bands still operated as clutches, thus offsetting the advantage of the added gears. Six changes took place on the frames used for the Alcos, geeps, and electrics in the eight years that Lionel produced the line.

In addition to reworking Hobbyline dies, Lionel created its own dies for 1959. The Lionel dies produced models with thin plastic walls, while Hobbyline dies produced models with much heavier cross sections. The collector can distinguish models made in the Lionel dies from models made in the Hobbyline dies by examining the heaviness of the casting. Hobbyline dies were used for the new 0605 Yard Switcher, Alco diesel, tank cars, gondolas, flatcars, the new Alaska hopper cars, and Lionel Corporation–stamped boxcars.[26] The Texas Special sets (0704–0707) and tuscan Pennsylvania sets of passenger cars remained available from earlier Athearn production (until 1960, when Lionel began to produce its own cars).

It is interesting to note that many illustrations in the 1959 consumer catalogue depict Athearn pieces, such as the 0865 gondola with canisters. The actual 1959 version produced by Lionel is a brown Hobbyline 40-foot gondola with Athearn canisters. Numbered 0865-200, the gondola has yellow/gold lettering and five unmarked red canisters — it can definitely be called "transitional"! Note that the catalogue tag-line "new" often appears next to items that had been available for at least a year.

Other pieces produced in 1959 include the new 0561 Minneapolis & St. Louis rotary snow plow with revolving blade — a Lionel copy of Athearn's little Hustler locomotive — and the 0056 AEC Husky with headlight; both were produced with gear drives. The revolving blade on the 0561 was a separate, newly made Lionel piece, too. The 0591 New Haven rectifier with pantograph had a band drive, as did the 0596 New York Central GP-9. The new 0625LT Pacific steam locomotive, still pictured with the Walschaerts valve gear that it never had, was a gear-driven work horse. The ex-Hobbyline Alco locomotives included A-B-A lash-ups decorated for the Santa Fe, Texas Special, and Alaska Railroad. New in the accessory line were the 0050 Gang Car, 0145 Automatic Gateman, and 0494 Rotary Beacon. A variety of Plasticville HO buildings, girder bridges, billboards, trestles, and the 0197 Rotating Radar Antenna enabled enthusiasts to make their layouts into miniature replicas of larger O Gauge layouts.

John English initially manufactured the A-5 Yardbird as a cast-metal kit under the English trade name. Later, he manufactured the same locomotive as a plastic static model (shown here) under the Hobbyline trade name. Lionel acquired the die work for this model in its deal with Hobbyline.

By December of 1959 Lionel had made the transition from "early" HO, when manufacturing was contracted to outside suppliers, to the intermediate period when Lionel produced its own equipment based on its O Gauge heritage. No other manufacturer could boast of blinking 0805 AEC cars (the nuclear reactors in the canisters glowed red), illuminated poultry cars, maintenance cars, circus cars, missile carrier flatcars, or — the prize of any Lionel HO collection — the 0808 and 0807 flatcars with "Matchbox"-series tractor and bulldozer, respectively. These were the only Lionel cars that ever had Matchbox models as loads.

Collector Geoffrey Bunza comments:

> It is possible that the order from Lionel in (presumably) early 1959 for the #4 tractor and #18 bulldozer might have spurred Lesney to actively solicit business from the model railroad community. Coincidentally in 1959, Mr. Peter Webb joined Lesney Products (England) as manager of advertising and public relations. He reportedly had a "keen interest in model railways," according to *Collecting Matchbox Diecast Toys, the First Forty Years*, by Kevin McGimpsey & Stewart Orr (Great Britain, 1989: Major Productions Limited), and began advertising in journals such as *Railway Modeller* (July 1959). Reviews of new

Matchbox cars appears in *Model Trains* magazines into 1960. Whether the Lionel order or Mr. Webb appeared first on the scene is not known to me.

By 1960 the inventory of discontinued Athearn and Rivarossi items had been depleted. Lionel's own production of HO continued until 1966, and then resumed in 1974, under the General Mills agreement (Model Products Corp., or MPC), as described in Volume II. The 1960-1966 production is described in Chapter V of this book. As one of the main purposes of this volume is providing guidance in identifying a piece as Rivarossi-, Athearn-, or Lionel-produced, we will next give an overview of the characteristics of each line and subsequently devote chapters to detailed study of each manufacturer's models.

NOTES

1. T. McComas and J. Tuohy, *A Collector's Guide and History, Vol. III: Standard Gauge*, TM Productions, 1978, p. 99.
2. Ron Hollander, *All Aboard! The Story of Joshua Lionel Cowen and His Lionel Train Company.* New York: Workman Publishing, 1981, p. 54.
3. McComas and Tuohy, ibid.
4. Telephone interview with Sam Belser by V. Rosa, August 14, 1984.
5. Hollander, p. 225.
6. McComas and Tuohy, p. 103.
7. Belser, ibid.
8. Interview with Lenny Dean, June 1984.
9. *Railroad Model Craftsman,* October 1957, p. 54.
10. McComas and Tuohy, ibid.
11. *Railroad Model Craftsman*, ibid.
12. Belser, ibid.
13. *Railroad Model Craftsman*, pp. 53-54.
14. Lionel HO catalogue, 1957.
15. Hollander, p.224.
16. McComas and Tuohy, ibid.
17. Letter from Rivarossi president Alessandro Rossi to Vincent Rosa, March 7, 1984.
18. McComas and Tuohy, p. 105.
19. Hollander, p. 232.
20. Interview with Dallas J. Mallerich III, September 8, 1983.
21. Ibid.
22. Telephone conversation with Lenny Dean; V. Rosa, July 1984.
23. Telephone interview with Sam Belser; V. Rosa, August 14, 1984.
24. Ibid.
25. J. Sadorf, telephone conversation, January 27, 1985.
26. McComas and Tuohy, p. 105.

CHAPTER II
Identifying Rivarossi, Athearn, and Lionel Items

This chapter presents guidelines and tips to help you differentiate production by Rivarossi, Athearn, and Lionel.

GEORGE HORAN ON THE TRAIL OF LIONEL HO

Having been a collector of Athearn and Hobbyline models for quite a few years before Lionel entered the HO market, I had little difficulty recognizing an open locomotive or car when I began to hunt down Lionel HO models. No color pictures or listings were available to me — as they are to you in this book — except for the catalogues, which left something to be desired and which can be misleading at times.

While searching for the models covered in the first edition of this volume, I used the same approach I had always used. First, I knew the **road names available** in a particular type of car or locomotive; keeping that information in mind, I found I could always recall the **colors** the car should be. With these two points of information, the type of construction was also easier to remember.

Many times at meets in the 1970s I would spot open cars by their colors. With the car laying on its side I could see the metal weight on the car floor (Athearn), or the heavy oversized detail and heavy steps (Lionel/Hobbyline), or the clean, smooth look with no detail of the Rivarossi cars sold as Lionel. And this was all before I ever picked up the model.

After picking up a model, I then checked the finer points that should be present. You can consult the detailed listings in Chapters III, IV, and V to acquire this information. Before turning to them, however, review the summaries of identifiers provided below.

This book should facilitate your own identification of specific pieces in several ways. Although many of the Lionel HO items, especially those produced by Rivarossi and Athearn, have a number on the car side that differs from the Lionel catalogue number, you can identify an unboxed piece by referring to the Index of this book to see whether the number on the car matches any entry (both catalogue and car numbers are indexed).

HOW TO RECOGNIZE LIONEL/RIVAROSSI HO

Rivarossi's production includes those items catalogued in 1957, and a few of the rolling stock pieces sold in 1958. This production is somewhat easier to identify than that of Athearn or the Lionel Corporation. The photographs, captions, and detailed listings in Chapter III document known models. In general, Lionel/Rivarossi HO can be differentiated from Lionel/Athearn and regular Lionel Corporation HO as follows:

- Rivarossi pieces have the Rivarossi name stamped underneath.
- Most Rivarossi pieces also have the Lionel "L" (as do Lionel/Athearn production pieces). This will differentiate Lionel pieces from *regular* Rivarossi production. However, in the rush to supply Lionel, Rivarossi packaged some items which did not have the Lionel logo. In this case, boxed items without the Lionel logo could then be accepted as a model sold by Lionel.
- Most numbers and lettering appearing on the Rivarossi-manufactured items were applied using the silkscreening process (the only known exceptions to this are two FM units) — quite new at the time, and very expensive. Today, this step in production helps to make these models collectors' delights because of the clear, sharp image the model presents. One drawback to this type of lettering was the thickness of the paint forced through the screen and onto the side of the model. It left a thick raised and glossy letter or number that would never rub off but could chip off.
- Rivarossi cars are extremely lightweight; no metal weight is used on Rivarossi rolling stock.
- Rivarossi boxcars have "model quality" detailing, such as separate roofwalks and fragile ladders. (See the comparison of the ends of State of Maine boxcars and photographs.)

Four known types of frames used on the FM units. Far left is sheet brass with metal weight fixed at its center, carrying the manufacturer's name and part number. The second unit is early plastic power A unit. Note that the metal weight has no name or number while the last two shown are later plastic dummy B and A units, both showing name and "Como–Italia". No metal weights were used on these. Note how truck side frames are fixed on both power units.

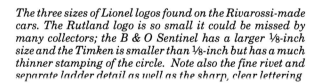

The three sizes of Lionel logos found on the Rivarossi-made cars. The Rutland logo is so small it could be missed by many collectors; the B & O Sentinel has a larger ⅛-inch size and the Timken is smaller than ⅛-inch but has a much thinner stamping of the circle. Note also the fine rivet and separate ladder detail as well as the sharp, clear lettering

The shells from the Lionel Rivarossi FM units of 1957. Center: The early Bakelite shell, flanked by plastic A and B. Note the much larger die marks left on the Bakelite roof; this shell also holds all lettering in print and has thicker walls. It used a brass frame, very rare with Lionel decorations and the Lionel logo. Both A units carry part #305, while all B units carry #1373.

- The two Rivarossi steam engines are the 0600 Dockside Switcher and the 0610 LT Consolidation. (See pages 24 and 25 for photographs.) Notes on this engine, according to the ones personally observed, are:

    The single cab window has an arched top, typical of European-style locomotives.

    Has turned-brass bell; cab, boiler, and tender shell are black-painted plastic; frame is sheet metal.

    Full working valve gear.

    Engine frame reads (see photographs):

    "Rivarossi
    Como — Italia
    1515
    Made in Italy"

    Tender number 280 in ⅝16-inch lettering (catalogue shows no number on tender).

    Tender frame is die-cast, lettering on bottom reads:

    "Rivarossi
    Como — Italia
    1370
    Made in Italy"

    Motor is in tender with drive shaft to engine.

    Castings on the tender were poor. This piece is extremely hard to find in good condition; it is a very scarce engine. It is advisable to purchase one in a Lionel/Rivarossi box, although there are not many to be found.

- See 1957 catalogue selling sheet for list of diesel road names.

Note: Some of the FM units were definitely sold as Lionel in early 1957, but do not carry the Lionel logo on their shells. It now appears that most of these units were found as separate pieces. All other identifying information listed for FMs should be present if indeed it is a 1957 Lionel model.

HOW TO RECOGNIZE LIONEL/ATHEARN PRODUCTION

See the groups of comparative photos in this chapter.

- Athearn pieces are not marked with the Athearn name anywhere on the model, but, on most rolling stock and engines, there appears the Lionel logo — an encircled "L". Some Rivarossi pieces have this logo too. However, the Rivarossi pieces are distinguished by the appearance of that company's name on the underside of all rolling stock and locomotives.

- All Athearn lettering is always in flat rubber-stamping method.

- Athearn boxcars have a higher profile than the Rivarossi cars do, and all cars have a metal weight between floor and frame.

The two known sizes of Lionel logo used on Athearn cars 1958–1959. The Wabash 0864-250 (bottom) sports the ⅟16-inch logo in the second panel to the right of the door. The 0864-50(A) (top) has the same size logo located at the corner of the car, and the 0864-50(B) (middle) has the logo in the same corner location but in the larger ⅛-inch size. Rivet detail is not as good as the Rivarossi-made cars shown. Speculation has it that the smaller logo was used in 1958 with the larger ⅛ inch appearing in 1959. Note the flat smooth finish to the lettering.

- Use Chapter IV and the 1958 consumer and advance catalogues as reference sources. If you have "mint" or boxed pieces, it will be very easy to cross-reference the catalogue numbers with those on the box. Only Athearn's road number appears on the piece.

Athearn produced HO for Lionel from 1958 to 1960. The 1958 catalogues (advance and consumer) provide a useful guide. The airplane car, Lionel 0800, was shown in both the 1958 and 1959 catalogues; evidently, either production had continued or a quantity remained available. Some collectors have mentioned that Lionel/Athearn HO has also been known to come through without the Lionel "L" stamped on it. A collector should consider these pieces as genuine Lionel products only if he saw them in mint condition in an unopened Lionel box. Undoubtedly, some regular Athearn (not marked with "L") did slip by the factory workers and into Lionel boxes. But one problem remains. If we allow all Athearn pieces (unboxed, for example) to be considered Lionel, then who is to stop the unscrupulous individual from putting a 1950s Athearn caboose worth $8 into a Lionel box and getting $25 for it?

Athearn made some pieces, or at least catalogued some pieces, in their own consumer catalogue that were also made for Lionel. Some recognizable pieces are the 0800 airplane car, 0590 Virginian Rectifier, and the 0866-25 Santa Fe stock car to name a few. Also, there is an 0864-50 State of Maine boxcar catalogued in 1957-1958. This "mint" boxed piece is clearly Athearn production. While Athearn and Rivarossi did duplicate some familiar paint schemes, such as that on the colorful State of Maine boxcars, in and after 1958, we are reasonably certain that all of the items depicted in Lionel's 1957 catalogue were produced by the latter.

Lionel/Athearn HO boxcar characteristics are easily recognized. Look for separate roofwalks (not molded in the roof), sprung trucks, black spray-painted weighted underframes, plastic "short pin" NMRA couplers rather than finger tab couplers (which have an extended piece of plastic to make manual uncoupling easier), thin plastic simulated steel doors, and separate plastic door guides. (See the section below which compares State of Maine boxcars.) Typical Athearn production boxcars are not numbered with the Lionel catalogue number. Examples: 0864-225 Central of Georgia and 0864-200 Monon.

Lionel/Athearn cabooses have many revealing characteristics. Underframes, trucks, and couplers are screwed in place. Many do not have a "tab-slot" (visible tab which holds caboose body to frame). All have body-mounted couplers. The Lionel name and logo do not appear on the bottom of the split frame. The Athearn name does not appear anywhere on the piece either. Usually there is a "Built by Lionel" or a Lionel "L" logo on each side of the piece.

Other characteristics to look for are plastic brakewheels, metal railings, and plastic smokejacks. Lionel numbers were stamped on some cabooses but not all. For example, one Rio Grande caboose is stamped "01439" on the side, but the number on the Lionel box is "0817-50". By the way, this is a mint piece; it clearly came with all railings, etc. but no smokestack. The Lionel Corporation often advertised in its instruction sheets that, for five cents or so, you could buy modeling parts to give your cabooses more detail. Many late Lionel Corporation HO cabooses, such as the 0837 M & StL, came without any detailing parts near the end near the end of production in 1965.

A "gray" area for collectors is the Lionel/Athearn NH passenger car series released in 1958. In this series, the numbers on the car sides are not the same as those used in the catalogues and on the cartons. (See the Index for all numbers.) For example, the 701 Pullman was actually numbered 3150. There are no Lionel logos reported on the pieces. Yet, the two F-7 New Haven diesels are numbered 0272 instead 0533, as found in the catalogue and on the box. Both have the Lionel "L" on them. Use extreme caution when purchasing Athearn pieces without a box. If the piece is "unboxed," only consider it a Lionel piece if it has the Lionel "L" (within a circle) on it.

All F-7s (1958) are clearly Athearn products with rubber belt drives. Of the rectifier locomotives, only the 0590 is a product of the Athearn shop. Actually, the locomotive is a joint product, as Lionel had created the dies for the body shells. Subsequent releases of the Virginian

locomotives feature a Lionel Corporation drive. The 0615 Boston & Maine Pacific would have been a Lionel/Athearn, but Athearn did not produce it in 1959, as scheduled. However, Athearn did release this model under its own label in 1962.

HOW TO RECOGNIZE LIONEL CORPORATION PRODUCTION PIECES

See the comparative photos in this chapter.
- Lionel Corporation pieces generally have the Lionel catalogue number on their sides and are lettered "The Lionel Corporation/Made in the U.S. of America" on the frame. Check Chapter V of this book.
- Lionel-manufactured cars all have hot-stamp-type lettering.
- The cars are least likely to have broken steps because of their thick construction.
- All operating rolling stock that mirrors the late 1950s through 1960s O Gauge line is clearly Lionel Corporation HO. Examples: The 0805 Atomic Energy Disposal Car, 0333 Satellite car, 0850 Missile Launcher, etc. This also applies to accessories such as the 0145 Gateman.
- Rolling stock produced until 1962 has sprung trucks and the finger-tab version of the NMRA couplers. After 1962 these items were produced with solid frame trucks, which do not have real coil springs as found on the earlier metal sprung trucks.
- There are two kinds of boxcars — early production and late production. *Early* boxcars were made from Hobbyline dies. Examples: 0864-900, 0864-700, and 0864-325. *Late* boxcars resulted from Lionel's attempt to create a new boxcar with its own die work. A late boxcar is the green 0874 New York Central. The late boxcars have the Lionel number and steel bottoms similar to the 6464-100 O Gauge boxcars. These two cars are quickly becoming two of the most difficult cars to locate, since they were more cheaply made and easily broken. There are no Lionel Corporation markings, just the Lionel number.
- Lionel produced all of the Pacifics, as well as all Alcos, like the Alaska Railroad 0567, and all motorized units like the 0050 gang cars. Plastic components were made from the old Hobbyline dies for all but the four-wheel power units.
- Bachmann "Plasticville" items were also packaged by Lionel.
- Atlas also made track and bridges that were boxed by Lionel.
- Track manufactured by Lionel bears the lettering "The Lionel Corp." on the underside.

DETERMINING MANUFACTURER BY COMPARING STATE OF MAINE CARS

Consider a State of Maine boxcar you might find at a local meet, unboxed. It has a low profile. The car is very light in weight and has high gloss, thick silkscreen lettering and it has the proper red, white, and blue decorated shell. You have found a Rivarossi-made Lionel car. The next step is to check for the manufacturer's name on the frame. Check the listing for that car in the appropriate chapter.

Undersides of boxcars from all three early Lionel HO producers. Top: Rivarossi — note rivet detail, metal sprung trucks, but no brake or air reservoir; Rivarossi name and part number present. Middle: Athearn — also equipped with metal sprung trucks, metal weight between frame and inner floor, reservoir and brake housing cast onto frame; no manufacturer's name present but cars do carry Lionel logo. Bottom: Lionel — sprung trucks along with good rivet detail; note reservoir and brake housing cast into floor. Lionel name present under truck.

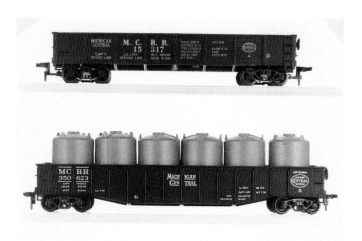

Rivarossi (top), 40-foot car with straight side sills; Athearn (center), 50-foot with "fishbelly" sides; Lionel model (bottom), 40-foot cars with straight side sills and ribs that are spaced more closely than those on the Rivarossi model.

The State of Maine boxcar as produced by Rivarossi, Athearn, and Lionel. Note the differences in door, rails, and steps. The Lionel shows the full catalogue number and has a much higher profile, with all detail cast in place (which represented a saving in assembly line work). Note the separate ladder on the Rivarossi car (top) and the Lionel Logo on the Athearn car (middle) at the handrail.

If this car had been an Athearn-made model, it would have been a higher-profile car, with flat rubber-stamped lettering on its shell. The car also would have been heavier, having a metal weight hidden but seen between the outside floor and the frame. No manufacturer's name is present on Athearn-made models. It should show the Lionel logo on its side.

If this same car were of Lionel's own manufacture, it would be as heavy as the Athearn car but only because of its much thicker wall, roof, and floor construction. The lettering, having been hot-stamped, has an edge to it that one can see and feel and it has a slight shine to it. All of the Lionel cars carry the Lionel name on the outer floor — with the exception of the later 0874-type boxcars.

I have used this method time and time again. You can rely on this approach, starting with type of car, road name, color, and number.

CARTONS AND PACKAGING

Separate Items

In 1957 the first cartons used for separate HO-scale items differed little in appearance from Lionel's classic orange and white packaging. However, the HO cartons featured a plastic window, which allowed the consumer to see the contents quite clearly. An engineer's face, pictured in black and white, appeared at the top of the window and on one side of the box; all other printing was black. A listing of items then available

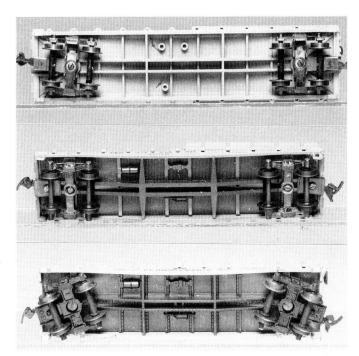

Top to bottom: Rivarossi, Athearn, and Lionel derrick cars, undersides. All three used sprung trucks and NMRA couplers. Note the Athearn car (center) was the only one to have a metal weight. The Rivarossi and Lionel cars have manufacturer's name on frame, a step Athearn had not used since later 1950 — and then only on its cast frames for their power units of that period.

Rivarossi, Athearn, and Lionel derrick cars, side views. Note the Rivarossi car on top has the main boom cast into car floor while Athearn and Lionel both use separate castings that snap into floor holes. Also note position of Lionel's logo and car numbers, which do not match Lionel's catalogue number on the first two cars.

appeared on the back of the box. A dull white cardboard liner provided a nest for the item in each box. Catalogue numbers appeared in black numerals on each end. The Rivarossi models were packaged in this type of box, which then had "Made in Italy" on the back. Only slight changes were made when Lionel production shifted to Athearn in 1958. The words "HO by Lionel" were added above the picture window on the front, and an illustration of HO accessories replaced the catalogue listing on back. The Lionel name and "U.S.A." first appeared on these cartons.

Some of the printing changed when Lionel assumed production of the line in 1959. The lettering and the illustrations were changed from black to bright blue, and the dull white liners were replaced by brighter white liners. Some of the later cartons featured written descriptions of the products. A blue band with the phrase "The Leader in Model Railroading" was added to both sides. The rear of the carton now featured a picture of an F-unit diesel and caboose. "Lionel" and "Hillside, NJ" also appear on the carton. The catalogue numbers on the box ends were changed to black. However, many of the cartons made for one product were used for another. In most cases, the original stamping was covered with a white paper sticker, which was stamped with the new number. Other times, a long blue line covered the old number, so that a new number could be stamped above or below it. Cartons for accessories were generally similar to those used for rolling stock items.

Set Boxes

Lionel employed a wider range of colors, shapes, and sizes in creating the boxes for its train sets. In 1957 the company packaged sets in a dull yellow box with black printing. Then, in 1958, it switched to a gaudy orange, yellow, and green box, which also had black printing. The sets contained individual cartons for each component; these cartons contained yellow liners, rather than the white liners used for individual

items. The boxes had a fold-back top (for countertop display), with the words "LIONEL HO" and the slogan "The Leader in Model Railroading". Set numbers appeared on the outer box. In 1959 Lionel again changed the boxes, this time to a bright yellow with a smaller "LIONEL HO" printed in red letters on the box top. The box top illustrations depict a Santa Fe Alco crossing a trestle and a steam locomotive and snow blower operating on a lower track. The 1959 box retained the fold-back design and black printing.

In 1960 the company changed the color of the box to orange and white and added a large white "HO" with a black "LIONEL" stamped across it. An illustration of a Pacific steam locomotive, printed in gray, appeared on the top; all other printing remained black. Some of these cartons had orange or gray liners with holes punched to accept the items of the sets. Others continued to house separate boxes for the individual components. The box design changed in 1964, when Lionel discontinued the two-part design. The company continued to use the "Lionel HO" logo and the illustration of the Pacific locomotive, however only the box top remained orange. The remainder of the box was flat off-white. A white liner with punched holes held the components of each set.

Some of the early passenger sets with Athearn cars and Lionel locomotives were packaged in bright yellow boxes approximately one foot square and six inches high. Very few sets of this period were packaged in the flat freight set-type box, which had "LIONEL HO" in red letters and the set description and catalogue number in black. The front and back of this carton were imprinted with the illustration from the cover of the 1957 catalogue. Later passenger sets were packaged in bright orange cartons approximately the same size. The printing on these boxes was all black, and only the lion's head illustration and the slogan "An Investment in Happiness" appeared on the box top. Individual component boxes were included in each of the foregoing box types.

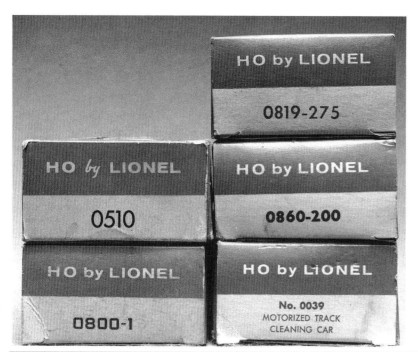

Top left: Rivarossi box with its large thin black stamping. Bottom left: Athearn box. Both have off-white end flap with black printing. Individual boxes on right are Lionel, with brighter white carton and blue lettering; note only one carries the model description. Note that the bottom carton has a replacement label glued over original item number; Lionel was known to have done this frequently. It can cause confusion when the glued-on label falls off.

First HO set offered as Lionel, made by Rivarossi in 1957. Set #5700, the 0600 Dockside Locomotive, headed the three-car set. Yellow cardboard filler held the five individual orange cartons, one of track that was included.

One of the early set boxes used for the Athearn-made Lionel items of 1958-1959. The box itself is rare! Set #5714, the New Haven, is described in Chapter VI.

Lionel-type set box used from 1960 to 1964. Used for many sets, with and without individual cartons for components. The carton shown holds the uncatalogued "Space Prober" set of 1963.

Top: Original box for catalogued set #5770, Texas Special passenger set from 1960. Bottom: Carton for set #14280, available 1964-1966; it is a light orange carton with catalogue number stamped in black.

Several variations of the basic designs were used throughout Lionel's production of HO. For example, set #14310 had an orange and gray box with black lettering. This box, circa 1965–1966, depicts an O Gauge steam locomotive with a square tender pulling a 6464-475 boxcar and a 6631 log car.

A paper tag with a description and illustration of the set contents is located on the side of the box. Santa Fe freight set 14310-502, with a 0595 diesel, was sold in a square cardboard box with "LIONEL TRAINS" stamped on it in black; the box is also lettered "Guaranteed and Manufactured by the Lionel Corp., N.Y., N.Y." in black letters. Vincent Rosa notes that the latter set may have been one of the last to leave the Lionel plant at Hillside, New Jersey.

Reproduction Boxes

As we completed the previous edition of this book, it came to the attention of both authors that an unscrupulous dealer had made a box which very closely reproduces the original Lionel cartons. The reproduction cartons have lighter construction (thinner cardboard and clear plastic) than the originals, but they are in no way marked to indicate that they are reproductions.

These boxes, which are used for single items, are rubber stamped such that they may be differentiated from the original cartons. The originals have thin lettering with crisp edges, whereas the reproductions have fat lettering with weak edges. Most of the original boxes are metal stamped. Lionel did rubber stamp a few boxes, but items like the 0057 Air Force switcher did not come in rubber-stamped boxes. The boxes first appeared in mid-1985, and they add to the price being asked for the items. The reproductions we saw have cardboard liners inside and the late-style picture, showing the diesel, caboose, and the Pacific set going through the girder bridge, on the back. *Collectors must inspect the cartons before making a purchase.*

I see nothing wrong with repro boxes if they are properly marked as such. Open models also need protection, but not at artificially raised prices.

CHAPTER III
Lionel/Rivarossi Trains

As chronicled in Chapter I, when Lionel entered the HO market in 1957, all of its HO products were manufactured by Rivarossi of Italy. Rivarossi was then almost unknown in the United States, as very few dealers carried their products, which included individual model kits as well as complete, ready-to-run train sets that sold in the $25 range. Even then the models were superior in workmanship. All power units had frames of cast metal, sheet metal, or, occasionally, brass. The body shells were molded very solidly with an extra-heavy type of plastic, and the mechanisms used excellent motors. Rivarossi identified the products that it sold in the United States, which were compatible with American-made models, with its Red Line label. Today, all of these, including those produced on behalf of Lionel Corporation, are rare and desirable to the HO collector. For Rivarossi, the brief engagement with Lionel provided prepaid exposure of their line to the large American market.

At present Rivarossi enjoys a large share of the U.S. market. The company produces not only trains in HO and other popular scales, but also trackside and electrical accessories as well. Furthermore, Rivarossi's market includes countries across Europe and other continents. One wonders what might have happened if, in 1957, Lionel had made an investment in the production capability of Rivarossi.

In describing certain variations in the production of Rivarossi models, it is necessary to distinguish between phenolic plastics and thermoplastics. Reader Lou Bohn, a professional engineer, has offered the following information.

Phenolic plastics, of which Bakelite is just one brand, are thermosetting plastics which cannot be heated and remelted once molded. These plastics withstand higher temperatures without deforming. The phenolics are brown, dark brown, and black in color, and they are always opaque. Commonly used in electrical insulation and normally found in relatively thick sections, Bakelite is brittle. Thin sections are easily broken.

Thermoplastics, on the other hand, can be heated, softened, and remelted. They withstand a lower operating temperature before deformation occurs. With plasticizer, these can be "softened" so that they will not crack as easily. Most plastic model train bodies are made of polystyrene with varied amounts of plasticizer added to make them less brittle. The plasticizer dessicates in time, and thus the body cracks around screw-mounting holes. This class of plastics is also available without pigmentation (clear). It yellows in time due to ultraviolet degradation. Very fine molding detail is possible, as are heat-stamped graphics.

STEAM LOCOMOTIVES

Lionel's first HO catalogue, a four-page color folder, showed a 4-4-2 Atlantic locomotive on its cover. This particular locomotive was sold in the early 1960s under the Aristo Craft trade name, but never under the Lionel name. The Atlantic locomotive and the two that *were* sold as Lionel, in 1957, were originally marketed in the U.S.A. in 1955 under the name Rivarossi "Red Line." The information on the two sold under Lionel's name is provided in the following listings.

	Gd	Exc	Mt

280: See (0610)

(0600) B & O-TYPE DOCKSIDE SWITCHER: Black, painted plastic body; unlettered; cast steam chest; brass bell; wire handrails at the cab doors, boiler front, and along the length of the boiler sides; full working valve gear; drivers are nickel-plated brass tires with plastic centers, the same type used on the 0610 Consolidation; lighted. A ¾" cast weight is located at the front of the boiler, ending at the center of the first driver. The size of this weight can help differentiate the Lionel locomotive from those imported in the 1960s. The later locomotives have a much larger weight that extends to a point just in front of the second driver. "1050" and "R.R. Italy" appear on the plastic section of the frame; "Rivarossi", "COMO, Italy", and "1051" appear directly below the motor. The rear of the motor housing is constructed of heavy white plastic; post-1958 models have black Bakelite instead. In 1956 this particular locomotive was sold in the Rivarossi packaging and identified on the carton as 1018. In 1960 AHM also imported this same locomotive with some small changes in boiler detail. They are all very much alike with few small changes. The Rivarossi builder's plate appears on all Lionel versions. The boiler must be removed to replace the light bulb. Catalogued in 1957 at $12.95 as a separate item and also with one three-car set, number 5700, which sold for $25. Lionel's 0600 is quite difficult to find.

	50	75	100

(0610) LIGHT CONSOLIDATION: (2-8-0); black plastic cab and boiler; European-type, arched windows; wire handrails on boiler front, pilot, and length of boiler; nickel-plated brass driver rims with plastic centers; sheet metal frame; cast-metal pilot truck; larger metal weight in boiler; headlight located behind removable boiler front; turned brass bell;

The very first steam unit introduced as Lionel HO in 1957. Note wire handrails at door, boiler front, and side — as well as the brass bell and full working valve gear. No lettering or numbers were used.

No. 0610, for the collector, the most challenging of all the Lionel steam locomotives. Note European-style windows, wire handrails on boiler, and working valve gear. Drive shaft and electric pickup wires can be seen for the motor located in the tender. Very fine window struts, almost always found broken.

	Gd	Exc	Mt

three pop-off valves; the Rivarossi signature, "COMO, Italy" and "1515" appear under the cab on the bottom of the frame. Two small jumper wires, as found on multiple-unit diesels, connect the locomotive and tender for electrical pickup, while a metal drawbar, attached with a screw at either end, provides a mechanical connection. The tender houses the motor, the power of which is transmitted to the locomotive gearbox by means of a flexible shaft. Plastic tender body, lettered "280" in heavy white printing, although this is not shown in the catalogue; wire handrails at the cab end; cast-metal tender frame, with lettering matching that on the locomotive frame. The arched cab windows help to distinguish the locomotive from Rivarossi Consolidations sold by other firms. Later, non-Lionel versions feature rectangular windows and different types of coal piles. Lionel's model was catalogued in 1957 as a separate item for $33.50; it also headed one freight set, number 5704, with six cars, which sold for $49.95. It carried no Lionel catalogue numbers or logos anywhere on the locomotive, however the number did appear on the carton. It is possible that the tender was available as described with the exception of a sheet-metal frame; verification of this variation is requested.

(A) Painted body.	100	175	250

Note: Mint in box seen by R. MacNary for $500.

(B) Unpainted body.	100	150	225

FAIRBANKS-MORSE DIESELS

A note on the prototype: the Rivarossi diesels are models of Fairbanks-Morse Company C-Liners. (The Fairbanks-Morse Company was famous for its World War II submarine diesels.) These diesels had an unusual design with opposed pistons. This apparently increased the amount of power available for a given volume. FM recognized that its diesel motor could be applied to locomotives. Eventually they offered three lines: 1600-, 2000-, and 2400-horsepower engines.

Frames and Motors

The frames on the earliest FM units are sheet-brass or steel, painted flat black (some blued). Both have a cast-metal weight riveted to the center. Fixed between the frame and weight is a strip of spring steel bent outward. The ends snap into the holes in the side of the shell to secure it to the frame. The frame itself has at its end two tabs that slide into holes in the rear of the shell. The jacks for the jumper wires are also present, but there is no window material. The front truck is bolted in place, and there is a solder joint for lighting purposes. The frame is actually a continuation from the early locomotive sold in the U.S. under

the Red Line name, which again shows the rush Lionel made to enter the HO market. The shells for frames of brass are made of Bakelite rather than polystyrene, as found on most other models. This appears to be the first type of the locomotive sold under the Lionel name. In the Richard Kughn Collection there is one A unit with WP markings; I have seen B units in WP and Wabash markings. All carry the Lionel logo, but no Lionel numbers are used. All other information listed on the FM units applies here, with the exception of truck side frames which are cast metal on the brass frame models. *Rare.*

The following information can be used to identify all Rivarossi diesel FM units catalogued as Lionel in 1957 (with the exception of the few brass frame models known to exist).

All powered A units with plastic or sheet-metal frames are equipped with hinge-mounted, articulated, gear-driven rear power trucks. All trucks have machined steel wheels with good electrical contact; all wheels are flanged, and two are equipped with rubber tires. They are good performers with good pulling power. The body has one-piece plastic construction with excellent rivet detail. The Rivarossi signature, the words "COMO, Italy", and the mold number 305 appear on the inside roof of each power unit as seen on p. 16. The units have no steps or ladders except on the pilot. The steps on the pilot help to distinquish Lionel units from models sold under the AHM label in the 1960s.

The late plastic frame of each unit is molded in clear plastic, with the floor being painted black. The inch-high, clear sides served as side reinforcement and as lenses for the number boards and headlights and as window glass for the doors of the unit. There is no window material in the cab itself. In the A unit a large lead weight is located at the very rear of the frame, and another weight made of ten or so thin metal plates rests in the middle of the frame just in front of the motor. These plates are riveted in place. The truck frames are plastic, with metal axle covers holding each axle in place. All units carry NMRA-type couplers at both ends. Each powered A and dummy A is lighted with one screw-based bulb, which is easily replaced. The body is fastened to the frame by four tabs built into the frame. They fit snugly into receiving holes in the side of each body. There are also two metal sockets on either side of the frame at the rear of each unit. These sockets accept small electrical jumper wires that transmit the power from the powered A through the B and into the dummy A for lighting purposes only.

The dummy B unit has much the same construction, with only minor changes. Trucks are bolted in place, and there are four electric sockets — one in each corner of the frame. With the exception of the rear power truck on the A unit, all trucks are fastened with a nut and bolt. The wire from one end to the other is bare of insulation. The Rivarossi signature and "COMO, Italy" are also in the roof of these units and the mold number is 1373. The B unit also has the painted black floor with clear sides. The B unit carries no weights and thus derails easily. The body fastens to the frame in the same manner as that of the powered A.

Comparison of the four frames found on the Rivarossi-made FM unit of 1957. Top shelf: The early and rare brass frame with cab-mounted weight, only found on Bakelite shells. Middle shelf: Plastic versions of frames used on dummy A and powered A units. Bottom: Frame for dummy B. Note the high clear plastic sides on these three units; they acted as windows. "Rivarossi" is found on all plastic frames but is covered by metal plate on some power units. Note: No weights found on dummy units.

Closeup of direct-drive Rivarossi motor, fixed and part of the truck. Note jumper wires (found on all FM units) to carry electricity to B unit. Note groove in lead weight that is part of shell.

Comparison of brass frame and plastic one with high plastic sides. See difference in motor and lead weight, with brass frame version having part #699 cast into its top.

Dummy A units are the same as powered A units with the exception of the weights; dummy A units carry none and also derail easily. There is a screw-based bulb at the front of the cab and the same two electric sockets. It has no electrical pickup of its own. Since no weights are riveted in the center of this unit, the Rivarossi name is visible on the outside frame without having to remove the shell.

Note: The wire handrails shown clearly in the 1957 catalogue did not appear on any FM unit with the exception of the two small rails on the nose of each A unit. This, it seems, is the reason why most units will be found with nose decals intact. All units did carry cast-on handrails at all door openings.

The following models are grouped in A(powered)-B(dummy)-A(powered) sets for each of the alphabetically listed road names. Remember that all numbers in parentheses indicate a catalogue number that does not appear on the car. All FM units listed as carrying the Lionel logo on their sides have the larger ⅛-inch-diameter logo.

CHICAGO AND NORTH WESTERN

(0500): Powered A unit; battery boxes, pilot, top row of side panels, and roof painted green; yellow lower side panels and nose; black pin

stripes separate colors; road name spelled out in reddish-orange lettering on the lower yellow side panels; wire handrails and the CNW winged decal herald appear on the nose; another logo decal appears under the first cab window; lighted; two decorative horns on roof; green, painted plastic truck side frames; no number on unit; catalogue number appears on carton; catalogued in 1957 as a separate unit at $15.95 or in A-B-A sets at $27.85; not catalogued in any set; very rare and prized.

	Gd	Exc	Mt
(A) With Lionel logo.	75	125	150
(B) Without Lionel logo.	65	100	125

(0520): Dummy B unit; painted to match the powered A unit; road name spread from door to door in the lower side panels; not lighted; no

Comparison of rear of FM shells, with Bakelite on left, showing two slots under the door for inserted tabs. Note also the rear of the truck of the plastic unit on the right, with cross brace of truck (not present on early truck frames). Each carries the Rivarossi name and part number on the frame.

The wire handrails on the nose of the FM unit protected the decal. Note rivet detail at top of pilot area and absence of windows in the cab.

	Gd	Exc	Mt

Lionel logo; no number on unit; catalogue number appears on the carton; catalogued in 1957 separately at $4.95 and as part of an A-B-A set; very rare and highly prized.   **60 80 150**

(0510): Dummy A unit; painted exactly as powered A unit; lighted; no Lionel logo; catalogued in 1957 as a separate item at $6.95 and in an A-B-A set at $27.85; not catalogued in any set; very rare and highly prized.   **60 80 150**

ILLINOIS CENTRAL

(0505): Powered A unit; light brown, painted body; ½" orange band on the lower side panels and nose; two yellow pin stripes separate the band from the floor and the brown portion of body; road name appears in brown lettering; black truck side frames, pilot, and battery boxes; no

Closeups of the only two models produced by Rivarossi not to have used silk screen-type lettering in the decoration of the shell. These two road names appear over gray cardstock with rubber-stamped lettering; the cardstock was glued to each of the A-B-A units. Truly rare.

	Gd	Exc	Mt

numbers; green IC logo decal appears on the nose, with wire handrails on either side; Lionel logo, also in brown, appears in the second orange side panel from the rear of the units; two black decorative horns on the roof; lighted; catalogue number appears on carton; catalogued in 1957 as a separate unit, in A-B-A sets, and at the head of set 5701 with five cars at $29; scarce but obtainable.

(A) Plastic body and frame. G. Horan Collection.
   80 90 100

(B) Bakelite body metal frame; rest of shell decoration as described. G. Bunza and K. Fairchild Collections.   **90 100 125**

(C) Plastic body, sheet-metal frame. G. Potts Collection.
   90 100 125

(0525): Dummy B unit; matches A unit, except orange band appears only on side panels; brown ends; no light; Lionel logo situated as described for A unit; no number on unit; catalogue number appears on carton; catalogued in 1957 as a separate unit at $4.95 and in an A-B-A combination; scarce but obtainable.   **50 70 90**

(0515): Dummy A unit; matches description of powered A unit; catalogue number appears on carton; catalogued in 1957 as a separate unit and in an A-B-A combination; very rare. **60 80 100**

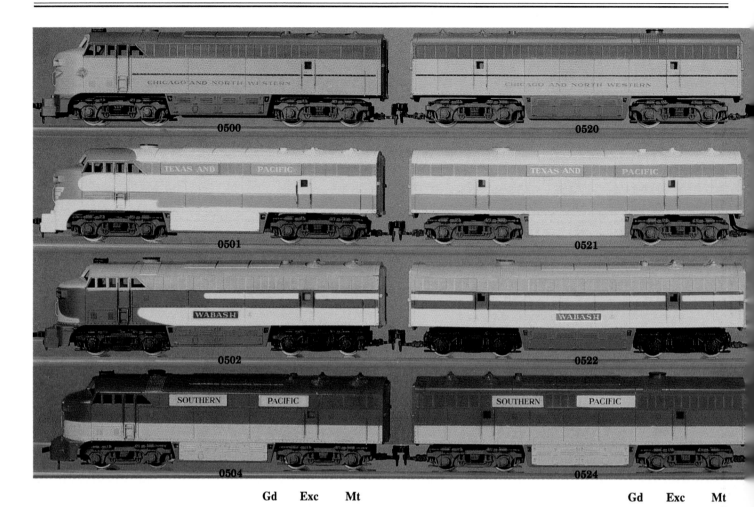

	Gd	Exc	Mt			Gd	Exc	Mt

SOUTHERN PACIFIC

(0504): Powered A unit; painted deep red; ½"-wide light gray stripe begins at the handrails on the nose and covers the bottom row of side panels and battery boxes; "Southern Pacific" decal under the headlight, protected by the wire handrails; road name printed in black letters on two gray cardstock boards, which are glued in place on the top row of side panels; stamped lettering; two black decorative horns; lighted; no number; darker gray truck side frames; catalogued in 1957 as a separate unit at $15.95 and in an A-B-A set. It is shown in the catalogue with black truck side frames, but they are found only in painted gray; very rare and highly prized.

	Gd	Exc	Mt
(A) With Lionel logo.	100	150	200
(B) Without Lionel logo.	90	100	125

(0524): Dummy B unit; painted to match exactly the A unit; lettering appears on two cardstock letterboards, as found on A unit; no light; no Lionel logo; catalogue number appears on carton; catalogued in 1957 at $4.95 and in A-B-A sets; very rare and highly prized.

	Gd	Exc	Mt
	90	125	150

(0514): Dummy A unit; all information regarding description of powered A unit applies here; catalogued in 1957 as a separate unit at $6.95 and in A-B-A sets; very rare and highly prized.

	Gd	Exc	Mt
(A) With Lionel logo.	90	125	150
(B) Without Lionel logo.	65	80	95

TEXAS AND PACIFIC

(0501): Powered A unit; very pale, painted bluish-gray body; flat white roof, pilot, battery boxes, and middle row of side panels; dark gray truck side frames; road name printed on two cardstock panels, glued to the top side panels; yellow "TP" winged herald decal on nose, just under

headlight; wire handrails; two black decorative horns; lighted; catalogue number appears on carton only; catalogued in 1957 as a separate item and in an A-B-A set; very rare.

	Gd	Exc	Mt
(A) With Lionel logo.	100	150	200
(B) Without Lionel logo.	80	100	125

(0521): Dummy B unit; painted to match powered A unit; road name appears on cardstock panels on top row of side panels; no light; catalogue number appears on carton; catalogued in 1957 as a separate unit and in A-B-A combinations only; very rare.

	Gd	Exc	Mt
	90	100	125

(0511): Dummy A unit; painted and decorated with decals exactly the same as powered A unit; lighted; catalogue number appears on carton; catalogued in 1957 as separate unit and in an A-B-A combination; very rare.

	Gd	Exc	Mt
	90	100	125

WABASH

(0502): Powered A unit; dark blue, painted body; light gray rear of unit, roof, nose, and top row of side panels; white band on lower side panels from just behind the front cab door to the rear of unit; ⅛" white stripe above the white band from just in front of the rear cab door to the rear of the unit; road name and Lionel logo appear in gold silkscreened lettering on the second and third panel in the white band; two wire handrails and the Wabash flag appear on the nose; excellent rivet detail; black plastic truck side frames; two black plastic decorative air horns; lighted; catalogue number appears on the carton; no number on unit itself; catalogued in 1957 as a separate item at $15.95, in an A-B-A set at $27.85, and in set 5702 with five cars at $39.95.

	Gd	Exc	Mt
	80	100	125

(0522): Dummy B unit; painted to match A unit; gray ends; white striping along the full length of unit; road name and Lionel logo appear

0510

0511

0512

0514

The last four road names offered as Lionel in A-B-A combos. All are of the plastic shell and frame variety and are not known to have ever come with brass frames. Note that the first, second, and fourth shelves show painted truck side frames, while the Wabash only came with black unpainted frames. The Texas and Pacific and the Southern Pacific are the only two units to have the road names in other than silkscreen lettering. Separate decorative horns are present on the cab roof with the only window glazing found on the unit side windows. All are very collectible.

	Gd	Exc	Mt

in the fourth and fifth white side panels; no other detail, number, or light; catalogue number appears on the carton; catalogued in 1957 in set 5702, as a separate item, and in an A-B-A set.

(A) Bakelite body; sheet-brass frame; rare. **NRS**
(B) Polystyrene plastic body; standard frame. **40 60 90**

(0512): Dummy A unit; all information regarding the powered A applies here, with the exception of the weights; no number on unit; catalogue number appears on carton; catalogued in 1957 as a separate unit and in an A-B-A set. This road name is somewhat common, thus variation (B) is fairly plentiful in the lower grades.
(A) Bakelite body; sheet-brass frame; rare. J. Jerome Collection.
50 125 150
(B) Polystyrene plastic body; standard frame. **40 60 90**

WESTERN PACIFIC

(0503): Powered A unit; body and truck side frames painted light semi-gloss gray; nose of unit, from below the windshield to the top of the pilot and the middle row of side panels, is deep orange; winged herald decal appears on nose just below headlight; wire handrails on nose; road name, in crisp black lettering, appears on the lower gray side panels; Lionel logo, also in black, also appears in these panels just in front of the rear door; lighted; two black decorative horns on the roof; no number on unit; catalogued in 1957 as a separate unit at $15.95, in an A-B-A set and in a five-car set, 5703, with A-B-A locomotives, at $45; scarce but obtainable.
(A) Light gray truck side frames, plastic frame. **75 100 125**
(B) Dark gray truck side frames, sheet-metal frame, plastic shell. J. Jerome, G. Potts Collections. **90 125 150**

	Gd	Exc	Mt

(0523): Dummy B unit; painted to match exactly the A unit; road name and Lionel logo appear in black lettering on the gray side panels; no light; no number; catalogue number appears on carton; catalogued in 1957 separately at $4.95, in an A-B-A set, and with set 5703 at $45; scarce.
60 80 100

(0513): Dummy A unit; description of powered unit applies here.
(A) Bakelite body; sheet-brass frame; rare. **NRS**
(B) Polystyrene plastic body; plastic frame. **60 80 100**
(C) Polystyrene plastic body, sheet-metal frame. G. Potts Collection.
60 80 100

BOXCARS

The boxcars sold in 1957 by Lionel were fine-looking models precisely engineered by Rivarossi of Italy, and they are among the scarcest of Lionel HO items. There are a total of *eight different boxcars*. With the exception of the 0864-1 Seaboard boxcar, all of the cars are standard 40-foot steel-type cars. All have metal door runners, sprung trucks, roofwalks (almost always matching the painted roof), plastic ladders, with NMRA-type couplers, crisp silkscreened lettering, and fine rivet detail. They are assembled of plastic parts. None are weighted for operation. The catalogue clearly shows under-the-floor detail, but none came with any car sold by Lionel. The eighth car, the Seaboard boxcar, reproduced a 40-foot wooden boxcar with outside bracing, and it carries all of the other detail previously mentioned.

None of the cars carry a Lionel catalogue number, but all of them have the Lionel logo, which appears in three different diameters on the car sides. The logo varies in diameter from $1/16$ inch to just

	Gd	Exc	Mt

over ⅛ inch in size. Another interesting distinction between Lionel and Rivarossi are floors. Rivarossi floors have detail, the words "COMO, Italia   Made in Italy" and the Rivarossi signature on the outside of the floor. The Lionel floor carries no detail parts, although there are cast-on receptacles to receive them. The words "COMO Italia", mold number "1228", and the Rivarossi name *in print* also appear on some of the floors, but there is no signature. There are also coupler pockets cast into the floors of both Lionel and Rivarossi cars. These pockets are not used on the Lionel cars, as they are equipped with the talgo trucks and couplers. It is believed that the State of Maine, B & O, Timken, Pacemaker, and Rutland boxcars are the only cars made exclusively for the Lionel Corporation. The other three road names were sold in the Rivarossi line before 1957 and can be found with the detail parts, with the exception of the Lionel logo. The cars sold for $3.75 each in 1957, but range in value now from $40 to $100 depending on condition. All are most difficult to find and much sought after by HO collectors. Lionel's catalogue number does appear on the cartons.

104   See (0864-125)

(0864-1) SEABOARD: Painted tuscan body; white lettering; "15412" to the left of door, under road name; ⅛"-diameter Lionel logo appears to the right of door, in the last panel "LIONEL"; catalogue number appears on carton; catalogued 1957; catalogued again in 1958, without illustration; rare. This car is the only wooden-type boxcar offered in the Lionel HO line.   **75   95   125**

(0864-25) NEW YORK CENTRAL "PACEMAKER": Painted gray and red; solid red door; white lettering; ¹⁄₁₆"-diameter Lionel logo appears on the fourth gray panel to the left of the door; "NYC / 174478" on car side; catalogued in 1957 and shown without steps, although steps are found on car; catalogued also in 1958, during Athearn's production, but no longer available then.   **80   100   120**

(0864-50) STATE OF MAINE: Painted in the well-known red, white, and blue paint scheme; black door guides and ladders; blue and white lettering; ¹⁄₁₆"- diameter Lionel logo on red portion of the third side panel to the right of the door; red, white and blue door; blue roof and roofwalk; blue "2300" to the left of door; the car does have steps, although none are shown in the catalogue. By 1958 Athearn was making Lionel HO, but the Rivarossi car was still depicted in the catalogue.

(A) Extremely rare variation with a decal showing a potato on the white panel to the left of the door.   **NRS**

(B) No potato decal.   **70   95   125**

(0864-75) BALTIMORE & OHIO SENTINEL: Beautifully painted in the silver and blue Sentinel colors with matching striped door; one of three boxcars to carry a decal; "Sentinel / FAST FREIGHT SERVICE" logo appears on a bright yellow decal to the right of the door; a white, ⅛"-diameter Lionel logo appears next to the ladder and just below the decal; "466464" on car side; catalogued for only one year, 1957; very difficult to find in good condition.   **75   125   150**

(0864-100) NEW HAVEN: Black; orange door; large, white lettering; "36409" at right of door; Lionel logo appears to the right of the door in

The top two shelves show two of the more readily found road names of the A-B-A combos available as Lionel models in 1957. Lucky are the collectors who are able to collect all eighteen models. On the bottom shelf: The first stage of production (with the first stage of decoration above) of an unoffered unmarked Santa Fe A-B, which shows that Lionel was thinking of adding more road names to its line. The Western Pacific is known to have been available with a brass frame and Bakelite shell. Note color matching side frames on these units.

	Gd	Exc	Mt

the second panel; catalogue number appears on carton; catalogued in 1957-58.

	Gd	Exc	Mt
(A) Dull, painted black body; solid orange, painted door; large Lionel logo.	75	100	125
(B) Similar to (A), except smaller logo; sometimes this logo is hidden by the door guide.	50	75	100
(C) Unpainted, glossy black body; solid orange, unpainted door; large Lionel logo.	50	75	100
(D) Similar to (C), except smaller logo.	50	75	100

(0864-125) RUTLAND: Painted yellow and green body; solid yellow door; darker green lettering on yellow portion of side; small Lionel logo appears on the fourth green panel to the right of door; small "104" to the left of door; with steps; catalogued in 1957-58 and shown without steps. The color of the car as shown in the two catalogues is quite different, but it was the Rivarossi car pictured in 1958. There is some question whether Athearn may have made this car in 1958-59; neither author has seen such a car.   **75   100   125**

(0864-150) MINNEAPOLIS & ST. LOUIS: Bright red; heavyweight lettering; "54652" in the second and third panel to the left of the door; unpainted, black plastic door, roofwalk, and ladders; Lionel logo appears in the second panel to the right of the door. The car has steps, though none were shown in the catalogue; catalogued in 1957. This boxcar and the NYC Pacemaker cars were the only boxcars lettered with only a road name, number, and herald. The lack of other markings gave these cars a very plain appearance. In 1958 Athearn reproduced this car with the same catalogue number; the Athearn car appeared in set 5709, and it is described in Chapter IV.

	Gd	Exc	Mt
(A) Painted body; road name spelled out across body is outlined in thin white striping; small Lionel logo, less than 1/16" diameter.	50	60	80
(B) Unpainted body; road name spelled out across body is outlined in thin white striping; larger 1/8" diameter logo.	40	55	65
(C) Same as (A) but solid white stripe with red lettering including herald. Rare. G. Bunza Collection.	60	80	100
(D) Sames as (A) but with red painted doors. J. Jerome, T. Armenti Collections.			NRS

(0864-175) TIMKEN: Painted bright yellow; 1/2"-wide white band on side and door; black and dark blue lettering; third car to have a decal; "ROLLER / FREIGHT" on a red and white decal to the right of the door; 1/16"-diameter Lionel logo appears just below the decal in the fourth panel; "646450" appears to the left of the door; catalogued in 1957; also pictured in 1958 and 1959, during Athearn production years. The

Timken and B & O Sentinel cars are the only boxcars that come close to carrying a Lionel catalogue number on the car side.

	Gd	Exc	Mt
	75	90	125

2300:	See (0864-50)
15412:	See (0864-1)
36409:	See (0864-100)
54652:	See (0864-150)
174478:	See (0864-25)
466464:	See (0864-75)
646450:	See (0864-175)

CABOOSES AND CRANE CARS

These cars are grouped together (as flats could be also) because these are all based on the same design, are made from the same mold, and differ only in the type of car they eventually became. Each car is molded in plastic of the same color the car is painted; however, the undersides are not painted. The cast-on steps are lighter and much smaller in width and length than those found on the boxcars. "Made in Italy" and "Rivarossi" also appear on these cars, but in much smaller lettering. The mold number, too, appears, as do the receptacle for the brake and valve, but once again no detail came with the cars. The red Reading and the black Illinois Central car body, no matter how they were used, were the only two cars in the entire line that did not have a road name spelled out on their sides.

Toward the end of 1957 some of these cars appeared as uncatalogued items. We attribute this fact to Rivarossi's knowledge that they would soon lose their contract to supply Lionel, their biggest American buyer. It was less expensive for them to add sidewalls, stakes, and pipe loads from their own line of cars to the cars made for Lionel and to ship them as uncatalogued items. These uncatalogued cars are all highly prized with their loads included.

Although an eight-wheel red caboose with Lionel lettering appears on the cover of the 1957 catalogue, this type of car was neither made nor sold by Lionel in 1957. The Reading bobber caboose, like the Seaboard boxcar, never appeared in the catalogue after 1957. Strange as it may seem, there were six road names used on the diesel units in 1957, but only two road names used on cabooses. Neither matches a locomotive road name. This oversight, like the others, can be attributed to Lionel's hasty entry into the HO market. The derrick, flatcars, and work cabooses manufactured by Rivarossi used the arch bar-type sprung truck, while the other types of rolling stock used the Bittendorf metal sprung truck. G. Bunza comment.

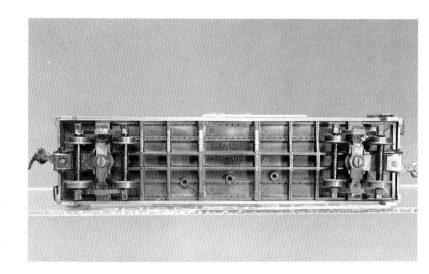

Underside of Rivarossi boxcar. Note talgo trucks screwed on with Rivarossi name and part number present, as it is on all Rivarossi rolling stock. Note also rivet detail and absence of air cylinders and brake valves.

Eight of the most attractive Rivarossi boxcars — the most sought after by Lionel HO collectors. The first and only wooden-type car offered by Lionel, the 0864-1, can be considered one of the rarest, followed by the State of Maine with the potato logo. The two cars on the bottom left are shown without the Lionel logo. Note the clear gloss lettering and the detailing of the ladders and roofwalks.

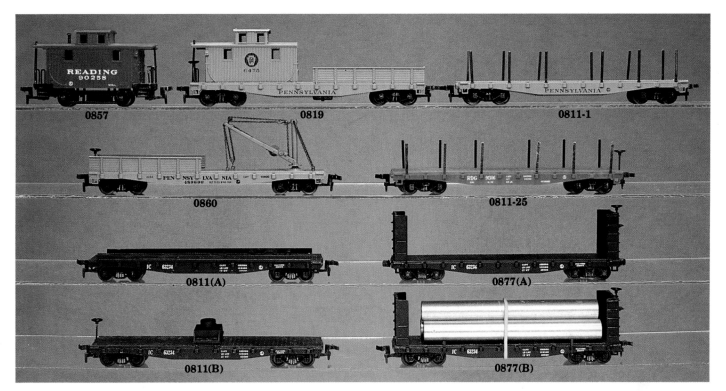

Shown are all the cabooses, flatcars, and work cars of Rivarossi make, including the only four-wheeled caboose and the only 40-foot flatcar. This long flat was used for all of the cars on the bottom three shelves, with only color or load changing; the derrick boom was added for the gray 0860, while stakes made the difference in the red 0811-25. The black IC had sidewalls or mounting block added and became the 0811(A) and (B), with the same body having bulkhead walls added to its end, with or without pipe, to become the 0877(A) or (B). Lionel was also to utilize this one car, with small changes, to create many different models.

	Gd	Exc	Mt

(0819) PENNSYLVANIA WORK CABOOSE: Painted gray; black lettering; road name, herald, Lionel logo, and "6475" appear on car side; separate brakewheel, ladder, grab-irons, and smokestack in black; marker lights cast onto the end of the cab; same body used on the 0811-1 gray flatcar; catalogue number appears on carton; catalogued in 1957 only. **35 50 65**

(0857) READING BOBBER-TYPE CABOOSE: Red, painted body; unpainted, black plastic and metal frame; white lettering; "READING", "90258", and the Lionel logo appear on side; wire handrails; separate ladders at each end, brakewheel, and smokestack; cast-on marker lights; mold number "1118", "Rivarossi" and "COMO, Italy" appear at one end of the plastic frame; this is the only car with body-mounted couplers, although the pockets are cast into the floor of every Rivarossi car; catalogue number appears on carton; catalogued in 1957. **35 50 60**

(0860) PENNSYLVANIA CRANE CAR: Painted gray; heavy black lettering; Lionel logo and "489690" on side; no toolboxes; plastic side fences run half the length of the car, opposite the crane end; highly detailed crane, with cranks, cogs, and hooks; fine chain from the top of the boom and back to the floor, secured in place with small wire eyelets; catalogue number appears on carton; catalogued in 1957-58, at $4.25; because of the delicate detail on the car, it is most difficult to find with the boom unbroken and the chain intact. The car is the only one of the three offered as Lionel to have its main boom cast into the floor of the car. **60 90 125**

6475: See (0819)

90258: See (0857)

489690: See (0860)

	Gd	Exc	Mt

FLATCARS AND MISCELLANEOUS CARS

(0811) ILLINOIS CENTRAL FLATCAR: Uncatalogued; standard flatcar also used as 0877 miscellaneous car; black, painted body; white lettering, with the initials "IC" and the number "63234"; Lionel logo appears to the right of the lettering; standing brakewheel; "0811" appears on the carton; the liner of the carton points to the fact that there was no load with the car; first appeared at the end of 1957; extremely rare.

(A) ⅛"-high sidewalls the length of the car; four pockets to accept a truck trailer. **35 45 60**

(B) Black plastic mounting platform with square base and round top held on the car with four steel stakes; this platform may have been intended for some other load never actually made for the car. **35 45 60**

(0811-1) PENNSYLVANIA FLATCAR: Light gray, painted body; "PENNSYLVANIA" in heavy black lettering; black Lionel logo appears in the neighboring side panel; no additional lettering; twelve black plastic stakes; floor has four pre-drilled holes to accept the work caboose cab, which is used with this same flatcar body to produce the gray work caboose; catalogued in 1957 only, at $2.25; hard to find with the stakes. **30 45 60**

(0811-25) READING FLATCAR: Bright red, painted body; heavy white lettering, with "RDG" initials; numbered "91306"; Lionel logo appears in the third side panel on the right side of the car; separate brakewheel and twelve black plastic stakes; no load; catalogued 1957-58 at $2.25; very rare in mint condition. **30 40 50**

The gondolas, reefers, and stock cars offered in 1957 present challenges to today's HO collector. The gondolas on the top shelf were one-piece castings that never included a load. The silver IC reefer on the bottom shelf is a striking car, but the second shelf holds what now seems to be a harder-to-find car, the orange SF, with the "all the way" markings, followed by the yellow FGE. The yellow MKT stock car was the only stock car available. Note the slanted steps of these cars with sprung trucks, separate ladders, roofwalks, and Lionel logos clearly seen. Only two of the reefer names were available in the 1958 Athearn production: 0872-1 and 0872-50.

	Gd	Exc	Mt

(0877) ILLINOIS CENTRAL MISCELLANEOUS CAR: With the exception of the bulkhead ends added to the car, it is exactly the same as the black 0811; separate brakewheel; catalogue number does not appear on carton; catalogued in 1957 at $2.50 without a load.

(A) Early 1957; no load.   30   40   50

(B) Late 1957; three silver metal pipes held in place with four steel stakes and a yellow rubber band; extremely rare with load intact.
                                                40   50   75

63234: See (0811)
91306: See (0811-25)

GONDOLAS

Returning to the cover of the 1957 catalogue folder, we can plainly see a yellow gondola, but there were no yellow gondolas sold that year. There were only two gondolas available in 1957; both were the 40-foot cars. There were changes in the mold used on these cars, which have one-piece plastic construction. There are only five floor braces. The fine rivet detail remains, as does the cast-on receptacle to receive the valves, reservoir, etc. These receptacles are much thicker than those found on any other car. The steps are much heavier than those used on the boxcars. The underside of the cars read "Made in Italy" and "Rivarossi". The same trucks and couplers used on the boxcars are found on the gondolas. Both cars were molded in colored plastic, with each shell being the same color as it would be painted.

(0862-1) PENNSYLVANIA: Tuscan red, painted body; heavy white lettering; PRR herald; Lionel logo appears in the center of the last panel, just above the floor line; separate brakewheel; numbered "357843"; no load; catalogued in 1957 only at $2.25. Fairly common.
                                                30   40   60

(0862-25) MICHIGAN CENTRAL: Flat black, painted body; white, stamped lettering; "M.C.R.R."; Lionel logo appears in the last side panel; numbered "15317"; no load; catalogued in 1957 only, at $2.25. This particular car has lettering in seven of eight side panels, thus having a very crowded appearance; it is also the only car not having silkscreened lettering.
                                                20   30   40

15317: See (0862-25)
357843: See (0862-1)

REFRIGERATOR CARS

Because Rivarossi produced trains for Lionel for only one year, it is difficult to locate the three reefer cars and one stock car carried in the 1957 line. The information regarding trucks, couplers, and construction, which was used to identify the boxcars, applies to reefers. The floor, trucks, and printing on the floor are exactly the same. Of course, the colors, the road names, and the car numbers differ. All of the lettering is silkscreened. Information received from many collectors seems to indicate that the 0872-1 is the most difficult of the three reefers to locate.

(0872-1) FRUIT GROWERS EXPRESS: Bright yellow, painted sides; tuscan ends, roof, and roofwalk; black plastic brakewheel and ladder; heavy black lettering; 1/8"-diameter Lionel logo appears in the last panel to the right of the door; doors do not open, but the handle and hinges are raised and outlined in black, thus giving the appearance of operability; "39783" on car side; catalogued in 1957-58 only; very difficult to find.   50   75   125

(0872-25) ILLINOIS CENTRAL: Bright silver, painted body and roofwalk; deep, glossy green lettering, including road name, herald, and car number "51604"; thin green pin stripes along sill; 1/8"-diameter

Speculation has it that the cars shown here were being considered in a possible expansion of the Lionel line. The handmade mock-up of the crane, made of sheet styrene, was never made, while the blue car could have been part of a girl's train in HO but also was never made. The wooden-type boxcar was already in the line, apparently new road names were being considered. The next boxcar could have been a Monon under consideration; one did appear in the Athearn production. The green stock car could have been a Santa Fe 1958-1959 while the three-dome tank did not appear as Lionel until 1974 in the MPC HO line. Last but not least, the bay window caboose. The Varney shell would have been a snap for Lionel to copy, and add to their HO line. No further information could be obtained from Lionel or Rivarossi; this information remains speculation.

	Gd	Exc	Mt

Lionel logo appears in the last panel to the right of the door; catalogued in 1957-58 at $2.95 and $2.50, respectively; this car has an outstanding appearance, and it would certainly delight any collector to find it at or near the original price. **40 80 100**

(0872-50) A.T.S.F. EL CAPITAN: Dark orange, painted sides; black roof, roofwalk, and ends; heavy black lettering; "El Capitan" slogan on one side of car, "SHIP AND TRAVEL" slogan on other; black and white Santa Fe cross herald located in the fourth panel to the left of door; "8175" appears directly below herald; 1/8"-diameter Lionel logo located in the last side panel to the right of the door; door and hinges outlined in raised black; separate brakewheel and ladders; catalogued in 1957; Rivarossi car shown again in 1958 catalogue, although Athearn had assumed production; illustration shows no steps. Most common of the three. **40 60 80**

8175: See (0872-50)
39783: See (0872-1)
51604: See (0872-25)

	Gd	Exc	Mt

STOCK CARS

The MKT cattle car is the only cattle car that Lionel sold in 1957. Although some other companies marketed much the same car, even down to the same number, it is nevertheless a desirable piece for the HO collector and as difficult to find as the other Rivarossi pieces.

502 See (0866)

(0866) M K T: Bright yellow, painted sides and ends; tuscan roof and roofwalk; black lettering; unpainted black plastic brakewheel and plastic ladders; working door with steel guides; "The Katy" on letterboard at one side of door; "502" on letterboard on opposite side of door; black Lionel logo appears at floor line in the third panel to the left of the door; catalogued in 1957-58 at $3.25 and $2.50, respectively; Rivarossi car illustrated in 1958; steps shown. The Lionel logo is the only difference between this car and those sold under different brand names. **40 60 90**

CHAPTER IV
Athearn to the Rescue: HO In 1958

Lionel's logo does appear, in either of two sizes, on most of the Athearn items made from 1958 to 1960, although there are some cars that do not have a logo. These cars typically appear in 1958 train sets. The first runs of Lionel/Athearn had such a small logo that it hardly could be seen. It measured only $\frac{1}{16}$-inch in diameter. On later cars, a larger, $\frac{1}{8}$-inch logo appears. The position of the logo varies somewhat. The Athearn name itself did not appear on any model manufactured by Athearn since the early cast-metal power frames used in their own line of HO in the early 1950s. The following cars can be found in early 1958 Lionel sets without the logo on them:

• Black Erie Flatcar with two automobiles
• Blue Wabash Boxcar
• Brown LV Hopper
• Orange El Capitan Reefer
• Orange Gulf Tank
• Red UP Crane
• Tuscan Michigan Central Gondola
• Tuscan Reading Flatcar with stakes
• Yellow Fruit Growers Express Reefer

The 1958 catalogue clearly shows Lionel numbers on the Athearn cars, but only a few passenger cars were made that way. All other items carried only Athearn numbers on the items and Lionel numbers on the cartons.

Lionel cars have other features not found on the cars sold under the Athearn label. Both Lionel and Athearn reefers have operating doors and ice hatches (contemporary Athearn reefers do not have operating doors). The boxcars all have an early door that rides inside separate door guides. The Athearn claw foot-type door appears only on one Lionel car, the 0866-25 Santa Fe stock car. The simple sliding door used on Lionel cars operates more freely than the claw foot door, but the latter is still used on current Athearn models. The brakewheels, roofwalk, and external door guides are press-fit into holes in the body and sometimes painted to match the body color. Steps, grab-irons, and ladders are details in the body casting.

The Athearn cars have good rivet detail, and they are weighted with a metal strip held between the floor and the undercarriage of the car. All of the Athearn cars sold as Lionel products have sprung metal trucks and body-mounted NMRA couplers. The boxcars have doors that slide inside external guides, while the refrigerator cars have working plug doors and ice hatches. The cabooses are detailed with metal ladders and wire handrails. Athearn really cannot take credit for introducing most of these external details as most were on the market in wooden kits from many manufacturers as far back as the early 1940s. The trucks and couplers are screw-mounted on all the Athearn-made cars for Lionel.

Motive Power

Athearn's 1958 HO line provided many of the familiar Lionel road names and paint schemes. F-7 diesels in separate A-B-A combinations were available in road names that included Denver and Rio Grande 0530, Milwaukee Road 0531, Baltimore and Ohio 0532, and New Haven 0533. Also new were the Virginian rectifier 0590 and the GP-9 in Milwaukee Road 0585 and Wabash 0580 liveries. Later, the rectifier was decorated by Lionel for Pennsylvania (1960) and New Haven (1959–1960) liveries.[1]

The 1958 consumer catalogue states that the Virginian rectifier is a model of GE's type El-C 3300 electric locomotive. This is one piece that was produced under both corporate names, Lionel and Athearn. The Athearn 1958–1959 catalogue flyer clearly shows the Virginian rectifier and states: "New, the Virginian Rectifier, a kit with power, is $7.95." It has number "0590" on the cab. Close scrutiny of the picture in the Athearn catalogue reveals a faint "Blt. by Lionel" on the cab. If Athearn made the piece, then why did they use Lionel's photo? Our research has shown that Athearn did not make the cab for the Virginian rectifier — Lionel did. The Lionel part number "0590-5" is on the inside of the cabs of both the Athearn and Lionel/Athearn pieces. In 1958 Athearn made the motor mechanism and frame. The version sold under the Athearn label came with silver trucks and frame, no herald decal, no lights, and no reflective material inside the body. Athearn's model featured wire handrails, whereas Lionel had none. The Athearn version, which carried "0590" at the end of the long hood, was not heavily advertised; it disappeared from the market in late 1958 or early 1959.

The Lionel/Athearn version (the model sold under the Lionel label) differs somewhat from the Athearn version. It has chemically blackened trucks and frames in some cases, though it may be found with the silver trucks and frames. (Trucks and frames are interchangeable between these models.) The road name on Lionel's model appears lower on the side and in lighter yellow print than on the Athearn version. A herald decal appears on its front hood just below the headlight. The Lionel version also has a headlight and reflective material in the headlight area. A black horn appears above the cab headlight. "Blt. by Lionel" (often in capital letters and on two lines) is rubber-stamped on each side of the short hood; however, there is no Lionel logo per se. Both versions feature the Athearn Hi-F rubber band drive. Later, Lionel introduced its own mechanism for the New Haven (1959–1960) and Pennsylvania (1960) rectifiers. Since 1958 Athearn has not produced any rectifier locomotives, which probably indicates that Athearn does not have the dies. Whether or not the tooling has been preserved was unknown until 1991 when I discovered Lionel still held the tooling. General Mills' attempted reuse of the die in 1973 met with failure.

The 1958 rectifiers, GP-9s, and Husky-type switchers, 0560 D & RG and 0570 Navy Yard, were all belt-driven locomotives. Although Lionel promoted the idea that belt-driven locomotives were super quiet, the company did not convince consumers that belts were better than gears. The "neoprene belts" were O ring transmissions positioned between the motor shaft and the drive axles. They were not consistent with the quality that Lionel usually produced, and they caused headaches for service stations. The rubber belts, Lenny Dean explained, "went bad and expanded as we tried to store them in our warehouses." They were a "severe service manager's nightmare, not knowing whether the shipment

A comparison of Hi-F drives used on the Athearn-manufactured power units of 1958-1959 (none were marked with the Athearn name). Top: GP-9 and rectifier, unfinished metal 90 percent of the time but blackened in small number of cases. All units shown are lighted (power transmitted by four rubber bands). Bottom: Husky drive with same light and motor but using only one shaft.

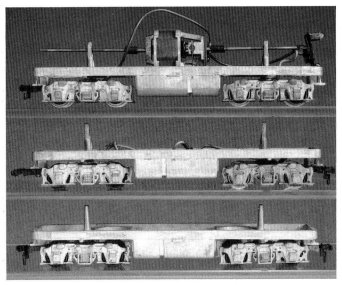

1958-1959 Athearn F unit frames as found on A-B-A combination. Top: Power A frame, lighted. Middle and bottom: Dummy B and A frames. Trucks were held with rubber washers on the dummy units. Neither were lighted. The Athearn name is not present on frames used for Lionel models. Dummy F unit trucks were equipped with thin metal axles and plastic wheels.

Different types of black plastic frames used on the Athearn-built 40-foot and 50-foot flatcars. Left to right: 40-foot 0800 airplane car, 50-foot 0830 piggyback, two road names for the 0801 boat car, with same frame. These frames were slightly different from those used on the Lionel-made cars.

of neoprene drive bands to a service station was a fresh or shopworn, dryrotted batch of rubber belts."[2]

The Athearn line continued with a little 0570 Navy switcher (black shell painted blue; Hi-F drive) and a Denver & Rio Grande 0560 snowplow. The Lionel logo (L within a circle) distinguishes the Lionel/Athearn piece, which has black and yellow or black and orange cab sides and blade. In 1958 both yard switchers had Athearn rubber band drives. By 1959 Lionel had begun to produce its own gear-driven mechanisms, along with a pretty close copy of the Athearn Husky-type shell. The road names of 1958 were not used again.

The Boston & Maine 0615LT (4-6-2) Pacific with full Walschaerts valve gear, which Lionel catalogued in 1958, has eluded HO collectors for good reason: it was never made. Athearn designed this piece, with a Hi-F rubber band drive, for its own line, but preproduction showed the drive to be terribly inappropriate for a steam locomotive. Athearn also found that the plastic drive wheels originally designed for the locomotive would collect metal from the rails and become too slick for sufficient traction. Unsatisfied with the samples, Athearn removed the locomotive from the production schedule. The company later designed a gear-driven mechanism for this locomotive pictured in Chapter VI, but Lionel had begun its own production by that time. There is no evidence that preproduction samples were made for Lionel. It is interesting to note that the engine depicted in Lionel's 1958 catalogue with "full Walschaerts valve gear" is actually a Fleishmann HO Pacific made in Germany.

Rolling Stock

New rolling stock made by Athearn in 1958 included a 0800 flatcar with airplane, 0801 flatcar with boat, 0879 Wrecker Crane, 0815 Gulf Chemical car, 0860 derrick car, 0814 Auto-Loader (which Lionel requested from Athearn), 0824 flatcar with two automobiles, 0817 Milwaukee caboose, 0865 gondola with canisters, 0819-100 Boston & Maine work caboose which also came in other road names, 0866-25 Santa Fe cattle car, 0836 Lehigh Valley hopper, 0877 miscellaneous car, and 0872-1 Fruit Growers Express. The 0864 Lionel HO boxcar series was introduced with all the O Gauge 6464-series road names such as State of Maine, Monon, Minneapolis & St. Louis, Timken, Rutland, etc., and a line of New Haven passenger cars (0700-0703). Track for 1958 train sets was produced by Atlas Tool & Die Co., while all of the accessories were produced by Lionel.

The 5714 New Haven passenger set released in 1958 has different numbers on the boxes and cars, similar to some of American Flyer's practices. In other words, the number on the car is different from the catalogue or order number that appears on the box end and in the catalogue. Athearn usually decorated rolling stock with prototypical numbers, while Lionel used their catalogue number, which was part of a series for order and inventory control. This inconsistency was resolved after Lionel began to produce its own line in 1959. The New Haven F-7s had a Lionel catalogue number of 0533. The Athearn number on the side was "0272". An orange Lionel "L" also appeared on the sides. The set also came with a Lionel number 0700 baggage which was numbered "3406" in black on the side. A Lionel 07011 Pullman actually numbered "3150", an 0702 vista dome numbered "500" on the side, and a 0703 observation car numbered "3246". There are many inconsistencies with Lionel/Athearn lettering. The Athearn-made passenger cars are the only models never to carry the Lionel logo.

Some mint pieces have shown up in Lionel boxes without the logos in freight-type rolling stock. But — a word of caution to the novice — if a piece of Athearn equipment is not in its original box, it should be accepted as Lionel only if it has the Lionel logo on it. **Note:** the suffix numbers used in the Athearn models listings only appeared on the cartons.

Many Lionel/Athearn items fall into the "scarce" or "rare" categories of Lionel HO models, and although one might expect to pay dearly for a particular item, it may still elude the collector.

LIONEL/ATHEARN LOCOMOTIVES

The following describes the mechanisms used in these locomotives, so that the detailed descriptions of individual units may be limited to body shell, trim, paint scheme, and lettering. See Chapter IX for illustrations of trucks, frames, and mechanisms.

Lionel/Athearn Mechanisms

The F-7 Mechanism

All of the Athearn locomotives sold by Lionel in 1958–1959 were powered with the Hi-F rubber band drive, which Athearn had introduced in 1956. This includes the F-7 units in four road names, one rectifier, one Hustler, one snowplow, and two geeps marketed in Lionel packaging.

The frame of the F-7 is a one-piece metal casting; the trucks are also cast in metal with drum-type axles approximately 3/8-inch in diameter. The five-pole, double-shaft motor is fastened to the center of the frame with a single screw. The frame also has two vertical lugs cast into it, both above and below the floor of the frame. The bottom portion of the lug passes through the truck frame and acts as a pivot for the trucks. On dummy A and B units the trucks are secured to these lugs with a small rubber washer that slips over the tip of the lug. The top portion of the lug has a small drilled hole in it and acts as a guide for the motor shaft extension. This extension is a length of steel rod held to the motor shaft with a rubber coupling. The wire extensions and lugs are found on all Lionel band-driven units built by Athearn, with the exception of the Hustler locomotive. Four black neoprene rubber bands couple the shaft and the four drum-type axles to drive all eight wheels on all power units. The models have electrical pickup in both trucks; they have metal wheel sets and plastic axles. All powered units are lighted with a bulb that is retained by a metal clip fastened to the front of the frame with a single screw.

The frame also has cast-on coupler pads at each end below the floor line and tabs at either side. The tabs hold the shell to the frame while the

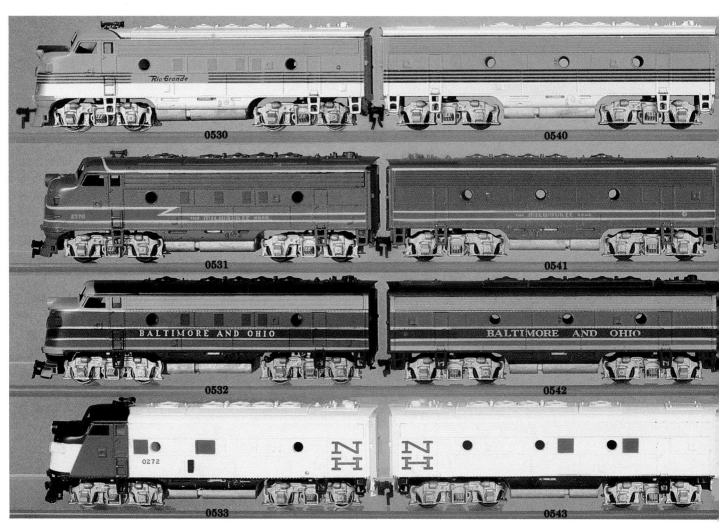

coupler pads accept both the coupler and coupler housing, again fastened with one screw. Except those used to mount the couplers, there are no screws in dummy A or B units. Most dummy models have thin metal axles and plastic wheels. To service the A units, the front coupler must be removed through the opening in the front of the shell. On powered units, the trucks must be disassembled in order to replace the rubber bands. This is accomplished by removing two small screws at the top of the truck frame, slipping the top of the band over the drum axle, and reassembling the truck. It was a tedious job for a new modeler. The very early Athearn frames carry the Athearn name cast onto the bottom, but they were never used on units sold as Lionel. Lionel units came with both silver and blackened trucks and frames.

The Rectifier and GP-9 Mechanism

The same frame appears on both the electric and GP-9. It is square at both ends, and it has a ½-inch extension to support the platform and steps at each end of the locomotive shell and to hold the coupler pad. The headlight fixture is fastened under the front of the frame with the same screw that holds the front coupler. The two round tabs on each side of the frame secure the shell. The coupler pockets and covers on these frames are cast metal. Just to the rear of the fuel tanks, there are two black plastic air tanks pressed into a hole in the top of the frame. The motor and drive shaft are the same as those used on F units. The frame and trucks are unpainted silvery metal, with a small number blackened.

Hustler Mechanisms

The Hustler frame and motor designs follow the basic pattern of the other mechanism. The frame is cast metal, and there is the same

0550

0551

0552

0553

five-pole double-shaft motor. Drum-type axles and metal wheel sets are driven by rubber bands mounted on the drive shafts. No wire extensions appear. The model is equipped with the same type of light fixture as found on the F-7; it is located in the cab end of the locomotive. The couplers are slightly different, in that they are mounted in notches in the frame; however, they do have a metal cover, which is attached with a screw. To replace the rubber band, one has to remove the two screws from the right side of the frame, but first the body shell must be removed to reveal these concealed screws. The mechanism for the Rio Grande snowplow is blackened, but otherwise similar.

Listings of EMD F-7 Diesels

The following locomotives are grouped in A-B-A sets for each of the road names, which are organized alphabetically. These are followed by individual powered units.

51: See (0570)
0272: See (0533)
452: See (0580)

BALTIMORE AND OHIO

(0532): Powered A unit; flat black, painted roof; gray nose and windshield extending past the cab windows to the end of the body; royal blue nose and side panels; herald appears on decal located under the lower headlight on a black stripe that runs back to the rear of the unit and separates the blue panel; all colors separated by gold pin stripes; cast-on number boards; two headlights and decorative horns; ¹⁄₁₆"-diameter Lionel logo located on the black stripe between the cab door and end of the body; these are the most common of the F units; catalogue number appears on carton, but not on unit. The gray and blue used on units sold by Athearn of the same period are much darker in shading. Catalogued in 1958 only for separate sale and in set 5713. Ken Fairchild comment.

	Gd	Exc	Mt
	40	60	100

(0542): Dummy B unit; flat black roof and ends; sides match those on powered A unit; ¹⁄₁₆"-diameter gold Lionel logo located above ladder in last side panel; road name in gold lettering on black stripe. Catalogued same as 0532.   35   45   65

(0552): Dummy A unit; matches description of powered A unit; catalogued in 1958 for separate sale or in A-B-A combination and in set 5713, with A-B diesels.   35   45   65

(DENVER &) RIO GRANDE

(0530): Powered A unit; roof painted silver, from above the cab windows back to the end of the roof, and matching lower side panels, air tank covers, and ladders; pale, flat orangish-yellow cab roof, end, headlight area, and top two sets of side panels; single black pin stripe between orange and silver at roof line; four black pin stripes on the side panels; black nose top; lower side striping broken approximately 1½" above the air tanks, where the road name appears in black; road name appears a second time in black on a decal located just above the pilot; two clear

The twelve F-7 units made by Athearn and available as Lionel in 1958-1959. Close inspection of the photo shows the Lionel logo appearing in the same ¹⁄₁₆-inch size on all units with that logo. Some F units did come in the 1958 sets and did not show the Lionel logo — such as the two B & O units pictured, along with the NH B unit on the fourth shelf or the Rio Grande B unit on the first. Note different areas where logos appear. These sets were part of the George Horan Collection in 1986. I leave it up to the buyer to accept or reject a model as Lionel if the logo is not present; I would reject it if not in its original box.

Gd Exc Mt

plastic headlight lenses; two black plastic horns, number boards, and steps; available for separate sale in A-B-A combinations or in set 5715, with an A-A combination; Lionel catalogue numbers appear only on the carton; catalogued in 1958 only.

(A) Lionel logo 1/16", on lower side panel just above last cab ladder. **35 50 100**

(B) Lionel logo appears above the black striping in the last orangish side panel; logo is larger and more easily seen; uncatalogued; 1959. **35 50 100**

(0540): Dummy B unit; fully painted silver roof and matching lower side panels; black striping as described for A unit; eight cast-on steps; no lettering or numbers.

(A) Lionel logo 1/16", on lower side panel just above last cab ladder. **40 50 70**

(B) Lionel logo appears above the black striping in the last orangish side panel; logo is larger and more easily seen; uncatalogued; 1959. **40 50 70**

(0550): Dummy A unit; matches powered A unit, as described. **35 45 70**

THE MILWAUKEE ROAD

(0531): Powered A unit; painted dark semi-gloss gray; yellow pin stripe across cab roof continues down the sides to the end of the unit at the roof line; bright flat orange nose, enclosing both headlights but not the number boards; nose coloration outlined with yellow pin stripe above and below the orange patch; "2376" in yellow on the side, below the cab window; road name appears between the two portholes on the side stripe; 1/16"-diameter Lionel logo in the last orange side panel, just behind the rear cab door; road name appears a second time on a silver and black decal just above the pilot; two decorative horns and headlight lenses; no Lionel numbers appear on the unit; catalogued in 1958 only. **40 60 100**

(0541): Dummy B unit; painted to match the powered A unit with corresponding striping; road name appears in the last orange stripe; no numbers; Lionel logo located as described for A unit. **35 50 70**

(0551): Dummy A unit; matches powered A unit as described. **35 50 70**

NH (NEW HAVEN)

(0533): Powered A unit; flat white, painted body, including roof and side panels from just behind the cab windows to the rear of unit; flat black cab roof, pilot, ladders, windshield area, nose, and air tanks; flat orange cab sides; one small black square and two orange squares appear on white side panel; orange "N" and "H" appear in the last two white side panels; no road name; "0272" directly under first porthole and Lionel logo under the rear porthole, both in the white portion of the lower side panel; catalogued in 1958 only, for separate sale, and in passenger set 5714 with A-A diesels. A similar model was sold in the Penn Line HO range of the period; in fact, the model featured the same paint scheme and road number. Of course, the Penn Line unit has no Lionel logo, and the paint is glossy rather than flat. Still, the Penn Line model could be mistaken for Lionel at first inspection. **40 60 100**

(0543): Dummy B unit; entire body painted white; flat black air tanks, ladders, and floor sill; orange "NH"; no road name; no road number.

(A) 1/16"-diameter Lionel logo between rear door and end of unit; two small orange squares and one black square on side. **35 45 60**

(B) Lionel logo between two side doors; Ken Fairchild Collection. **35 45 60**

Gd Exc Mt

(0553): Dummy A unit; matches description of powered A unit. **35 45 60**

(0560) (DENVER &) RIO GRANDE "SNOWPLOW": Powered; flat black, painted body; light, semi-gloss yellow cab sides; road name and 1/16" Lionel logo appear in black on cab side; Lionel logo directly under "R" in "Rio Grande"; black decorative horn on each side of hood; darker, yellowish-orange non-operating snowplow blade snaps onto the front of body; cast-on headlight housing at each end, but only cab end lighted; no headlight lenses; no road number; catalogued in 1958-59 as a separate item; Lionel number appears on carton only; snowplow often missing. Athearn sold the same unit in the same period with orange cab sides and a yellow plow blade.

(A) Yellowish-orange blade. Very rare. **100 200 250**

(B) As described but with darker orange blade and cab sides. Verified by G. Horan and J. Otterbin at Greenberg Show, Philadelphia, August 1990. **Note:** This color is extremely rare. The one seen in Philadelphia was for display only and was not for sale. Ken Fairchild Collection. **NRS**

(0570) NAVY YARD SWITCHER: Powered; same body as 0560 snowplow; painted light blue; two black plastic horns and headlights; the headlight housing on the Athearn units is very small, while the later Lionel locomotive has a much larger light casting; white, stamped lettering on cab sides; "NAVY YARD / NEW YORK" and "51"; 1/16" Lionel logo; "HUSTLER" runs vertically on the front radiator and is part of casting; Lionel numbers on carton only; catalogued in 1958 only, as a separate item and with set 5705; it was not reintroduced in 1959 when Lionel made their own switchers; difficult to find and considered rare.

(A) Logo under "N" in "NAVY". **75 100 150**

(B) Lionel logo under letter "K" in "NEW YORK". G. Bunza Collection. **80 100 150**

(0580) WABASH GP-9: Powered; tri-color body; light gray cab and upper portion of body; dark blue lower portion trimmed in white; four blue fans on roof; road name, in white lettering, on blue portion of long hood; 1/8"-diameter Lionel logo appears just before the road name; "452" on blue portion of short hood; four headlight inserts; no handrails; blue Wabash flag on gray portion of cab; two brass decorative horns; separate cab casting snaps onto body shell; Lionel numbers appear on carton only; catalogued in 1958 as a separate item and in set 5707; very rare. The Athearn Wabash unit of the period had a blue cab with a white flag and no Lionel logo. The unit was also available with black plastic decorative horns. G. Bunza comment.

(A) Brass horns. **100 150 200**

(B) Black plastic horns. **100 150 200**

(0585) THE MILWAUKEE ROAD GP-9: Powered; flat black cab, upper portion of body, pilots, and floor sill; bright flat orange roof fans and lower portion of body; only the road name appears on long hood; white logo on cab side; no other markings or numbers, except Lionel logo on the orange side panel just past the rear cab door; wire handrails and decorative horn present; Lionel number on carton; catalogued in 1958 only as a separate item; rare. This locomotive also exists in the collection of K. Fairchild with the Lionel logo appearing on the short hood on one side and at the very end of the long hood on the opposite side. It appears in the 1/8" size and is factory.

(A) Logo at cab door. **100 125 175**

(B) Logo appears in two locations. **NRS**

(0590) VIRGINIAN RECTIFIER: Powered; painted light blue; yellow, 1/4"-wide band around the entire locomotive at roof line; "Blt. by Lionel" stamped in yellow on the short hood just in front of the cab door; road name spelled out and centered on the long hood; brass pantograph

Top: Two Hustler-type switchers sold as Lionel in 1958-1959 — the Navy Yard and the 0560 Rio Grande snowplow with yellow sides and blade (this locomotive has been found with orange sides and blade very close in color to the Milwaukee Road GP-9 on the middle shelf). Middle: The Lionel logo is located on the front of the long hood on the Wabash while the Milwaukee GP-9 has the logo stamped on the short hood. Bottom: Both variations of the Virginian shown were available as the 0590 and carry the "BUILT BY LIONEL" on the front hood; they were available in black (C) or silver (A) frame, as shown. Both are rare. Note that both have a decal on the nose with decorative horns on the front roof and wire handrails (one is shown without). No Lionel logo was ever used on these units. 0585: Ken Fairchild Collection.

	Gd	Exc	Mt

mounted on roof with four metal pins; single black ornamental horn in front of pantograph; light insert at each end, but only cab end lighted; Virginian logo decal on the front of shell. The Virginian disappeared in 1959. It was replaced with Lionel's 0591 New Haven rectifier using the same shell, which has the part number cast into the inside roof; this part number appears in all rectifiers whether sold by Lionel or Athearn. It was always assumed that the Virginian was an Athearn locomotive, because of the rubber band drive used to power it. However, the model is actually a combined effort: Lionel manufactured the body shells, while Athearn decorated the body shells and manufactured the mechanism.

(A) No number on end of long hood; silver frame and trucks.

	65	90	200

(B) Lionel number on end of long hood; darker blue body; sold by Blum's Hobby House in the early 1960s in Athearn sets; as far as can be determined, this locomotive was never sold by Lionel. K. Fairchild, G. Bunza Collections. **NRS**

(C) Similar to (A), but black frame and trucks. G. Bunza Collection.

	65	90	200

(D) Similiar to (A), but with no nose decal.

	65	90	200

Note: While researching the Kader-made items offered in the 1974–1977 Lionel HO line, all covered in Volume II, I received a letter from Lee Riley of "Kader" Bachmann Corporation, Philadelphia, Pennsylvania. Lee stated, in answer to one of my many questions, that the original tooling for the rectifier was available and that in 1973 a test run of fifty pieces was made by Kader Industries. Lee consulted with Lionel on this project but could not recall if the tool was damaged while in use or just worn out. He also stated that the tool itself is not worth fixing. This information — not given for this reason, I am sure — will certainly have a bearing on the future prices of any Lionel HO rectifier a collector is lucky enough to find in the 1990s.

We may all be assured, however, that we will not soon see another rectifier of Lionel manufacture.

2376: See (0531)

BOXCARS

In almost every case, Lionel/Athearn rolling stock is identical to the items sold under the Athearn label at the time. Only the Lionel logo on the car or a Lionel package distinguishes the items from regular Athearn production. Except those cars found in the early-1958 Lionel sets without the logo. All of the Athearn cars have sprung metal trucks and body-mounted NMRA couplers.

88: See (0864-175)

(0864-25) NYC (NEW YORK CENTRAL): Red and gray, painted body with matching door and door guides; unpainted black rootwalk and brakewheel; white lettering; numbered "174477"; Lionel numbers appear only on the carton; catalogued in 1958 only; very rare.

(A) 1/8" logo appears in the gray portion of the first panel to the right of the door.

	40	55	90

(B) 1/16" logo, corner of shell. G. Potts Collection.

	40	50	90

(0864-50) STATE OF MAINE: Red, white, and blue, painted body, with matching door; four-letterboard door; three boards carry the lettering "OF" and the letters "D" and "U" from "PRODUCTS"; white stripe on door seldom matches white of car side; black and white lettering; numbered "5206"; Lionel logo appears in the last panel to the left of the door; catalogued in 1958; Lionel's own version replaced it in 1959.

(A) 1/16"-diameter Lionel logo; "AND" on door. 40 60 95

The five road names shown were never produced for Lionel or by Lionel for that matter but seem to show that plans were afoot to increase the production of the F unit. Why, then, when Lionel offered their first power units, were only Alcos and Geeps offered? The units shown were in the Vincent Rosa Collection and clearly show "BUILT BY LIONEL" and the "0000" I have seen on all the Lionel mock-up power units I have held in my hands. A collector owning this type of model has no way of knowing just how many such units were made up and thus true value is not known. The top three shelves hold the A-B units lettered for the Atlantic Coast Line, Southern Pacific, and Great Northern, while B units lettered for the Santa Fe and Union Pacific appear on the bottom. Decal lettering

	Gd	Exc	Mt

(B) ⅛"-diameter Lionel logo; no "AND" on door.

| | 40 | 60 | 95 |

(0864-150) MINNEAPOLIS & ST. LOUIS: Dull orange, painted body; white lettering; numbered "52673"; Lionel logo appears just above the door guide in the second panel to the right of the door; unpainted black door rails, roofwalk, and brakewheel; four-letterboard door as found on the State of Maine car; Lionel number appears only on carton; catalogued in 1958 only; very difficult to find.

(A) ¹⁄₁₆"-diameter Lionel logo; unpainted door. 40 60 90
(B) ⅛"-diameter Lionel logo; painted door. 40 60 90
(C) Same as (B), but bright red body door rails. G. Potts Collection. 40 60 90

(0864-175) TIMKEN: Bright yellow, painted body; ½" white band on side; matching door and door guides; unpainted black brakewheel and roofwalk; brown "ROLLER FREIGHT / TIMKEN R.B.X. 88" on the white band at the upper left of the door; ¹⁄₁₆"-diameter brown Lionel logo appears just below the road number; red "ROLLER / FREIGHT" logo

at the right of the door; catalogued in 1958 and 1959; no Lionel number on car; discontinued in 1960; extremely hard to find.

| | 50 | 90 | 150 |

(0864-200) MONON: Brown, painted body; white lettering; numbered "3029"; ¹⁄₁₆"-diameter Lionel logo appears in the fifth panel to the left of the door, just below the grab-iron; Lionel number appears only on carton; catalogued in 1958 only. The catalogue illustration depicts a black car with "THE HOOSIER LINE" appearing in black letters on a white stripe at the top of the car; however, the car was not made this way. Rare.

(A) Brown door, roofwalk, and door guides, painted to match car sides. 50 60 80
(B) Unpainted black roofwalk and brakewheel. 35 40 60

(0864-225) CENTRAL OF GEORGIA: Tuscan, painted body; silver side panels and door; silver and tuscan lettering; red "CENTRAL / OF / GEORGIA" on a yellow square; unpainted black roofwalk; numbered

0864-50(B)   0864-150(A)

0864-50(A)   0864-200

0864-50(B)   0864-250(B)

0864-175   0864-250(A)

Eight of the Athearn-made boxcars with both sizes of Lionel logo appearing in different locations on their sides. The 0864-50(B) (top left) shows the word "AND" on its door, while the 50(A) below shows the smaller Lionel logo with the "AND" on its door; the third 0864-50 shows a thicker Lionel logo with no "AND". The Timken (bottom left) has the $\frac{1}{16}$-inch logo at the left of its door. The 0864-150(A) is the only car shown with unpainted door rails; it has the $\frac{1}{16}$-inch logo at the right of the door. The 0864-200(A) also has the $\frac{1}{16}$-inch logo at its corner step and painted roofwalk. Compare the Lionel logos on the 0864-250s.

	Gd	Exc	Mt
"7402"; $\frac{1}{16}$"-diameter Lionel logo appears in the last side panel to the left of the door; catalogued in 1958; discontinued in 1959.			
(A) Unpainted black, brakewheel.	30	40	50
(B) Painted brakewheel to match car. G. Horan, G. Bunza Collections.	35	45	60

(0864-250) WABASH: Light blue, painted body, with matching door and door guides; unpainted black brakewheel and roofwalk; white lettering; red Wabash flag appears in a white heart-shaped background at the right of the door; numbered "6287"; Lionel number appears only on carton; catalogued in 1958 only; discontinued in 1959. Unlike the O Gauge counterpart, this car does not operate.

	Gd	Exc	Mt
(A) Without Lionel logo; found in early 1958 sets.	25	35	45
(B) $\frac{1}{16}$"-diameter Lionel logo appears in the second panel to the right of the door.	35	45	60
(C) Roofwalk, and brakewheel painted to match car. G. Horan, G. Bunza Collections.	30	40	50
(D) Same as (B), but $\frac{1}{8}$" logo. K. Fairchild Collection.			

3029: See (0864-200)

	Gd	Exc	Mt
5206: See (0864-50)			
6287: See (0864-250)			
7402: See (0864-225)			
52673: See (0864-150)			
174477: See (0864-25)			

CABOOSES AND WORK CABOOSES

Cabooses

(0817) THE MILWAUKEE ROAD: Silver, painted body; separate smokestack, handrails, and additional details as found on other offset-cupola cabooses; black lettering; "THE MILWAUKEE ROAD" across body above windows; numbered "01924"; Lionel logo appears below grab-iron at end of car; catalogue numbers appear on carton only; catalogued in 1958 only in set 5709; scarce.

	Gd	Exc	Mt
(A) Semi-gloss paint finish.	15	25	45
(B) Flat finish.	15	25	45

Top: Both have painted roofwalks and door rails; left car has large Lionel logo to right of door while the other has ¹⁄₁₆-inch logo at the left corner steps. Second shelf: Same size logo, same location. Third: To the left, the Santa Fe with the side showing the "El Capitan" motto; the Lehigh Valley from an early set has no logo. Fourth: Cattle car, with logo in the same spot as on the three reefers, and the Gulf tank less the Lionel logo. As a collector I have never seen this car with the Lionel logo. Note that the black area shown on the Fruit Growers Express is not Lionel decoration! 0864-25, 0872-50, 0836(A), and 0866-25: Ken Fairchild Collection.

	Gd	Exc	Mt

(0817-25) VIRGINIAN: Deep blue, painted body and roofwalk; unpainted black plastic floor, end platform, and smokestack; separate brakewheels, wire handrails, and stamped metal ladders; white lettering; "VIRGINIAN" appears below cupola; numbered "1217"; catalogued in 1958 only with set 5711; illustration shows "VIRGINIAN" appearing below the windows, but the car was never made this way; catalogue numbers appear on carton only; discontinued 1959.

	30	40	75

(0817-50) RIO GRANDE: Silver, painted body; black unpainted plastic end platform, smokestack, and roofwalk; brakewheel at each end; wire handrails; stamped-metal ladders; black lettering; "Rio Grande"; numbered "01439"; name and number appear within black pin stripes on side; ¹⁄₁₆" Lionel logo appears below grab-iron at end opposite cupola; catalogued in 1958 only in set 5715; Lionel did not sell the car in the gray and yellow scheme depicted in the catalogue illustration, however Athearn later sold that scheme in its own line. 30 45 60

0817(-200) A.E.C.: Athearn shell; flat white, painted body and roofwalk; wire handrails; metal ladders; bright red lettering; "A.E.C.", "0817," and "BLT BY / LIONEL" appear on car side; "-200" suffix appears only in catalogue; catalogued in 1959 in set 5719; discontinued in 1960, then replaced in 1963 by Lionel's 0827-50.

	30	40	50

0817(-225) ALASKA RAILROAD: Athearn shell decorated by Lionel; painted dark flat blue; wire handrails; metal ladder; yellow lettering; "ALASKA RAILROAD" spelled across car side; illustration of Alaskan Boy appears between windows; "BLT BY / LIONEL" and "0817" also appear on car side; catalogued in 1959 only in set 5729; "-225" suffix appears only in catalogue; very rare.

	30	40	60

0817(-250) THE TEXAS SPECIAL: Athearn shell decorated by Lionel; painted bright red; wire handrails; metal ladders; white lettering;

0817(A)   0817-200

0817-50   0817-250

0817-225   0817-25

0817-275   0817-300(B)

All of the cabooses shown here are Athearn-made shells, but only three were decorated by Athearn — 0817(A), 0817-50, and 0817-25, all carrying the Lionel logo at the right lower corner. The remaining five cars were all decorated by Lionel and carry "BLT BY / LIONEL" at the corner opposite the cupola. All carry the 0817 catalogue number, with three having the road name spelled out. 0817(A): K. Fairchild Collection.

	Gd	Exc	Mt

"BLT BY / LIONEL" and "0817" stamped on sides; "-250" suffix appears only in catalogue; very rare.

	25	30	60

0817(-275) NH (NEW HAVEN): Painted flat black, with matching roofwalks; wire handrails; metal ladders; New Haven initials only, orange "N" and white "H"; initials approximately ½" tall; catalogue number "0817" and "BLT BY / LIONEL," appear on side; catalogued in 1959 in set 5725 with the New Haven rectifier; discontinued in 1960; this car is an Athearn shell decorated by Lionel; Lionel introduced its own model with the same catalogue number in 1963.

	30	40	45

0817(-300) SOUTHERN PACIFIC: Athearn shell decorated by Lionel; painted maroon body and roofwalk; two brakewheels; metal ladders; wire handrails; black unpainted plastic end platforms and frame; Lionel sprung trucks; yellow lettering; "SOUTHERN PACIFIC", "BLT BY / LIONEL", and "0817" appear on car side; no Lionel logo; catalogued in 1959 only in sets 5731 and 5717; in the illustration of set 5717, car is shown with black cupola, but it was not made that way; discontinued in 1960.

	Gd	Exc	Mt
(A) With window inserts.	25	35	45
(B) Without window inserts.	20	30	40

Work Cabooses

17: See (0819-75)

24: See (0829-100)

615: See (0819-50)

(0819-1) PENNSYLVANIA: Entire car, including roofwalks, painted dark gray; sprung metal trucks; wire handrails; metal ladder; black letter; "Maint." and "MW1741" appear on cab side; Lionel logo appears just above the grab-iron at the ladder end of cabin; catalogued in 1958 only; discontinued in 1959; very rare.

	25	35	45

(0819-25) U.S. NAVY: Painted light blue to match 51 U.S. Navy Switcher; black roofwalk, brakewheel, and smokestack; metal ladder; wire handrails; white lettering; "U.S. NAVY" between cab windows; "1013" directly below road name; Lionel logo appears below the grab-

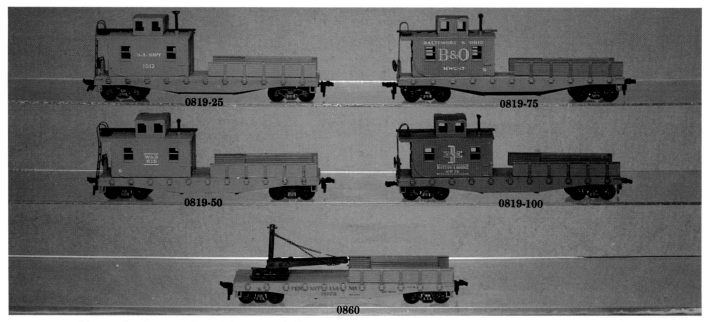

Blue work cabooses in four of the six available road names; the U.S. Navy and B & M cars are from early sets of 1958 and do not show the Lionel logo, but they do exist with the 1/16-inch size logo on the cabin. The car was also available in a light gray Pennsylvania version. The 0819-200, the first hybrid-type work caboose, is found with an Athearn flatcar but Lionel-made cabin, carrying "BLT BY / LIONEL" and catalogue number; the car is covered in Lionel production. It reappeared in 1961 in set 5762. Bottom: The only derrick car of Athearn manufacture for Lionel; its 40-foot body carries the number "489711" and the Lionel logo appears under the black derrick, on the body side, in the 1/16-inch size. This car was copied in Lionel's 1960 line. Note: The fine chain on the boom of the derrick does not extend down to the floor of car.

	Gd	Exc	Mt

iron at the ladder-end of car; catalogue number appears on carton only; catalogued in 1958 only; rare. **35 40 60**

(0819-50) WAB (WABASH): Light blue, painted body, toolboxes, and cabin; unpainted black plastic roofwalk, brakewheel, and smokestack; metal ladder; wire handrails; single brakewheel; white lettering; overscore and underscore enclose "WAB" and "615"; 1/16" Lionel logo appears between the grab-irons at the end of the car; catalogued in 1958 only in set 5707; illustration shows larger lettering than that which actually appears on car; discontinued in 1959. **20 30 45**

(0819-75) BALTIMORE & OHIO: Painted blue car body, cabin, toolboxes, and fence; unpainted black plastic smokestack, brakewheel, and roofwalk; single brakewheel at cabin end; "BALTIMORE & OHIO" above windows; large "B & O" betweeen windows; "MWC17" below initials; Lionel logo appears on cab by the grab-iron at the fence-end of the car; no catalogue numbers on car; catalogued in 1958 only in set 5713; discontinued 1959. **20 30 40**

(0819-100) BOSTON & MAINE: Deep blue, almost purple, body, cabin, fence, and toolboxes; black roofwalk, brakewheel, and smokestack; metal ladder; wire handrails; white lettering; approximately 1/2"-square "B&M" logo between cabin windows; solid white "B" and white-outlined "M" comprise logo; road name appears below the windows; "MW24" below name; overscore and underscore enclose name and number; Lionel numbers appear on carton only; catalogued in 1958 as a separate item and in set 5717. This car was catalogued again in 1959 in sets 5723 and 5727; the former had the Athearn car, while the latter had 0819-200 from Lionel's production; the catalogue shows both cars with a two-color B.M. logo, but neither car was made this way. **20 30 40**

1013: See (0819-25)
1217: See (0817-25)

	Gd	Exc	Mt

01439: See (0817-50)
1741: See (0819-1)
01924: See (0817)

CRANES AND DERRICKS

787: See (0879)

(0860) PENNSYLVANIA DERRICK CAR: 40' car; light gray, painted body; black lettering; "PENNSYLVANIA"; numbered "489711"; 1/16"-diameter Lionel logo appears at the toolbox end of car; sidewalls and toolbox also finished in gray separate casting of black plastic derrick with fine metal link chain; sidewalls, toolboxes, and derrick snap into holes in car floor; one brakewheel; derrick usually broken; catalogue number appears only on carton; catalogued in 1958-59; very difficult to find. **35 40 60**

(0879) UNION PACIFIC CRANE: Red, painted cab; white lettering; "U. P." in white lettering; "03043" between the last door and end of cab, directly below the single smokestack; "Bucyrus Erie" appears at the roof line, next to the center cab door; 1/16"-diameter Lionel logo appears on the cab skirt below the road number; unpainted black frame, roof access door, and boom; boom operated with metal crank that came with car; two metal hooks and brass pulleys on boom; catalogued in 1958-60 and illustrated with the red, white, and blue UP shield on the car frame, but not made this way; catalogue number appears on carton only; replaced in 1960 by Lionel's Illinois Central crane.

(A) Without Lionel logo; found in 1958 Lionel train sets.
30 40 50

(B) 1/16"-diameter Lionel logo appears on the cab skirt below the road number. **35 50 65**

Four variations of the 0879 Athearn-made "Bucyrus Erie" crane car. Top: 0879(A), from early set, without Lionel logo. Second: New variation (C) from the Ken Fairchild Collection, with the number "787" and the "U.P." appearing between the last two side doors, with the ¹⁄₁₆-inch Lionel logo on the front side door. Third and fourth: (B) variation (model on third self has much thinner circle around the letter "L"). All are equipped with metal hooks and brass pulleys with six-wheel trucks.

	Gd	Exc	Mt

(C) ⅛" Lionel logo on front cab door "U.P." and number "787" in white stamping between last door and middle window. Note the "Bucyrus Erie" name is also missing. Original box, K. Fairchild Collection; verified by G. Horan.   **NRS**

03043: See (0879)
489711: See (0860)

FLATCARS

See page 37 for photo of plastic frames of Athearn-made flatcars.

	Gd	Exc	Mt

(0800) NICKEL PLATE ROAD FLATCAR WITH AIRPLANE: 40' flatcar painted black; white lettering; "NICKEL PLATE ROAD"; numbered "1958", the year the car was introduced; ¹⁄₁₆" diameter Lionel logo appears in the second side panel; plastic single-engine Beechcraft airplane with landing gear and prop; separate wings carried alongside airplane body; black plastic mounting carriage snapped onto floor of car; load often broken in some way; catalogued in 1958-59.

(A) Airplane with unpainted black underbody; dull orange, painted top portion, tail, and wings. Much harder to find than silver plane.

	30	50	70

(B) Airplane with unpainted black underbody; silver, painted top portion, tail, and wings.

	25	30	40

0800(A)

0865(A)

0800(B)

0865(B)

0801

0824(A)

0811-25(A)

0877

Top two shelves show both of the 0800 airplane flats, along with both variations of the 0865, 50-foot gondola, with original loads. Pictured on third shelf is the 0801 flat with boat and the 0824 auto flat that also exists with a brown car body and same number. Shown last is the 0811-25 flat with steel stakes. This car was also available with a black body. It is followed by the 0877 bulkhead car that is one of the few Athearn flatcar types not to have a load. The cars were available as Lionel in 1958-1959.

0814(B)

0814(A)

0830(B)

0830(A)

Four of the 50-foot flatcars made by Athearn. The two Auto-Loaders were made to reflect the same car in the O Gauge line, as were the piggyback cars on the second shelf. Both cars were available using the Reading name and the number of 40125. The second road name used on both cars was the New York Central, numbered "499300". Lionel logo in 1/16-inch size, although the cars can be occasionally found with 1/8-inch logo. The cars on the auto car came in many colors, while the piggyback flat is known to have the two trailers as shown but with orange or gold arrows holding the Cooper-Jarrett name. All four flats are difficult to find with loads in place.

	Gd	Exc	Mt

(0801) SEABOARD FLATCAR WITH BOAT: 40' flatcar; dark brown, painted body; blue and white plastic boat, same as that used on the O Gauge counterpart; white lettering; "SEABOARD"; numbered "42806"; black plastic brakewheel; Lionel logo appears near end of car; two black plastic carriages snap onto car floor and retain load; Lionel number appears only on carton; catalogued in 1958-59; replaced in 1960 by 0801-200. Reportedly, this car has been seen with a different road number; verification of other road number(s) requested. **NRS**

(0811-25) READING FLATCAR WITH STAKES: White lettering; "READING"; numbered "9440"; black plastic brakewheel; $1/16$"-diameter Lionel logo appears just before the road name; one dozen steel stakes; Lionel number appears on carton only; very difficult to find with original steel stakes.

(A) Painted brown; 1958.	15	25	45
(B) Painted black; 1959.	20	35	50

(0814) EVANS 50' AUTO-LOADER: Tuscan, painted flatcar; black automobile rack superstructure; loaded with two white station wagons and two red sedans; white lettering; automobile rack lettered "EVANS AUTO-LOADER"; Lionel logo appears in the second side panel; catalogue number appears on carton only; catalogued in 1958-59; illustration does not show station wagons as part of the load, but they were available in at least five colors including tan.

(A) Flatcar lettered "READING" numbered "40125"; $1/16$"-diameter Lionel logo; 1958.	25	40	60
(B) Flatcar lettered "NYC"; numbered "499300"; $1/8$"-diameter Lionel logo; 1959.	30	45	65
(C) Same as (B), except for $1/16$" logo.	30	40	60

(0824) ERIE AUTO FLAT: Flatcar with two automobiles; white lettering; "ERIE"; numbered "74286"; $1/16$"-diameter Lionel logo appears in the side panel just before the road name; Lionel number appears on the carton only; catalogued in 1958-59; replaced in 1960 by Lionel's 0824-200.

(A) Black car, as shown in catalogue illustration for separate item and set 5713; small Lionel logo.	20	30	45
(B) Red car, as shown in catalogue illustration for set 5709. Harder to locate than the black car.	25	35	55

(0830) READING PIGGYBACK FLATCAR: Same body as used for the 1958 Auto Loader; tuscan; white lettering; "READING"; numbered "40125"; Lionel logo appears in the second side panel; two white plastic trailers; "COOPER-JARRETT, INC." on orange or gold arrow on trailer side; black plastic trailer rack snaps onto car floor; catalogue number appears on carton only; catalogued in 1958-59.

(A) $1/16$" Lionel logo, orange arrow. R. Kughn, G. Horan Collections.	15	25	50
(B) $1/16$" Lionel logo; gold arrow. G. Bunza Collection.	20	30	60
(C) $1/8$" Lionel logo, orange arrow. R. Kughn Collection.	15	25	50

(0877) ILLINOIS CENTRAL MISCELLANEOUS CAR: 40' bulkhead flatcar; painted flat black; white lettering; "ILLINOIS CENTRAL"; numbered "63210"; $1/16$"-diameter Lionel logo; one brakewheel; no load came with car; catalogue number appears on carton only; catalogued in 1958 only; available uncatalogued in 1959; discontinued 1960; much scarcer than the similar Rivarossi car.

	20	30	55

1958:	See (0800)	
9440:	See (0811-25)	
40125:	See (0830) and (0814)	
42806:	See (0801)	

	Gd	Exc	Mt

63210:	See (0877)
74286:	See (0824)
499300:	See (0814)

GONDOLAS

(0865) MICHIGAN CENTRAL GONDOLA: White lettering; "MICHIGAN CENTRAL" and "MC RR"; numbered "350623"; $1/8$" Lionel logo appears at the floor line in the fifth side panel; loaded with six red unmarked canisters; catalogued in 1958.

(A) Tuscan body; $1/16$"-diameter Lionel logo; 1958 only.	15	20	30
(B) Black body; $1/8$"-diameter logo; uncatalogued; 1959.	15	20	30
(C) Same as (A) but with $1/8$" logo. D. Bunza Collection.	15	20	30

350623: See (0865)

HOPPER CARS

(0836) LEHIGH VALLEY: 40' car; brown, painted body; white lettering; "LEHIGH VALLEY" spelled across side; "L.V." and "4127" in first large side panel; diamond-shaped herald in third side panel; operating doors on all four bays; catalogue number appears on carton of cars sold separately; catalogued in 1958 only; replaced by Lionel's Alaska Hopper in 1959.

(A) No Lionel logo; found in early Lionel sets.	15	20	40
(B) $1/16$"-diameter Lionel logo near the ladder, just below herald in the third side panel; very difficult to find.	30	45	65

4127: See (0836)

REFRIGERATOR CARS

(0872-1) FRUIT GROWERS EXPRESS: Dull yellow, painted sides; tuscan roof and ends; unpainted roofwalk and brakewheel; black lettering; numbered "9253"; Lionel logo appears in the fifth panel to the left of the doors; operating doors and ice hatches; cast-on ladders and six steps; catalogue number appears on carton only; catalogued only in 1958; replaced in 1959 by Lionel's Railway Express refrigerator. Very difficult to locate.

	45	65	95

(0872-50) SANTA FE: Dull orange, painted sides; black roof and ends; black and white Santa Fe cross herald; black lettering; operating doors and ice hatches; cast-on ladders and six steps; catalogue number appears on carton only; catalogued in 1958; difficult to find with the door unbroken. Dallas Mallerich suggests that the variations found probably arose because of batches being mixed between the stages of this printing job which had different lettering each side. The same road numbers, and a variety of slogans, are found on variations in regular Athearn production.

(A) "El Capitan" slogan on one side, "SHIP AND TRAVEL" on other; numbered "8392" on both sides; Lionel logo appears at the left of the door below the grab-iron.	20	30	65
(B) Similar to (A); numbered "8293" on both sides; Lionel logo appears only on the "El Capitan" side.	15	20	50
(C) "THE ROUTE OF / THE / Super Chief" on one side, "SHIP AND TRAVEL" on the other; "8293" on both sides; $1/16$-inch diameter Lionel logo; see photograph; extremely rare. **NRS**

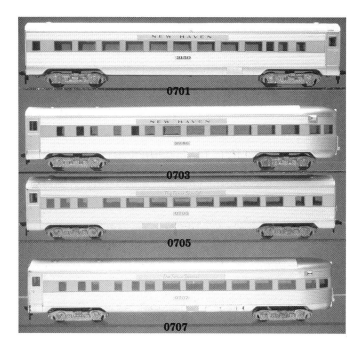

These two photos show the four types of passenger body styles sold as Lionel, 1958-1961 (there are also two types of construction). The Texas Special 0707 observation car with battery box area showing in center of floor (not present on the early 1958 cars)! The two road names shown were sold in sets and separately with the Pullman car being replaced in some Texas Special sets by a second dome car. The NH cars do not carry a Lionel catalogue number, while the Texas Special cars do (as do the tuscan and black Pennsylvania cars, not shown).

	Gd	Exc	Mt

8293: See (0872-50)
8392: See (0872-50)
9253: See (0872-1)

STOCK CARS

(0866-25) A.T. & S.F.: Light green, painted body, door and door guides; claw foot door; door guides cast into car side; two letterboards cast onto the left-hand side of the car; yellow lettering; "SANTA FE" appears on upper board; "50656" appears on lower board; 1/16" -diameter Lionel logo appears in the third panel to the left of the door; unpainted black brakewheel and roofwalk; catalogue number appears on carton only; catalogued in 1958 only; available uncatalogued in 1959; discontinued in 1959; replaced by Lionel's Poultry Car. This is the only Athearn stock car sold by Lionel.

20   30   50

50656: See (0866-25)

TANK CARS

(0815) GULF: Unpainted black frame, platform, and lower half of tank body; bright orange, painted top half of body, dome and ends; black band runs vertically under the platform down to the frame; lettered "GULF / OIL CORPORATION"; numbered "2605"; no Lionel logo; wire handrails on platform; stamped-metal ladders from platform downward to the frame; brakewheel; catalogued in 1958-59 as a separate item and in sets; Lionel number appears on carton only; discontinued in 1960. This is the first HO tank car sold by Lionel; none were sold in 1957.

30   40   60

2605: See (0815)

PASSENGER CARS

Between 1958 and 1961 Lionel catalogued a variety of three road names for the four types of streamlined passenger cars made by Athearn. The four car types had been made by Athearn as far back as 1956 and included a baggage, Pullman, vista dome, and observation. All have plastic bodies, clear plastic window inserts, and metal four-wheel trucks with NMRA-type couplers. Each truck is secured to the floor with one screw. During the period in which the Lionel/Athearn cars were catalogued, they were constructed in two ways. Each is considered rare. None of the cars ever carried the Lionel Logo.

Type I Construction: In 1958 the first cars have a one-piece body with a separate flat floor casting which snaps into the walls of the body. The only details on the outer floor are the coupler pockets and floor bracings. These early cars are found with part of the main bracing and coupler pocket removed (to accept the talgo-type truck used by Lionel). The trucks are silver. New Haven cars are found only with this type of construction.

Type II Construction: The second type of construction appeared in 1961. It was catalogued in the Pennsylvania set 5756. The main changes occurred in the floor design, which was revised to have a cast battery box in the center of the floor. The coupler pockets are absent, and the skirting of the car body is part of the floor, rather than the car side. A half-inch high wall was added inside to hold the car together. The trucks are black, and they have a pivot pin cast into them. The pin passes through the floor of the car, and it is fastened from inside with a single screw.

The Texas Special and Pennsylvania cars have both types of bodies. Early cars, like Type I, are not as difficult to find as the later cars, with the battery box area having been produced for a shorter time

	Gd	Exc	Mt

period. Type II cars were available in set 14054 in 1962. K. Fairchild comment.

500: See (0702)

NEW HAVEN: Painted silver; dull orange band through window area; black lettering; "NEW HAVEN" appears centered above windows; no Lionel numbers appear on cars; no Lionel logo; catalogue number appears on carton; catalogued in 1958 only, and never reintroduced in the Lionel line; catalogued in set 5714 and as separate items; prized when found in their original boxes; rare.

(0700) Baggage "3406" on car side.	40	60	90
(0701) Pullman "3150" on car side.	40	60	90
(0702) Vista Dome "500" on car side.	40	60	90
(0703) Observation "3246" on car side.	40	60	90

PENNSYLVANIA: Deep tuscan, painted body; black roof; yellow-gold lettering; road name centered above windows; Lionel catalogue number appears on number board below windows; first catalogued in 1960 in set 5742 with the Pennsylvania rectifier and three cars, the Baggage, Vista Dome, and Observation. In 1961 set 5756 featured the same consist and a 0635 Pacific. The 0711 Pullman was catalogued in 1960 as a separate item, and it is the most difficult passenger car to find of all the Athearn for Lionel cars. Discontinued in 1961, these are very attractive cars. With the exception of the road name and the colors of the cars, they are the very same type of car shown here in the New Haven and The Texas Special road names.

| 0708 Baggage | 60 | 85 | 100 |
| 0709 Vista Dome | 60 | 85 | 100 |

	Gd	Exc	Mt
0710 Observation	60	85	100
0711 Pullman	85	100	150

THE TEXAS SPECIAL: Painted silver; dark red striping in window area; red lettering; road name centered above windows; catalogued first in 1959 as separate items and in set 5732. The cars were headed by Lionel's new Alco units; two powered 0566s and a dummy B 0576 pulled the four cars. In 1960 the cars were catalogued in set 5770; this set consisted of the same A-B-A diesels, but the consist included two 0706 Vista Dome cars, one 0705 Pullman, plus one 0707 Observation. The cars were not shown in the 1961 catalogue, but they reappeared in 1962 in set 14054, which featured a powered 0566 and the same consist found in set 5770; the cars were never shown again after 1962.

500: See (0702)

0704 Baggage	50	60	95
0705 Pullman	50	60	95
0706 Vista Dome	50	60	95
0707 Observation	50	60	95
3150: See (0701)			
3246: See (0703)			
3406: See (0700)			

NOTES
1. McComas and Tuohy, p. 105.
2. Telephone conversation with Lenny Dean (V. Rosa), July 1984.

The very desirable Athearn-made passenger cars in the Pennsylvania road name, offered 1960-1961. Top: 0708 baggage and 0711 Pullman; Bottom: 0709 dome, 0710 observation. All four of the cars have the battery box area at the floor's center. Type II construction. The 0711 is the most difficult to find, having been offered for separate sale only in 1960. Ken Fairchild Collection.

CHAPTER V
Lionel Lines: 1959–1966

The models sold after the 1960 period were strictly Lionel-manufactured models. The following photos show the GP-9s and Alcos that Lionel produced using the old Hobbyline die work, and the electrics that were of the Lionel/Athearn joint venture of 1958, with all road names that were available until production stopped in 1966. This chapter covers all steam locomotives, rolling stock, and accessories of Lionel manufacture and will cover the Plasticville line of buildings made by Bachmann Bros., of Philadelphia, Pennsylvania, and marketed in Lionel packaging. *Greenberg's Guide to Lionel HO, Volume II: 1974–1977* covers all models made in the General Mills era of Lionel HO, as produced by six different manufacturers including Lionel. This era of Lionel history is also fascinating.

LIONEL EMPHASIZES PLAY VALUE

Josh Cowen once said, "after a kid watched a train go around more than three times, he would get bored with it, so give him plenty of action." Action is what the Lionel HO line got in 1960. The new personnel in Roy Cohn's group made some radical changes. Emphasis on scale quality, as seen with Rivarossi and Athearn, gave way to emphasis on the familiar "toy quality" and "play value" associated with Lionel trains. The 1960 consumer catalogue announced with fanfare: "A first in HO — Brand New Action-Packed Operating Cars." 1960 was the year of the 0319 Operating Helicopter Car, 0847 Exploding Target Car, 0850 Missile Launching Car, 0300 Operating Lumber Car, and the 0301 Coal Dump Car. There is a picture of the Lionel SP Helicopter Launch prototype in the March 1960 issue of *Railroad Model Craftsman*.

"The Father and Son Set," 225W, was heralded as one of the Lionel star performers in the 1960 advance catalogue. A product of the company's play-value marketing strategy, the set contained in two separate boxes identical "Super O" and HO sets. Some collectors call it the "over and under" set. While the components may be found for sale individually, the boxed set would be a very highly prized piece. The very rare 6357-50 Santa Fe red caboose came with the O Gauge portion of this set; the 0817-150 Santa Fe HO caboose matches it.

From 1960 through 1966 the HO line failed miserably, especially the military items. According to Lenny Dean, "The new strategy was to get as much of the younger, mass-market railroaders as they could to join the model railroading ranks. Then eventually, as they grew up with Lionel trains, the HO line would get more sophisticated as the line flourished." Apparently, Roy Cohn's objective was to get kids interested in HO trains. "They were the future of Lionel," Dean stated.[1]

Hobbyists scoffed at the new Lionel toy trains designed for play value, but today collectors find the ingenious operating locomotives, cars, and accessories to be very vital, exciting pieces. Lionel engineers almost literally shrank O Gauge operating cars to HO proportions. Many of the items produced from 1960 to 1966, such as the Sheriff and Outlaw Car, Operating Milk Car, and Giraffe Car, operate just as well as the O Gauge counterparts. Many of these items display a sense of humor unique to Lionel, while others exhibit remarkable technological advances.

It is interesting to note that between 1959, when Roy Cohn assumed operational control of Lionel, and 1963, when he left, the Lionel Corporation lost $14 million.[2] During these years of corporate turmoil, trains, as toys, were losing their popularity. Ultimately, the O Gauge line suffered and the fledgling HO line, especially the gimmick items, met disaster. Lionel also lost the HO enthusiast market. "How would you like a car to explode on a trestle bridge, handmade out of toothpicks that it took you four years to build?" queries one collector interviewed by McComas and Tuohy.[3]

1961

The 1961 HO line continued to sell play action. New were fifteen different train sets. The 0635LT Pacific became the new steam engine with headlight and smoke. The 0545 GE-44 switcher with headlight and the 0602 switcher with gear drive were also added, while the 0605 saddle tank locomotive remained in the line. A new four-wheel Canadian Pacific Husky 0054 appeared at the Toy Fair, though Lionel never made it for the U.S. market. Madison Hardware listed the piece on page 61 of their *Railroad Model Craftsman* ad in December 1961, but few if any seem to have been made. The *Lionel Service Manual* lists the piece and notes "no ornamental horn 1-62. Body assembly is $1, but there is no bin number." Perhaps Lionel made only a few mock-ups or a short production run for the Canadian market; additional information requested.

The new HO rolling stock for 1961 included the 0366 Operating Milk Can Unloading Car, 0333 Operating Satellite Launching Car, 0337 Animated Circus Giraffe Car, and the 0039 Motorized Track Cleaning Car. The 0068 Executive Inspection Car has a sedan shell similar to the body found on the O Gauge 6414 Auto Car. The HO accessories, which included the 0480 Missile Firing Range, continue the military-space theme along with the Exploding Target Car. The 0282 Gantry was another addition to the 1961 line. Today, it is particularly difficult to find unbroken.[4]

1962

The big news for 1962 was that Joe Bonanno had squeezed Lionel's O/O27 horn and whistle mechanisms down to HO size. For 1962 Lionel's Pacific 0645 had smoke, headlight, and whistle. The deluxe A-B unit also had an operating headlight and air horn. The biggest difficulty was retention of the authentic sound. Lionel also adapted the Mallory magnetic coupler to some of its HO sets. A two-inch magnetic bar sat between the rails in the heart of the new uncoupling system. The Mallory coupler, while not sanctioned by the NMRA, was a further development of the NMRA X-2f coupler, and was designed to couple with regulation NMRA couplers. A special feature of the new Lionel Mallory magnetic coupler was the extra-long lateral pin extending from the shank to facilitate easier uncoupling. The couplers are truck-mounted carry-overs from 1961. The 0771 Lionel trucks were packaged separately at $1.50 a pair.

Other items representing the 1962 line are the 0370 Animated Sheriff and Outlaw Car, the 0845 Gold Bullion Car, and the 0357 Cop and Hobo Car. The Cop and Hobo Car is a scaled-down reproduction of the O Gauge model. Every time the car rolls under a special trestle section a hobo and policeman jump on and off the car from the trestle. There is also a 0365 Minuteman Missile Launching Car and a 0349 Turbo Missile Firing Car. Indeed, these models reflect Lionel's ongoing desire to reproduce the highly imaginative O Gauge cars. According to Hal Carstens "model auto racing sets seemed to take some of the spotlight away from model trains that year, but it would take Lionel four more years to call it quits with the HO line and eight more years to sell out their declining O train line," and discontinue train production altogether.[5]

Even the day before the New York Toy Fair opened, Lionel's Board Chairman, Roy M. Cohn, showed great optimism. The executives at Lionel felt that both HO and O were going strong, with promise of steady growth in the future. (Cohn, Joshua Lionel Cowen's nephew, was better known for his role in the McCarthy hearings.)

1963

The performance of the HO trains continued to improve as Lionel replaced rubber band-driven locomotives with newer models that featured a Helic drive (a sprung steel band). The newer models include the 0571P Pennsylvania Alco diesel with headlight, the 0569P Union Pacific, and the 0536 Santa Fe Alco A-B multiple unit. Steam locomotives improved, too. The 0636 Pacific steam locomotive with headlight and smoke received a new gear ratio for smoother operation. The 0595 Santa Fe dummy A, 0575 B unit, and the new Santa Fe powered A unit with headlight and Helic drive are pictured in the catalogue as EMD F-3 or F-7 units, but they were actually produced as models of Alco diesels. In the GP-9 series, Lionel added the 0593P Northern Pacific powered unit, 0593T Northern Pacific dummy, and the 0594P Santa Fe. Both of the powered units feature dual front headlights.

In retrospect, the cover of Lionel's 1963 catalogue, which shows two model race cars and a train in an apparent race, seems quite appropriate. Eight pages at the rear of the catalogue describe motor racing sets. The fad had hit hard, and trains had fallen from popularity. Lionel attempted to follow the changes in the marketplace by offering its own race sets. Ironically, Lionel had created the first toy racing sets in 1912, long before the market desired such automotive toys.

Many of 1962's operating cars were continued in 1963. The only new 1963 items are the 0815-85 Lionel Lines chemical car and the Boston & Maine boxcar. It is interesting to note that the 0864-400 B & M boxcar is listed in the 1960, 1961, and 1963 catalogues. It is described as a new item in both 1960 and 1963, though it had the same number each year and no apparent change in design. The 1960–1961 car belongs to the early Lionel/Hobbyline group of boxcars. The 1963 car, we believe, is similar. It is in 1965 that the catalogue shifts to a new number, the 0874-60, although there is no reference to anything being new. This Lionel car is a cheapened version of the earlier Lionel/Hob-

The 0366 milk car features an ingenious mechanism to deliver cans, which are inserted in a device that resembles a cap gun bullet chamber.

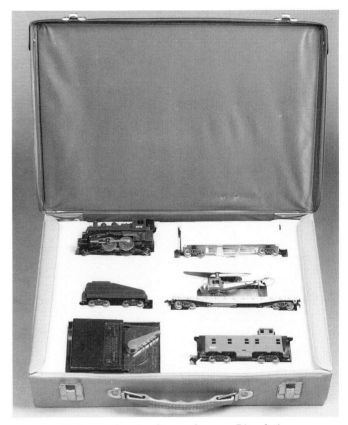

"Take me along" valise pack was a Lionel gimmick designed to create excitement and sales. "Have valise . . . will travel" touted the 1961 catalogue. The set came with a 0642LT steam locomotive and tender, the 0337 Giraffe Car, 0319 Operating Helicopter Car, 0841 unmarked caboose; eleven sections of 0989 18-inch radius track, one section 0975 18-inch radius curved terminal section, 0103 power pack, 5767-15 carrying case, wires, instruction sheets, and a 1961 pulp paper catalogue. Very rare, this set can bring as much as $500 in mint condition.

byline boxcar. It is smaller in height and very plain. It has a 6464-style steel plate on the bottom. The 0874-60 was also listed and, for the first time, illustrated in the 1966 catalogue.[6]

The 1962 0864-900 NYC boxcar was given a new number in 1963, without any indication of specific changes that may have been made. The hyphenated number most likely indicates that changes took place in either the truck or coupler design. The same car was renumbered 0874 in 1964, when Lionel began to replace the Hobbyline boxcars with a cheaper line of steel bottom cars. The 0874 NYC reappears in the 1965 and 1966 catalogues; again without reference to any changes.[7]

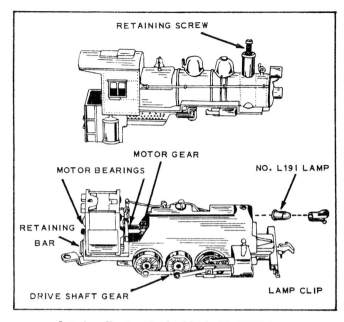

Interior of instruction booklet for No. 0602 steam switcher

Another interesting piece of rolling stock released in 1963 is the 0827 Illuminated Safety First Caboose, while the 0845 Gold Bullion Transport, 0810 Emergency Generator Transport Car, 0805 Illuminated Radioactive Waste Disposal Car, 0889 Illinois Central Crane, and 0813 Mercury Capsule Carrying Car are the premier pieces of collectible rolling stock produced in this year. The Northern Pacific 0593T and 0593P are very hard to find in new condition, while the 0571 Pennsylvania diesel and the 14163 four-unit Pennsylvania diesel passenger set are both extremely rare.

1964

By 1964 Lionel had begun to print its catalogue on a less-expensive, uncoated paper, yet the new catalogue devoted six pages to selling the HO line. With the return of the O Gauge 773 steam locomotive, Lionel seemed to be preparing to offer greater quality in its line. Apparently, the company wished to reduce emphasis on the lower-quality space age cars. The catalogue showed eight HO sets, with gear-driven steam and diesel locomotives. The locomotive range includes the 0055 Minneapolis & St. Louis Husky switcher with headlight, the 0594P Santa Fe GP-9, and a deluxe 0646LTS Pacific steam locomotive with tender and whistle. A three-unit Alco diesel with air horn could be substituted for the 0646LTS steamer in set 14310. Lionel pushed neither the HO nor the O Gauge space age cars, although a stock of each remained in inventory. Motor cars and other toys were listed in separate catalogues.

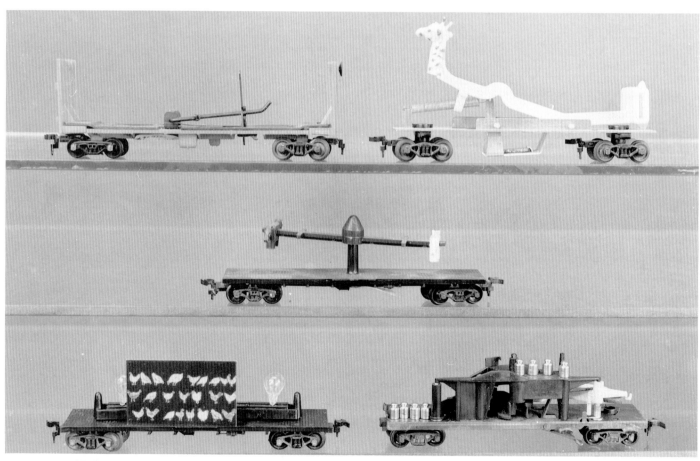

Mechanisms for operating cars produced by Lionel. Top: 0847 Exploding Boxcar and 0337 Giraffe cars. Middle: 0873 Rodeo Car; the motion of the car caused the horseheads to move back and forth. Bottom: 0834 Poultry Car and one of its four plastic sides (note two lights that make the chickens on these sides seem to move); 0366 Milk Car, with its eight steel cans. All were extremely simple in their operation.

1965

The number of HO catalogue pages decreased to four in the unusual 1965 consumer catalogue. Only a year remained before Lionel would discontinue the line. The equipment selection included the same fourteen action cars that had been offered in 1964. The 0646LTS continued to be the premier steam locomotive, and, once again, Lionel erroneously depicted the 0595 dummy A and the 0536 A-B combination as EMD F-units, rather than correctly as Alcos. The train set themes all seemed to indicate a return to the traditional railroading concept. During the year, the company also produced the 0874-60 Boston and Maine, which was not illustrated in the catalogue, the 0646LTS Pacific with smoke and whistle, the 0626 without smoke or whistle, and a 0535/0536 Santa Fe Alco with diesel horn. The 0626 is one of the rarest Lionel Pacifics of the late corporation run; this locomotive has a piston in its steam chest, although it was not equipped with a smoke unit until 1966, when a few were made up with smoke units from inventory. Both variations are difficult to locate, with the later being uncatalogued.

1966

This was the last year of HO. Lionel showed five complete sets in the catalogue, but none of them was a dynamic offering. The Pacific steam with smoke and whistle became 0647LTS. The Sante Fe A-B combination with the diesel horn became 0537 with 0535W. Lionel also produced the 0592 GP-9, which had the first direct-gear drive. The operating cars and space cars prevailed, most likely due to the large quantities remaining in inventory. The era for bobbing giraffes, guided missiles, helicopters, and see-through gold bullion cars had crested, and Lionel management threw in the towel, thus surrendering their battle in the HO market. Lionel filled all of its HO orders from inventory in 1967.

LIONEL STEAM LOCOMOTIVES, 1959–1966

With only small changes in their shells, all of the steam locomotives produced by Lionel were made from old Hobbyline dies. Locomotive shells and tender bodies were molded in black plastic. Locomotives had cast-metal frames, while most tenders had sheet metal floors. All of the locomotives were lighted; some had smoke and whistle units. None of the locomotives were very powerful. Lionel used a three-pole motor with band, worm, and gear drives. Current was collected by wipers that rubbed against the drive wheels. Wire handrails were applied to all Pacific locomotives. Sprung trucks were used on the tenders until 1963, after which solid frame trucks were used. Along with the change to solid frame trucks came minor changes in couplers and covers.

The first Pacific-type locomotive offered by Lionel in 1959 was the 0625. It replaced the never-delivered Athearn model shown in the 1958 catalogue. Lighted, the steel wire handrails were the only detail not cast into its shell. 1960 saw some small changes made to the locomotive, including a lower gear ration and larger motor.

Introduced in 1961, the first smoke unit worked well considering its simplicity. It had a cast-metal steam chest with an integral electric heating element. The unit used liquid to produce smoke, which was forced up the stack by a piston in the left side of the steam chest. The piston operated directly off the drive rod, which was stamped steel. Three plastic pouches of smoke fluid came with each locomotive. The whistle units were introduced in 1962 in the 0645 Pacific. The metal floor of the tender was replaced by a small plate fastened to the front of the tender. The truck fastened to the bottom of this plate, and the relay for the whistle was attached at the top. The rear truck was fastened directly to a plastic lug that was cast into the tender body. These trucks were the same type used on the later passenger cars made by Lionel. They were insulated with plastic wheels on one side. The motor for the whistle was the same type

0602: Lionel's first switcher with tender. The locomotive was lighted with all detail cast into its shell. Drive rods and oil linkage present, along with sprung trucks on tender. Note motor showing from rear of cab.

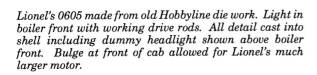

Lionel's 0605 made from old Hobbyline die work. Light in boiler front with working drive rods. All detail cast into shell including dummy headlight shown above boiler front. Bulge at front of cab allowed for Lionel's much larger motor.

New in 1963, though similar to the 0625, the 0626 had the thumb screw in its smokestack and a piston in the steam chest — but no smoke unit. In 1964 it was available in sets and did have a working smoke unit. Thought to have been made up from extra inventory parts.

0635: first Lionel Pacific with smoke unit, new in 1961 and dropped in 1963; it headed the 5756 set that year and pulled the three Athearn tuscan Penn passenger cars.

First catalogued in 1963, the 0636 was available until 1966, unchanged.

The uncatalogued 0637 Pacific was the first to have its number on a paper sticker under the cab windows and a brass bell on its boiler. The pilot also had steps cast into it — another first; the wire handrails ran down the boiler side to its pilot. Rare!

used on the Husky locomotives and was mounted vertically in the center of the tender with the whistle housing attached to the top shaft. A special button came with the locomotive to activate the whistle. A maintenance folder providing the "how to" on lamp change and lubrication came with each locomotive equipped with smoke and whistle units. All of the steam locomotives with these ingenious accessories are difficult to find.

0602 PENNSYLVANIA: 0-6-0 steam switcher with tender; painted flat black, white lettering; "0602" on cab side; "PENNSYLVANIA" on side of slope-back tender; cast-metal frame; 1960-type motor; plastic pilot and steam chest; valve gear includes wire guides, main rod, and drive rods; "LIONEL" appears on gear cover plate; cast-on handrails; two headlights, one with a bulb in boiler front and one dummy fixture above it; shell fastened to frame by one tab at the rear of frame and a screw passing through the smokestack; metal floor on tender; four-

	Gd	Exc	Mt

wheel metal tender trucks secured with screws to plastic studs extending from body casting through tender floor; catalogued in 1960 only; second most difficult to find of the steam switchers. **60 80 100**

0605: Tank-type steam switcher; painted flat black; "0605" in white numerals appears below the cab window; no lettering appears anywhere on the unit; cast-on handrails and steps; lighted; combination cast-metal and plastic frame; plastic pilot and steam chest; shell mounts to frame with two tabs at the end of frame, which pass through shell, and a screw passing through the smokestack into a weight at the front of frame; rear steps often broken after servicing; combination band and worm drive; easily bent side and drive rods made of very thin metal; coupler with top pivot pin used with metal cover; catalogued in 1959 for separate sale and in set 5723; catalogued again

0642: Lionel's first "Haybird," which appeared in the prized valise pack set of 1961. Lighted, with metal pilot; note steps, large motor in cab, and the extra-large drive wheels.

0643: same "Haybird" as 0642 with the exception of its "Helic drive," a spring drive belt. Unlettered tender with solid truck frames.

0645: the first Pacific to have smoke and a whistle in its tender. One of the few locomotives to have blackened wheels — which made it a poor pulling locomotive.

0646: Lionel's fifth steam unit to have smoke, and the second to have a whistle in its long haul tender. Lighted, with wire handrails, metal pony, and trailing trucks, it was also equipped with one rubber traction tire. Note wire to tender for whistle.

0647(A), top; (B) bottom: The last of the Lionel Pacifics and the second to have its number on a paper sticker. Catalogued in 1966 separately, and in one set, 14300-A. Also came with the heat-stamped number shown as (B), from Ken Fairchild Collection. Both have smoke unit, long haul whistling tender with plastic side frame trucks, wire handrails and the white stripe present. Both difficult to find.

	Gd	Exc	Mt

in 1960 for separate sale and in set 5737; (available separately again in 1961-62; the only tank locomotive Lionel produced.)

(A) 1959 motor; black drivers. R. Kughn Collection.

| | 50 | 75 | 90 |

(B) 1960 motor; different coupler; black drivers. R. Kughn Collection.

| | 50 | 75 | 90 |

(C) Highly polished nickel drivers and rods. G. Potts Collection.

| | | | NRS |

0625(LT) SOUTHERN PACIFIC: Pacific with tender; painted flat black locomotive and tender shells; short tender with high sides; white lettering; catalogue number on cab side; "SOUTHERN PACIFIC" across tender side; wire handrails; headlight; cast-metal frame, pilot, and steam chest; no smoke unit; cast weight screwed to frame; frame lettered "LIONEL N.Y., N.Y."; cast-metal pony and trailing trucks with plastic wheels; nylon gear drive; stamped-metal drive rods; sprung metal trucks on tender; catalogued separately in 1959-61 and in sets 5717 and 5731 (1959) and sets 5745 and 5771 (1960).

(A) 1959 motor with ball bearings; motor secured by black plastic gearbox cover.

| | 50 | 75 | 90 |

(B) 1960 motor with thrust plate; motor fastened to frame with a single screw; sold in 1960-61.

| | 50 | 75 | 90 |

0626(LT) SOUTHERN PACIFIC: Pacific with tender; flat black body and tender shell; white lettering; catalogue number appears on cab side; "SOUTHERN PACIFIC" on tender side; white stripe on boiler walkway; internally similar to 0625LT(B); slower gear ratio; no smoke unit, but locomotive does have a piston in the steam chest; thumb screw in stack secures shell; catalogued separately 1963-65 and in sets 14153 (1963) and 14270 (1964); very rare.

(A) Painted shell; 1963.

| | 85 | 100 | 150 |

(B) Unpainted shell; 1964-65.

| | 80 | 100 | 125 |

(C) With smoke unit; 1966. J. Otterbin Collection.

| | | | NRS |

0635(LT) SOUTHERN PACIFIC: Pacific with tender; painted flat black; white lettering; catalogue number on cab side; "SOUTHERN PACIFIC" on tender side; internally similar to 0625LT(B); heating

element in top portion of steam chest; plastic piston located in left side of chest to force smoke up the stack; larger smokestack hole for thumb screw to fasten shell to frame; stamped-metal valve guides; catalogued separately in 1961-62 and in sets 5756 with three tuscan Athearn passenger cars, 5757, 5762 (1961), and in 14043 (1962).

| | 60 | 90 | 125 |

0636(LTS) SOUTHERN PACIFIC: Pacific with tender; flat black, painted body and tender shell; white lettering; catalogue number on cab side; "SOUTHERN PACIFIC" on tender shell; white stripe on boiler walkway; with smoke unit; very similar to 0635LT; short tender with solid frame trucks; catalogued 1963-66; not easily found in good condition.

| | 75 | 100 | 125 |

0637(LTS) SOUTHERN PACIFIC: Pacific with tender; uncatalogued; painted flat black; white lettering; catalogue number on black paper sticker on cab side; "SOUTHERN PACIFIC" stamped on tender; white stripe along boiler walkway; turned brass bell (rather than molded plastic bell found on other Pacific shells); metal handrails with three cotter pins as stanchions; handrails extend to pilot; smoke unit and headlight; frame marked "BUILT BY LIONEL"; geared axle visible through opening in frame; traction tire on one rear driver; short box-type tender; 1960-type motor; steel worm drive; 1963; rare. This locomotive was the only steam unit known to have steps cast into its pilot until 1989 when the 0647 began to show up with steps on the pilot.

(A) Painted shell.

| | 80 | 95 | 125 |

(B) Unpainted shell.

| | 75 | 90 | 100 |

0642: 2-4-2 steam switcher with tender; painted flat black; "0642" in white numerals appears below cab windows; tender matches that found with 0602, but it is unmarked; larger cast-metal frame; plastic steam chest and gear cover; cast-metal pilot; larger drive wheels; sheet-metal lead and trailing trucks with plastic wheels; 1960-type motor; band and worm drive; separate drive and connecting rods found; Lionel name does not appear anywhere on locomotive; catalogued in 1961 separately and in sets 5752 and 5767; catalogued again in 1962 separately and in set 14023; discontinued 1963.

| | 60 | 75 | 100 |

0643: 2-4-2 steam switcher with tender; painted flat black; "0643" in white numerals appears below cab windows; very similar to 0642; sprung trucks replaced in favor of solid frame trucks; no connecting rods; Helic drive; unlettered tender; catalogued in 1963 only in set 14133; very scarce.

| | 60 | 90 | 100 |

0645(LT) SOUTHERN PACIFIC: Pacific with 0645-W long haul whistling tender; black; white lettering; catalogue number on cab side; "SOUTHERN PACIFIC" on tender; no stripe on boiler walkway; similar to 0635LT, but two electrical wires extend from the rear of cab to whistle in tender; blackened wheels on locomotive; long haul tender; catalogued separately 1962-63 and in sets 14074 and 14098 (1961); scarce.

| | 80 | 100 | 140 |

Alco diesel mechanisms. Top: The A-B-A combination shown is typical of the first drive and dummy units of 1959 to 1960. Note the thin drive shaft and black wheels on the power unit. Middle: The improved power unit of 1961, with larger motor and silver sheels. Note larger motor shaft present, with same dummy B and lighted dummy A as above. Bottom: The new Helic drive with larger weight at rear, followed by the 0535W B unit with horn unit that operated from two AA batteries. This frame is plastic; the metal A frame can also be found on some 1965 dummy A units. The last unit shown was produced in 1964 and was the first gearbox-type drive Lionel offered. Note double shaft motor with only one shaft in use.

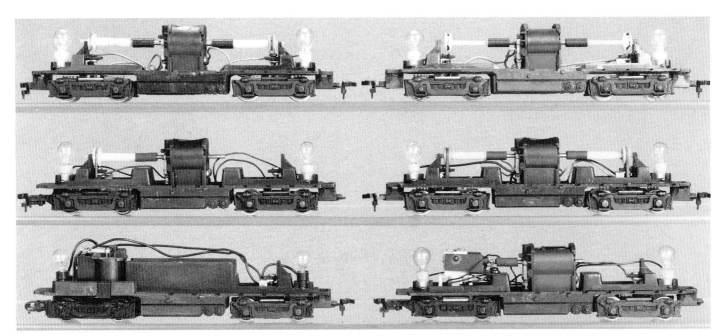

*Top: 1959 Geep and rectifier mechanism with thin shaft, followed by 1960 thick shaft with mill-finished frame.
Middle: 1963 Helic drive belt "A spring," followed by blackened frame 1960 with added weight and larger motor.
Bottom: The only direct drive offered by Lionel, used on the 0592 SF Geep only, followed by the single-truck
gearbox drive of 1965.*

*Six power units shown before the Decoration Department did its work in making the shells into Lionel models.
All detail work can be clearly seen before painting hid some of it, such as the fine rivet and louvers on the shell
sides. Few undecorated models are available to the average collector, with only so many shells sent to each
department to use in its specific step of production. The center cab on the second shelf and the rectifier both carry
paper labels that read "Non-production item," while the first GP-9 on the third shelf could very well have been the
preproduction run of the 0592 SF Geep from the Decoration Department.*

*Some of the unmarked shells found at Madison Hardware — most are from the old Hobbyline die work. As we all know, the
shells were used in a number of ways with many road names and numbers used in their decoration. Most of the caboose and
gondola shells were sold both painted and unpainted.*

Five Lionel mockup models, all of which became a part of pre-1966 Lionel HO. Top: An undecorated Pacific and the 0850 Missile Launching Flat, with wooden platforms. Middle: Mercury flat, with wooden capsule that has detail work hand-painted on its sides, and 0841 AEC caboose. Bottom: 0349 Turbo Missile Car mockup with non-working platform. The sticker labels read "This is a mockup — not a production line item".

	Gd	Exc	Mt

0646(LTS) SOUTHERN PACIFIC: Pacific with 0645-W long haul whistling tender; similar to 0645LTS; black; white lettering; catalogue number on cab side; "SOUTHERN PACIFIC" on tender; catalogued in one set 1963-65 and separately 1964-65; scarce.

| (A) Silver wheels. | 75 | 90 | 125 |
| (B) Blackened wheels. | 75 | 90 | 125 |

0647(LTS) SOUTHERN PACIFIC: Pacific with 0645-W long haul whistling tender; similar to 0637LTS, with headlight and smoke unit; white catalogue number appears on black paper sticker on cab side; long haul tender lettered "SOUTHERN PACIFIC"; solid-frame, six-wheel tender trucks; catalogued only in 1966 separately and in set 14300; very rare — the last steam locomotive produced.

(A) Paper sticker. K. Fairchild, G. Horan, and R. Kughn Collections.

| | 80 | 95 | 125 |

(B) Stamped number. K. Fairchild, R. Kughn, J. Otterbin, B. Juhasz, and G. Potts Collections.

| | 90 | 125 | 150 |

Note: George Horan has verified that the unit also exists with a pilot that included the cast-on steps and a heat-stamped white "0647" on its cab. The 0645-W Whistling Tender lettered for the SP and available with the last three listed locomotives was also available as a separate sale item. Packed in a separate orange picture-window carton bearing "0645-W" and "(Whistle Tender)". It is believed the tender was sold as a separate item to upgrade earlier steam locomotives. G. Bunza comment.

| | 20 | 35 | 50 |

DIESEL AND ELECTRIC LOCOMOTIVES

Frames, Motors, and Couplers Used on 0593, 0596, and 0591

When Lionel produced its first diesel locomotive mechanism, it attempted to combine features from the early Rivarossi gear-driven locomotives and the later belt-driven Athearn units. The hybrid mechanism worked so poorly that it only lasted one year in production.

The cast-metal frame (part number 0596-16) has integral coupler pads with pins that project downward through the metal cover; two raised areas support the one-piece nylon drive shaft and pulley that connects the motor shaft with a rubber coupling, much the same as the 1958 Athearn units. Neoprene O rings transfer power from the double-shafted, three-pole motor to the cast-metal trucks, both of which are powered. The motor, which sits on four raised areas in the well of the frame, is held together by a single screw. There is a white plastic electrical socket for a bayonet-base headlight at each end. A single screw secures each truck to the frame. Blackened wheel sets on some units contribute to poor operation, because they impede current collection. In 1960 the Service Stations were instructed to change the blackened wheel sets to the newer chrome wheels just introduced. The 1959 locomotives use a standard horn hook coupler.

1960 Frames, Motors, and Couplers

The 1960 frame is similar to the previous frame with the following exceptions: cavity beneath the motor on 1959 frames filled, two vertical extensions added to increase weight, larger nylon drive shaft with pulley, hole added to accept pin found on new coupler, chrome-plated wheel sets, and improved electrical conductivity. The 1960 motors have sleeve bearings, two screws, and interlocks (between the halves/pieces). Used on the 0581 Pennsylvania electric, 0597 NP GP-9, and 0598 NYC GP-9.

1963 Frames Used on 0593 GP-9

Identified as "Helic Drive" in the catalogue, the 1963 frame is fairly similar to that of 1960. Only one truck is powered. Lionel continued to use the double-shafted 1960 motor, although only one shaft transmitted torque to the powered truck with the new Helic spring drive belt. The trucks have cast-metal sides and chrome-plated wheel sets. The 1963 couplers have a ½-inch shank extending from one side. This coupler was also used on most rolling stock from 1963 to 1966. Both headlights remain from the 1960 design. There is no part number on the frame, but it is stamped "LIONEL N.Y., N.Y."

1965 Frame Used on 0594 SF GP-9

In 1965 Lionel reintroduced the 1963 frame with a different drive train. The 1965 frame has a larger motor and a single power truck with all-gear drive. A rubber coupling connects the motor shaft to the metal drive shaft of the truck. The truck is secured by a single pin that passes through the frame and the plastic truck housing. There is no part number on the frame, but it is stamped "LIONEL N.Y., N.Y."

1966 Frame Used on 0592 SF GP-9

Lionel modified the frame again in 1966 and added more weight to the center of the frame. The frame is solid metal from truck to truck. The rear axle of the cast-metal rear truck is driven directly by the truck-mounted, 1960-type motor. The dummy front truck is all plastic. Headlights and couplers are similar to those on the 1965 frame. There is no part number on the frame, but it is stamped "BUILT BY LIONEL". Minor changes in gear ratios occurred during production.

Alco Diesel Frames

The development of Alco frames follows that of the Geep frames. However, the shape is different, because of the difference in body contours. Unlike the underside of a Geep frame, the area between the trucks on an Alco frame is more exposed to show the battery box and ladder detail. Alco frames have only one headlight, which is located at the front of the unit. The changes to chrome wheel sets and blackened frames occurred in production of both the Alco GP-9 locomotives. Dummy A units have the same frame as found on the powered models, while the B units usually have a plastic frame. Very few B units were made with a cast frame.

Listings of Rectifiers

0581 PENNSYLVANIA: Painted flat tuscan; keystone herald stamped on each end and cab sides; gold striping and lettering; "0581" on cab side; "PENNSYLVANIA" on hood; single stripe over entire length, broken by cab; two smaller stripes on front end, just below the longer stripe; brass pantograph; clear headlight lens at each end; part number inside shell; sold without handrails, although stanchion holes present; black 1960-type frame; catalogued in 1960 only as a separate item and in set 5742 with three Athearn Pennsylvania passenger cars.

| | 150 | 200 | 225 |

0591 N.H.(NEW HAVEN): Painted black; bright orange cab roof and cab sides; white "0591" on cab side; ½" wide white band along length of body, broken by cab; white "N.H." on each end; larger New Haven logo, with white "N" and orange "H" on long hood; orange "BLT BY / LIONEL" on white stripe; one brass pantograph; clear headlight lens at each end; only cab end lighted; sold without handrails, although stanchion holes are present; part number inside shell; decorated by

	Gd	Exc	Mt

Lionel; introduced in 1959 as a separate item and in set 5725; also listed, without illustration, in 1960.

(A) Flat black, painted body; 1959-type frame with natural steel finish.

	150	200	250

(B) Gloss black, painted body; blackened 1960-type frame. Rare.

	150	200	250

Listings of EMD GP-7 and GP-9 Diesels

0592 SANTA FE: GP-9; painted medium blue body; bright yellow striping and lettering; "0592" on cab sides; yellow ends and dynamic brake housing; single stripe along floor line; "Santa Fe" on hood below brake housing; herald next to name; two white metal horns; clear plastic lens at each end; only cab end lighted; catalogued only in 1966, separately and in 14260; set number used again in 1966 with different locomotive; rare with the proper gear-driven mechanism. See information given above on frames and motors. **75 100 150**

0593 NORTHERN PACIFIC: GP-9; similar to 0597, except "0593" appears on cab side; different frame than 0597; catalogued separately in 1963 and in set 14193 with dummy 0593T; the dummy appears in the catalogue with the number visible in the illustration; it was not produced with the "T" stamped on the model, however the "T" does appear in the catalogue and on the carton. **50 90 120**

0594 SANTA FE: GP-9; similar to 0592, except for drive and "0594" appearing on cab side; catalogued separately in 1963 and 1965, in set 14143 in 1964 and in set 14260 in 1965. **50 75 100**

0596 NEW YORK CENTRAL: GP-9; painted dark gray; light gray band bordered by white pin stripes on side of long and short hoods; "0596" on cab sides; white lettering; "BLT BY / LIONEL" at the end of long hood; road name at center; two metal horns, one on the short hood and one just below the second fan on the side of the long hood; sold without handrails, although stanchion holes are present; 1959-type frame and drive; catalogued only in 1959 as a separate item and in freight set 5727; scarce. **75 100 150**

0597 NORTHERN PACIFIC: GP-9; black and gold, painted body; red pin stripe between principal colors; gold "0597" and "NORTHERN PACIFIC" on long hood; decal herald on cab sides; red "RADIO / EQUIPPED" on short hood; two metal horns; 1960-type motor and frame; catalogued in 1960 separately and in freight set 5743; catalogued again in 1961 separately and in set 14064; discontinued in 1963; scarce. **60 90 125**

0598 NEW YORK CENTRAL: GP-7; similar to 0596, less roof-mounted dynamic brake housing; "0598" on cab side; 1960-type frame and motor; catalogued in 1961 separately and in freight set 5755; catalogued again in 1962 only as a separate item; more common than 0596. **70 90 100**

Listings of Alco Diesels — Powered A Units

Note: All of the Santa Fe Alcos were decorated in the red and silver war bonnet scheme. These units headed most passenger sets from 1959 until the end of production in 1966. They were all made from the old Hobbyline dies. With the exception of road numbers, markings are the same on all units. The forward portion of the body is red, while the roof and sides are silver. Black and yellow pin stripes separate the principal body colors. "BLT BY / LIONEL" appears in the last lower side panel; the road name appears at the center. All lettering is black. The catalogue number appears just behind the cab door on each side. Each shell has one clear headlight lens, two metal horns on the roof, and a Santa Fe decal just below the headlight.

0535 SANTA FE: See "Note" above; catalogued in 1962 for separate sale with the 0535W B unit with horn; both units catalogued in set 14084; 1962-type frame; scarce. **50 75 100**

0536 SANTA FE: See "Note"; catalogued in 1963 for separate sale and with the 0535W B unit; also in set 14203 in an A-B-A combination; catalogued again in 1964-65 separately and in an A-B-A combination in set 14310.

(A) 1963-type frame; 1963-64. **50 75 100**
(B) 1965-type frame; 1965 only. **50 75 100**

0537 SANTA FE: See "Note"; direct-drive rear truck with two traction tires; 0537 B unit also catalogued, but made as 0535W; A-B-A combination sold separately and in set 14310; rare with right drive unit. **50 80 125**

0555 SANTA FE: See "Note"; Helic drive; 1963-type frame; catalogued in 1963 separately and in set 14173 with four red-striped passenger cars; catalogued again in 1964 in set 14290; catalogued also in 1965 in set 14320; discontinued in 1966; rare. **60 90 125**

0556 SANTA FE: See "Note"; direct-drive rear truck; catalogued only in 1966 in set 14320 with 0575 dummy B unit; very rare. Often confused with more common 0565. **50 75 100**

0564 CHESAPEAKE AND OHIO: Painted dark blue; bright yellow cab hood and lower side panels; blue lettering; "C AND / O" on nose and on cab sides just below windows; "BLT BY / LIONEL" does not appear on model; two metal horns; clear headlight lens; 1960-type frame; catalogued in 1960 for separate sale and in a military set 5739; catalogued in 1961 separately and in set 5733; discontinued in 1962; no C & O dummy units were made. **60 90 125**

0565 SANTA FE: See "Note" concerning Santa Fe units; 1959 catalogue incorrectly describes 0565 as a dummy A unit; catalogued again in 1960, for separate sale with 0575 dummy B unit and in set 5747 also with the B unit; catalogued again in 1961 in sets 5758 and 5759; catalogued again in 1963. **40 60 80**

0566 THE TEXAS SPECIAL: Painted red body; white lower side panels from cab side below windows to rear of unit; white star below headlight; red lettering on white panels; two metal horns; catalogued in 1959 separately and in two sets; catalogued in 1960 in an A-B combination for separate sale and in set 5770; sold only in A-B combination in 1961 and in set 14054 in 1962; the most frequently catalogued road name next to Santa Fe; all Texas Special passenger cars were produced by Athearn; very common.

(A) 1958-59-type frame; flat red. **40 75 100**
(B) 1960-type frame; semi-gloss red. **50 80 125**

0567 ALASKA RAILROAD: Painted dark blue; deep flat yellow from cab door to rear of unit; road name decal on nose; blue lettering; "BLT BY / LIONEL", road name and number on yellow band in lower side panels; two metal horns; clear plastic headlight lens; 1959-type frame with natural steel finish; catalogued in 1959 only in an A-B-A combination and in set 5729; rare. **90 100 150**

0568 UNION PACIFIC: Painted semi-gloss yellow; thin gray stripe centered from just behind the cab door to rear of unit; red lettering; "UNION PACIFIC" and "0568" appear in the lower side panels; light gray UP winged herald just below cab windows; two metal horns; plastic headlight lens; 1960-type frame; catalogued in 1962 only in set 14033; no dummy units made in this road name; rare. Available 1963 uncatalogued with Helic drive.

	Gd	Exc	Mt
(A) 1962.	75	100	125
(B) 1963; Helic drive.	80	125	150

0569(P) UNION PACIFIC: Similar to 0568, with new number; "P" does not appear with number on locomotive; "BLT BY / LIONEL" does not appear on this unit.

(A) 1962-type frame.	60	75	100
(B) 1963-type frame with Helic drive; two rubber tires.	60	75	100

0571 PENNSYLVANIA: Unpainted maroon body; keystone herald decal below headlight on nose; 1/8" yellow stripe from rear of unit to cab side and down to floor; road name on lower side panels; number on cab side; "BLT BY / LIONEL" does not appear on this unit; 1963-type frame with helic drive and two rubber tires; catalogued in 1963 only, as a separate item and in passenger set 14163; no dummy units made in this road name; very rare.

	125	150	200

Listings of Alco Diesels — Dummy A and B Units

The Dummy units were not made in all road names. Lionel had proposed many different road names (see photographs of B unit prototypes), but the lack of sufficient advance orders preempted several schemes. All A units have a headlight; one B unit has a horn.

0535W SANTA FE: Dummy B unit with horn; similar to 0575; battery-powered horn; metal truck side frames; 1963-type plastic frame; horn performs poorly; catalogued in 1962 in sets and in an A-B combination; continued in many combinations through 1966; difficult to find with horn intact.

	35	50	90

0575 SANTA FE: Dummy B; silver, painted body; red, yellow, and black striping; lettering as found on A units; plastic trucks screwed in place; no light; catalogued 1959-63 and 1965-66. Common.

(A) Cast-metal frame.	20	25	35
(B) Plastic frame.	15	20	30

0576 THE TEXAS SPECIAL: Dummy B unit; painted red body; white stripe; road name, number, and "BLT BY / LIONEL" on white stripe; catalogued in sets and separately 1959-61; common.

(A) Cast-metal frame.	20	25	35
(B) Plastic frame.	15	20	30

0577 ALASKA RAILROAD: Dummy B unit; painted and lettered per A unit; numbered "0577"; 1959 plastic frame; catalogued in 1959 only separately and in set 5729; rare.

	50	60	80

0586 THE TEXAS SPECIAL: Dummy A unit; painted and lettered like powered unit; numbered "0586"; 1958-type metal frame; blackened wheels; catalogued only in 1959 as a separate item.

	50	75	90

0587 ALASKA RAILROAD: Dummy A unit; similar to powered A unit, but numbered "0587"; 1959-type metal frame; catalogued in 1959 only as a separate item; rare.

	50	60	80

0595 SANTA FE: Dummy A unit; similar to powered A unit, but numbered "0595"; 1959-type metal frame; blackened wheels; catalogued in many sets and in multiple-unit combinations; catalogued 1959 and 1961-66; very common.

	20	30	45

SMALL MOTORIZED UNITS

With the exception of the Gang Car, which has a sheet-metal frame, all of the four-wheel diesels have a cast-metal frame with direct gear

drive to both axles. They can be found with either brass or nylon worm gears on the motor shafts. Similar to the design used for Alco frames, the two halves are secured by two screws; the motor is held in place between the halves, one of which is insulated. The bracket for the single headlight is held in place by one of the coupler-mounting screws. The frame is not an Athearn product, as some people believe. Rather, it is a Lionel item, which was introduced in 1959 and continued through 1966. A black plastic nameplate, which bears the Lionel name in white letters, is located between the two wheel sets; the Gang Car wheels are slightly wider than those used on the Alcos. The early plate reads " HUSKY SWITCHER, The Lionel Corporation, New York, made in U.S. of America". The later plate reads "The Lionel Corporation, New York, made in U.S. of America". The plate also serves to seal the motor and gears from dust and dirt. It is found on all Husky switchers. All of the small diesel units are scarce.

Geoffrey Bunza comments:

By my own observations, the older frame had four raised, flat oval surfaces, two each on the right and left sides. The two on the left side are somewhat obscured by the screws which secure the frame halves together. Athearn frames used on the 0560 DRG Snowplow and the 0570 Navy Switcher had the same ovals, as do Athearn hustler frames made today. The newer frames seem to have flattened rectangular surfaces where the ovals were on the old frame. The 0545 Switcher is listed as having "1959-type motor and frame." I have found the 0545 with the flattened frame sides, and only once with the 1959 (single-screw) motor. Since the 0545 was first released in 1961, might it not be less likely that one could find it with a 1959-type motor? My only conclusion: the flattened frames are the *later* variation. Note: my copy of the service manual does not differentiate among the listings of the frames for any of the small units.

1: See (0068-50)

7: See (0068) and (0068-100)

0050 LIONEL LINES SECTION GANG CAR: Unpainted plastic body; metal handrails; stamped-metal frame; chrome wheels similar to those found on Alco diesels; blue rubber man (the same used on the O Gauge piggyback platform accessory; blue rubber bumpers; "LIONEL LINES" and "0050" on side; shaft motor drives O ring, which drives axles; reverses when either bumper contacts a solid object; runs fairly well; catalogued 1959-63.

(A) All-orange body; white lettering; 1959-60.	30	50	90
(B) Orange top; gray bottom; black lettering; 1961.	30	50	90
(C) Similar to (B), but white lettering; 1962.	35	60	100
(D) Gray top; orange bottom; white lettering; 1963.	35	60	100

0055 M & StL HUSKY: Painted red; white trim at front of the hood; white lettering; road name and number on cab side; illustrated in the black and white catalogues with white cab sides, but not produced as shown; headlight; catalogued in sets and separately 1961-66; catalogued more than any other small locomotive.

(A) 1960-type frame with brass worm gear; two metal horns.	40	60	80
(B) Later frame with nylon worm gears; two metal horns.	40	60	80
(C) Similar to (B), but no horns; 1964-66.	35	40	75

0056 AEC HUSKY: Painted white body; red cab sides; red trim on front edge of hood; white lettering; "AEC" and "0056" on cab sides; clear lens at each end; operating headlight at front only; two metal horns; body shell as manufactured by Lionel may be differentiated from

0581

0591

0592

0594

0593

0597

0598

Top: Penn rectifier, catalogued in 1960 only, followed by the NH Electric of 1959 and 1960; the "BLT BY / LIONEL" is not present on the long hood of the 0581 unit. Second: 0592 GP-9, available in 1966 only with direct drive power truck, while the 0594 was available from 1963 to 1965 in sets and separately. Third: 1963 power Geep, followed by the 0597 of 1960-1962, known to have come with double-stamped numbers. Bottom: The NYC 0598 of 1961-1962 is shown, but its counterpart, the 0596 of 1959, is not pictured.

	Gd	Exc	Mt

Athearn product, as the Lionel unit has a much larger headlight housing; also, Athearn units have "HUSTLER" molded into front radiator, Lionel units do not; 1959-type motor; catalogued in 1959 in set 5719 and separately in 1959-60; scarce.

(A) Regular version, as described.	60	90	125

(B) Promotional model for NBC; painted and lettered as regular version; decal with "WNBC-660 N.Y." in black letters on side of hood; model displayed on desk-top display with a left-hand track switch, three short sections of track, and a bumper; a plaque on the front of the display is lettered "NATIONAL BROADCASTING COMPANY"; a plaque on the end is lettered "MADE BY / THE LIONEL CORPORATION"; the top of the display is lettered to indicate changes in the names of the New York television and radio stations; may be one of a kind. T. Shepler Collection. **NRS**

(C) Right side lettered "WNBC-TV / Channel 4 TV". G. Juhasz Collection. **NRS**

Note: Buck Buckley stated decal was poor and there could have been a "W" in front of "NBC 660 NY" on left side.

0057 UNION PACIFIC HUSKY: Painted yellow; gray cab sides; red lettering and trim on front edge of hood; road name and number on side of hood; two metal horns; headlight lens inserts; 1959-type motor; catalogued in 1960 only for separate sale; very scarce.

	50	75	100

	Gd	Exc	Mt

0058 ROCK ISLAND HUSKY: Flat black, painted body; bright red cab sides; white lettering; road name and catalogue number on cab side; white trim on front edge of hood; two metal horns; headlight lens inserts; 1960-type frame; catalogued in set 5735 in 1960 and as a separate item from 1960 to 1963, when it was discontinued.

(A) Brass worm gear.	40	75	100
(B) Nylon worm gear.	40	75	100

0059 U.S. AIR FORCE HUSKY: Painted white; blue and red Air Force herald on cab side; dark blue lettering; "MINUTEMAN" on cab side; two metal horns; headlight lens inserts; 1960-type frame with brass gears; catalogued only in 1962 for separate sale; second rarest of the Husky locomotives. **75 100 150**

(0068) EXECUTIVE INSPECTION CAR: Painted red body; light gray unpainted bumpers at front and rear; clear plastic one-piece window insert; white sidewalls stamped on the four cast-on wheels; two holes in the bottom of car doors mount shell to Husky frame; no couplers nor lights; no lettering nor numbers on body; catalogued for separate sale only in 1961-62; shown in 1962 catalogue with "7" on its door; the body shown was made for the Lionel race car sets of the same year. Some of these shells have turned up with the holes for mounting on the Husky mechanism.

(A) Frosted windows.	100	125	150
(B) Clear windows. T. Shepler Collection.			NRS

Gd   Exc   Mt

Note: The Lionel HO race car bodies had the same holes for chassis mounting as the 0068 Executive Inspection Car. One can also find a very nice picture of both race cars in *Greenberg's Guide to Lionel Trains, 1945-1969, Volume I: Motive Power and Rolling Stock*, p. 159. We include this comment and the following for reference:

(0068-50) LIONEL HO RACE CAR: Red car body with heat-stamped "1" on left and right side doors, catalogued 1961, set 6100.

(0068-100) LIONEL HO RACE CAR: Yellow car body with heat-stamped "7" on left and right side doors, catalogued 1961, set 6100. G. Bunza comments.

0545 ERIE LACKAWANNA GE 44-TON SWITCHER: Black, painted body; white lettering; road number and large diamond herald on side; white grid trim; one working headlight; cast-on steps and couplers at each end; only four-wheel diesel with body-mounted couplers; 1959-type motor and frame; catalogued in 1961 separately and in set 5751; catalogued in 1962 separately and in set 14013.   **50**   **75**   **100**

0561 M & StL SNOW BLOWER: Husky; bright red, painted body; white cab sides; red lettering; road name and number appear on cab sides; design similar to that of the O Gauge snow blower; red blower housing; black plastic plow blade; operates by metal shaft and rubber cap driven directly by the motor shaft; solid plastic headlight fixture cast onto top

Gd   Exc   Mt

of blower housing; no headlight bulb or fixture; 1959-type motor; rear coupler only; catalogued as a separate item 1959-60; rarest Husky.

              75   **150**   **300**

BOXCARS

The early boxcars introduced by Lionel are all products of the old Hobbyline dies. They have thick plastic shells and oversized detail in the casting. They are all rather high in profile. The cars are assembled from four separate pieces — with the roof and top door guide being one casting; the floor, sides, and ends as another; and a separate door on each side. They have sprung trucks, which are screwed in place. Most of the cars were catalogued for only one year, but a few of the cars reappeared with different numbers. Few of the cars were catalogued in sets.

Towards the end of production in 1964, there were a few boxcars made from a new Lionel die. These cars are few in number and very different in appearance from the earlier cars. They have much lighter shells, with a thinner section and a lower profile. Lionel continued to use operable doors, but the later cars had a claw foot-style door, which was easily damaged. They have metal floors; some have black plastic floor bracing beneath the floor detail. Others have a metal floor with only a plastic bolster to hold the trucks. All of these cars have plastic

Santa Fe Alcos. Top: Power A of 1959; dummy B, 1959-1966; dummy A, 1959-1966. Second: Power A of 1962, power A of 1963-1965, power A of 1966; the 0535 and then the 0556 are the hardest of the SF road names to find (the latter has a #1 direct drive rear truck). Third: Power unit with matching B unit with horn, offered in 1962. Bottom: Power unit available from 1963 to 1965 with Helic drive.

	Gd	Exc	Mt

talgo-type trucks. Produced for only two years, the later style boxcars are more difficult to find than the Hobbyline types.

0864-275 STATE OF MAINE: Similar to 0864-350, below, except number "0864-275" appears on car instead; catalogued in 1962 only.

	25	40	55

0864300 THE ALASKA RAILROAD: Painted dark blue to match the Alaska Alco diesels; ¼" yellowish-orange band on the side; yellow lettering; catalogue number "0864300" and outline of the Alaskan Boy appears to the left of the door; road name spelled at right; "BLT BY / LIONEL" on car side; all detail molded into body casting, including floor bracing, brakes, and valves; five-board door; sprung metal talgo-type trucks; "LIONEL" on cast floor; weighted with a metal slug above each truck; one of the first three boxcars introduced by Lionel; 1959 only.

	35	50	65

0864325 DSS and A: Painted red body; matching door; flat black roof; white lettering; numbered "0864325", "BLT BY / LIONEL" on car side; sprung trucks; molded detail as described for 0864-300; catalogued in one set in 1959, 5725, and as a separate item from 1959 until 1961; second of the HO boxcars. 20 30 45

0864350 STATE OF MAINE: Painted red, white, and blue; white lettering on blue and red portions of car side; black lettering on white

Top: Only four known variations of the 0050 Gang Car (1959-1960, 1961, 1962, 1963). Second: M & StL Husky, 1961-1966, in three variations of drive unit; AEC unit of 1959-1960, which came in two variations, one a special NBC-TV promotional model; 1960 UP; the Rock Island 0058 of 1960-1963, with blackened frame, found in two variations of power frame. Third: Air Force unit, 1962; Erie cab, catalogued 1961-1962; the rarest of all small units, the 0561 M & StL Snow Blower of 1959-1960 — a real prize to the HO collector. Bottom: Track Cleaning Car, that depends on another source of power to move, and the Executive Inspection Car of 1961-1962, known to have come in two variations.

	Gd	Exc	Mt

portions; numbered "0864350", "BLT BY / LIONEL" on side; details as found on all other boxcars from Hobbyline dies; sprung trucks; catalogued in set 5725 in 1959 and separately 1959-61; rare with this catalogue number. **25 45 55**

0864400 BOSTON AND MAINE: Painted light blue; unpainted black, four letterboard door; white lettering; "BLT BY / LIONEL" and full catalogue number "0864400"on car side; plastic wheels; talgo-type truck; made from Hobbyline dies; catalogued 1960-61 and 1963; catalogued in set 14203 in 1963 and said to be new, although car remained unchanged from 1961. Very rare. **50 75 100**

0864-700 SANTA FE: Painted bright red; white lettering; herald and catalogue number at left of door; "with . . SHOCK / CONTROL" and slogans at right of door; sprung trucks; made from Hobbyline dies; catalogued separately only 1961-62; rare. **20 35 45**

0864900 NEW YORK CENTRAL: Painted jade green; black and white herald at left of door; "NEW YORK" and "SYSTEM" appear in red lettering in herald above and below "CENTRAL" in white lettering; "NYC" appears in black lettering on a white square at right of door; catalogue number "0864900"in red lettering below square; "BLT BY / LIONEL"; catalogued separately 1960-62. **25 35 40**

0864-925 NEW YORK CENTRAL: Similar to 0864-900, except number "0864-925" appears on car instead; also, does not have "BLT

BY / LIONEL" as found on earlier car; plastic trucks; 1963-type couplers; made from Hobbyline dies; catalogued in 1964 only in three freight sets, 14270, 14280, and 14300; scarce. **25 35 45**

0864-935 NEW YORK CENTRAL: Similar to 0864-900; "BLT BY / LIONEL" absent; plastic trucks; 1963- type couplers; catalogued in 1963 separately and in sets 14183 and 14233. **25 30 35**

0874 NEW YORK CENTRAL: New car type; new Lionel dies; low profile; light construction; painted jade green; lettering as found on other NYC cars; "0874" in red lettering at right of door; "BLT BY / LIONEL" absent; new door type with four claw feet; door rides on external guides; no number boards on door; metal frame with no detail, except truck bolster; 1963-type talgo trucks; separate black floor bracing; spartan appearance; catalogued as a separate item in 1964-65, while 0864-925 NYC appeared in sets; rare. **20 30 40**

0874(-25) NEW YORK CENTRAL: Identical to 0874; truck bolster on bottom; no floor bracing; "-25" added to carton only; catalogued in sets 1965-66; rare. **25 35 40**

0874(-60) BOSTON AND MAINE: Same car type as 0874; painted medium blue; white lettering; "0874" (without suffix) on car side; "BLT BY / LIONEL" absent; catalogued 1964-65; rare. **25 35 45**

0586

0587

0571

Top: Texas Special Alcos. The dummy A was catalogued only in 1959; dummy B can be found with plastic or metal frames. Note blackened wheel sets. Second: Alaska A-B-A, catalogued in 1959 only; an uncommon road name in the three-unit combination. Third: C & O power A, catalogued for two years only (1960-1961); the Texas Special power unit of 1960, with nickel wheel sets; unpainted Pennsylvania power A, available in 1963 only with Helic drive. Bottom: Two UP powered A units, 1962 and 1963; both can be found with Helic or band drive power. No B units were ever offered in the C & O, Pennsylvania, or UP road names.

Top: The Alaskan of 1959; DSS and A of 1959-1961. Second: BAR, available from 1949-1961; BM, catalogued from 1961-1963. Third: SF of 1961-62; NYC, 1960-1962. All cars on top three shelves were made from the old Hobbyline dies, while Lionel's new die work of 1964 was used to make those on bottom shelf: NYC and BM, both available in 1964-1965 and not carrying the "BLT BY / Lionel" markings.

0864-300

0864-325

0864-350

0864-400

0864-700

0864-900

0874

0874-60

Four of the Lionel production work cabooses catalogued in sets and separately from 1959 to 1963 are shown on top two shelves. Top: The BM was the only work caboose not to have a locomotive with the same road name; catalogued in 1961 only. The SF was catalogued 1959-1960 separately and in sets and was available un-catalogued until 1962. Second: The NP and the C & O were both catalogued in 1960, with the C & O listed until 1962; it was catalogued in 1963 with the trucks changing to solid side frames. The suffix also changed to -285 but only on the box. All of these work cabooses carry the full seven-digit Lionel number on their sides. The bottom shelves show four of the caboose road names, with all carrying the 0817 number on their sides; again, the suffix was only used on the box or in the catalogue. Third: SF, followed by a NH which is part of the Ken Fairchild Collection. Bottom: UP and Rock Island. All except the black NH (only shown in 1963) first catalogued in 1960.

CABOOSES AND WORK CABOOSES

Shells

All of the Lionel cabooses follow the Santa Fe offset-cupola steel caboose design. The body shell is a one-piece casting, with the roofwalk molded in place and a tab at each end to secure the body to the frame. Few of the cabooses released after 1963 came with any separate detail parts.

Frames

The frame changed only slightly through the period. It is a one-piece black plastic casting with steps, toolbox, coupler pockets, valves, and floor bracing molded in place. All frames are marked "LIONEL" and "N.Y. N.Y." The frame also has a tab on each side for interlocking the body and frame. A few of the cars are illuminated; these have special trucks for electrical collection as used on the operating cars. It appears that the catalogue number 0817 covers the years 1959–1960, while 0827 covers 1961–1963. Several additional numbers — 0838, 0840, 0841, and 0873 — represent production from 1961–1966. The variety of road names, many of which were produced for only a year or two, presents an interesting challenge for the collector.

The early and late frame types may be distinguished as follows (note that 1962 cabooses may be found with either frame type):

Type I. Early frame, 1960–1961; part number molded on bottom; generally found with sprung trucks.

Type II. Later frame, 1963–1966; no part number; found with solid frame trucks.

Ten more of the cabooses offered from 1961 through 1963. Note that the first three illuminated cars shown carry detail absent on the other seven. These cars were only available for one or two years, with even the cheaper cars of 1963 being difficult to locate today. 0827-50 from the Ken Fairchild Collection.

	Gd	Exc	Mt		Gd	Exc	Mt
					10	15	25

Listings of Cabooses

0817(-150) A.T. & S.F.: Flat red, painted body; white lettering; only "0817" and "A.T. & S.F." on car side; "BLT BY / LIONEL" absent; Type I frame with sprung trucks; catalogued in 1960, separately and in sets 5745, 5747, and 5771, and in 1961, separately and in set 5758; scarce.

| | **10** | **15** | **20** |

0817(-275) NH (NEW HAVEN): Flat black, painted body; white lettering; "-275" does not appear on car side; decorated like 1959 Athearn caboose, which has the same stock number; Type II frame with solid frame trucks; no ladders nor railings; catalogued in 1963 separately and in set 14153. **15 20 25**

0817(-325) UNION PACIFIC: Painted flat yellow body; flat gray cupola; bright red lettering; "UNION PACIFIC" and "0817" on car side; "BLT BY / LIONEL" absent; two separate brakewheels; separate wire handrails and metal ladders; Type I frame with part number; metal sprung trucks; uncatalogued; only sold separately in 1960-61.

0817(-350) ROCK ISLAND: White lettering; "ROCK ISLAND", "0817", and herald appear on car side; "BLT BY / LIONEL" absent; separate wire handrails and metal ladders; Type I frame; sprung metal trucks; catalogued in 1960 only in set 5735.

(A) Red body; black cupola. J. Otterbin and J. Kimenhour comments.

| | **15** | **20** | **30** |

(B) Painted flat black body. **NRS**

0827 SAFETY FIRST: Painted flat red body; white lettering; "SAFETY FIRST" and "0827" on car side; catalogued in 1961, separately and in set 5757, and separately 1962-63; illustrations in the later catalogues incorrectly show the car with M & StL markings.

(A) Illuminated; separate smokestack; two separate brakewheels; wire handrails and metal ladders; Type I frame; collector trucks; frosted window shell insert. **20 25 35**

(B) Unlighted; no separate details; believed to have been made as an uncatalogued item in 1964. **Verification Requested**

	Gd	Exc	Mt

0827(-50) AEC: Unpainted white plastic body; red lettering as found on 0817-200 Athearn caboose of 1959, except number differs; separate smokestack; two separate brakewheels; Type II frame; solid frame trucks; catalogued in 1963 in set 14183.

	Gd	Exc	Mt
(A) "0841" on car side; no handrails; no ladders.	15	20	25
(B) "0827" on car side; handrails and ladders present; frosted window inserts. T. Shepler Collection.	15	20	25
(C) Same as (B), but lighted. G. Bunza, K. Fairchild Collections.	20	25	35

Note: Also available in Set 14183. R. MacNary-K. Armenti Collection.

0827(-75) A.T. & S.F.: Flat red, painted body; white lettering; "A.T. & S.F." and "0827" appear on car side; separate smokestack; two separate brakewheels; wire handrails and metal ladders; Type II frame; solid frame collector trucks; illuminated; catalogued in 1963 only, in set 14203; scarce.

	Gd	Exc	Mt
(A) Clear window insert.	20	25	35
(B) Frosted window insert.	20	25	30

0837 M & StL: Painted red body; white lettering; "M StL" and "0837" on car side; "BLT BY / LIONEL" absent; separate smokestack; two separate brakewheels; no handrails nor ladders.

	Gd	Exc	Mt
(A) Type I frame; sprung metal trucks; catalogued in 1961, in set 5750, and in 1962, in set 14003.	8	10	15
(B) Type II frame; solid frame trucks; identical to 0837-100; catalogued in 1964-66.	8	10	15

0837(-100) M & StL: Same as original 0837(A), except solid frame trucks and Type II frame; in 1964 the suffix disappeared, and the caboose became 0837 again; see 0837(B); catalogued 1963.

	10	15	20

0837(-110) M & StL: Exactly the same as 0837(B). Late-style box, new number stamped on box on paper label. G. Bunza, G. Potts Collections.

	10	15	20

0838 E (ERIE) Light gray, painted body; red lettering; only "0838" and diamond-shaped "E" herald appear on car side; "BLT BY / LIONEL" absent; separate smokestack; two separate brakewheels; no handrails nor ladders; Type I frame; sprung trucks; catalogued in 1961, in set 5751, and in 1962, in set 14013; not sold separately; scarce.

	10	20	30

0840 NYC: Painted flat black; white lettering; "NYC" and "0840" on car side; "BLT BY / LIONEL" absent; separate smokestack; two separate brakewheels; no handrails nor ladders; Type I frame; sprung trucks; catalogued in 1961 only in set 5755; no mention of item being new; scarce.

	10	15	25

0841: See 0827(-50)

0841 (UNLETTERED): Painted flat red; white "0841" on car side; no additional lettering; Type I frame; sprung trucks; catalogued in 1961, in sets 5734 and 5752, and in 1962, in five different sets; common; see also 0841(-125).

	8	10	15

0841(-50) UNION PACIFIC: Unpainted light yellow body; bright red lettering; "UNION PACIFIC" and "0841" appear on car side; "BLT BY / LIONEL" absent; separate smokestack; two separate brakewheels; Type II frame; catalogued in 1962 only in set 14033; one of the few unpainted cabooses; rare.

	Gd	Exc	Mt
(A) Entire body unpainted yellow plastic.	15	20	35
(B) Cupola painted gray; remainder of body unpainted.	15	20	35

0841(-85) A.T. & S.F. Painted flat red; white lettering; "A.T. & S.F." and "0841" on car side; separate smokestack; two separate brakewheels; Type I frame; sprung metal trucks; catalogued in 1962 only in set 14084; scarce; see also 0841(-175).

	10	15	20

0841(-125) AEC: Unpainted shell, red lettering as found on the 0817-200 and 0827(-50); "0841" on car side; solid frame trucks; otherwise identical to 0841, including number on car side; no detail parts; solid frame trucks; catalogued 1962 in set 15503. K. Fairchild Collection.

	15	20	25

0841(-175) A.T. & S.F.: Type II frame; solid frame trucks; otherwise identical to 0841(-85); catalogued in 1963 only in set 14143.

	10	15	20

0841(-185) A.T. & S.F.: Unpainted red body; white lettering; Type II frame; no brakewheel; no smokestack nor handrails; "0841-185" appears on end of box. J. Otterbin and J. Kimenhour comments.

	10	15	20

Listings of Work Cabooses

0819200 BM (BOSTON AND MAINE): Painted light blue; white lettering; "BM" logo on large letterboard between windows; "BLT BY / LIONEL" on the second letterboard closest to the window; "0819200" on third letterboard at other end of cab; separate black plastic smokestack; two separate brakewheels; wire handrails and metal ladders; weighted with a metal slug; "LIONEL" appears on frame; sprung trucks with plastic bolster; two holes in the floor at the open end of car, but car has no load or derrick; catalogued in 1961 only in set 5762. This is the only work caboose for which Lionel did not offer a locomotive in a matching paint scheme. A Boston & Maine Alco was considered but not made.

	15	20	35

0819225 SANTA FE: Entire car painted light flat gray; red and yellow herald on side of cabin; yellow lettering; "0819225" and "BLT. BY / LIONEL" on letterboards; separate smokestack and brakewheel; wire handrails and metal ladders; sprung trucks with plastic bolsters; catalogued in 1959, separately and in set 5733, and in 1960, in sets 5737, 5741, and 5749; sold uncatalogued in 1961-62.

	15	20	35

0819250 NORTHERN PACIFIC: Painted flat black; semi-gloss red cabin, fence, and toolboxes; black and white herald on cabin side; "0819250" appears in black letters on car side; "LIONEL" on frame and coupler pocket; one brakewheel; wire handrails and metal ladders; catalogued in 1960 only in set 5743; rare.

	15	20	35

0819275 C AND O (CHESAPEAKE AND OHIO): Painted semi-gloss dark blue; bright yellow lettering; "C AND / O" logo on large board between windows; "0819275" on second letterboard; separate smokestack and brakewheel; wire handrails and metal ladders; sprung metal trucks; catalogued in 1960-62, separately and in sets; see also 0819-285.

	12	15	30

(0819-285) C AND O (CHESAPEAKE AND OHIO): Solid frame plastic trucks; otherwise identical to 0819-275, including number on car side; catalogued in 1963, separately and in sets 14193 and 14233.

	12	15	30

FLATCARS, CRANES, AND MISCELLANEOUS CARS

200: See 0889

0800-200 SEABOARD RAILROAD FLAT WITH AIRPLANE: Painted flat black body; white lettering; "Seaboard Railroad", "0800-200", and "BLT BY / LIONEL" appear on car side; one-piece black

	Gd	Exc	Mt

plastic loading frame; not the same as that used on 1958 Athearn cars; separate brakewheel; sprung trucks; catalogued separately in 1960 only, but available as an uncatalogued item until 1963; difficult to find with unbroken airplane.

(A) Airplane with unpainted black underbody; dull orange, painted top portion, tail, and wings.   **20**   **30**   **50**

(B) Airplane with unpainted black underbody; silver, painted top portion, tail, and wings.   **15**   **20**   **35**

0801200 SEABOARD FLAT WITH BOAT: Painted flat black 40' body; white lettering; "SEABOARD", "0801200", and "BLT BY / LIONEL" appear on car side; separate brakewheel; made from Hobbyline dies; catalogued separately in 1960 only, but available as an uncatalogued item until 1962.

(A) Boat with red hull and white top.   **15**   **20**   **45**

(B) Boat with blue hull and white top.   **15**   **20**   **45**

0806 SOUTHERN PACIFIC FLATCAR WITH HELICOPTER: Painted flat black 50' body; white lettering; "SOUTHERN PACIFIC", "0806" and "BLT BY / LIONEL" on side; separate brakewheel; sprung

metal trucks; gray helicopter has single twin blade with turbo charger at each end; helicopter has yellow tail; "BLT BY LIONEL" on left side; helicopter secured with one black rubber band across its black landing gear; no platform on car. This helicopter also used on the 6819 O Gauge non-operating car. Heat-stamped "NAVY" in blue; door in black. Catalogued in 1959 separately and in sets 5717, 5719, and 5731; incorrectly illustrated in 1959 as a tuscan car loaded with a helicopter with double turbo blades; catalogued separately also in 1960 and shown again incorrectly as a blue flatcar.

(A) Helicopter lettered "NAVY" in blue; black door.   **20**   **35**   **50**

(B) Unmarked helicopter.   **NRS**

0807 NYC FLATCAR WITH BULLDOZER: Painted red 40' car; white lettering; "NYC", "0807", "BLT BY / LIONEL" and a NYC herald appear on car side; separate brakewheel; sprung trucks; Caterpillar Bulldozer made by Lesney; the bulldozer is Number 18 in the Matchbox series; it has a yellow body, green rubber treads (almost always missing), and gray wheels; a driver is cast onto the seat; secured to the car by a red

Ten of the flatcars offered by Lionel between 1959 and 1966, shown with original loads. Closeups of loads appear in Chapter VIII, in the section on forgeries, in hopes of discouraging the temptation of making up a rare car. Shown are seven of the 40-foot cars, along with three of the 50-foot type — all are rare today if complete with proper loads.

Gd   Exc   Mt

rubber band, the bulldozer came packaged in a Matchbox carton; flatcar is weighted and marked "LIONEL" on frame; catalogued 1959 in set 5727 and separately 1959-60; illustration incorrectly shows catalogue number in the center of car and tractor with black treads; number is actually between the third and fourth stake pockets; very rare in mint-and-boxed condition.   90   125   175

Note: Geoffrey Bunza, whose information on the Matchbox/Lionel connection appears in Chapter I, comments on the numbering of the car:

The Matchbox Bulldozer used as a load on the 1959-1960 cars is designated as No. 18-B1 Caterpillar in Nancy Schiffer's book, *Matchbox Toys* (Schiffer Publishing Ltd., West Chester, Pennsylvania, 1983). The number 8 was cast inside the body (which probably accounted for the original *mistake* of labeling it No. 8 in the series). Matchbox No. 8 during 1959-1960 was actually the same bulldozer tractor without the front blade attached. This version of the No. 18 Bulldozer was produced starting in 1958. Sometime between then and 1961, the casting was changed to reflect the accurate No. 18 inside the body, with no outward changes in appearance. It is *possible* that *both* were shipped to Lionel. My one mint car has the "No. 8" designation inside the bulldozer.

0808 NYC FLATCAR WITH TRACTOR: Painted red 40' car; white lettering; "NYC", "0808", "BLT BY / LIONEL" and NYC herald appear on car side; separate brakewheel; sprung trucks; Red Farm Tractor made by Lesney; the tractor is Number 4 in the Matchbox series; it has a red body and gray wheels; the large hollow wheels have painted gold centers; secured to the car by a red rubber band, the tractor came packaged in a Matchbox carton (its picture showed no fenders); the flatcar is weighted and marked "LIONEL" on frame; catalogued in 1959 in set 5723 and separately 1959-60; incorrectly illustrated with catalogue number at center of car; very rare in mint-and-boxed condition.   100   150   175

Geoffrey Bunza comments:

The number of the Massey-Harris Tractor is correct as shown. However, between 1957 and 1960 two versions of No. 4 were produced. The first version had a hollow body with "4" and "Lesney England" cast inside, solid front wheels with a "4" on one side, and large rear hollow wheels which had "No. 4" cast on the inner side of each, gold painted wheel hubs, and no fenders. The second version had the same body as the second with front and rear solid gray plastic wheels, with crimped axles (later rounded axles) and no fenders. The plastic unpainted gray

Five more Lionel-manufactured flatcars, along with two of the gimmick-type cars that first appeared in 1962 — the 0845 Gold Transport Car and two of the three known variations of the 0873 Rodeo Car. 0873(C), from the Ken Fairchild Collection, is almost transparent yellow and unpainted plastic lettered in a tuscan color.

	Gd	Exc	Mt

wheels had no numbers cast into them. (A pre-1957 tractor had a solid body, metal front wheels with four small holes, and solid red metal wheels *with fenders*.) My one mint car has the first 1957 version with hollow body, metal wheels, and no fenders. It is possible that different versions were sold by Lionel, but I have no way to confirm this. (See Chapter VIII's discussion of forgeries for further information on the Matchbox connection.)

(0809) HELIUM TANK TRANSPORT: Unpainted black 40' car body as used on 0861 log car; hopper car undercarriage; three wooden cylinders painted silver held in place with two black rubber bands; no lettering nor numbers on car side, although catalogue depicts a number board at car center; "LIONEL" appears on car frame; catalogued in 1961 separately and in sets 5753 and 5754; catalogued in 1962 separately and in set 14033; common. **10 15 25**

0810 SOUTHERN PACIFIC EMERGENCY GENERATOR TRANSPORT: Black, painted 50' flatcar; white lettering; "SOUTHERN PACIFIC", "0810", and "BLT BY / LIONEL" appear on car side; unpainted orange generator as found on the O Gauge 3520 Searchlight Car (held with one rubber band to car floor); metal sprung trucks; weighted; underframe marked "LIONEL"; catalogued in 1961 in set 5762, in 1963 in set 14183 and separately 1961-63. Load always missing. **20 30 45**

0813200 SEABOARD MERCURY CAPSULE CAR: Unpainted light blue, 40' flatcar; white lettering; "SEABOARD" and "0813200" appear on car side; two silver plastic capsules, the same as that used in the rocket on the O Gauge 3413 Capsule Launching car; two ¾" vertical tabs cast into the floor hold the two capsules; two gray rubber bands secure the capsules to the tabs; capsules are very fragile and difficult to find; solid frame trucks; catalogued in set 14038 in 1962 and separately 1962-66; a preproduction prototype with wooden capsules is shown in the photo section; this car is the most difficult to find with its load present and in good condition. **90 125 150**

Note: High-quality reproduction capsules now available are made of a slightly thicker plastic, with much more pronounced detail. See Chapter VIII on Oddballs and Forgeries.

0814200 SOUTHERN PACIFIC AUTO TRANSPORT: Painted flat red 50' flatcar body; painted flat black superstructure; white lettering; "SOUTHERN PACIFIC", "0814200", and "BLT BY / LIONEL" appear on car side; "EVANS AUTO- LOADER" on superstructure, which snaps into floor of the car and holds four plastic automobiles; automobile colors varied through the years; catalogued in 1960 only as a separate item, but available through 1962. G. Bunza comments: Autos (both station wagons and sedans) came in at least white, red, green, blue, yellow, and unpainted black. The Lionel service station manual also lists an unpainted tan station wagon, that I have recently authenticated (in T. Armenti, G. Bunza, G. Horan, and K. Fairchild Collections). **30 40 55**

(0821) PIPE CAR: Unpainted black, 40' hopper car undercarriage as used on the Log Car and the Helium Car; three plastic pipes; no lettering nor numbers on car; plastic pipes; catalogued in 1960 separately and in set 5737; see also (0821-50) and (0821-100).

(A) Sprung trucks; silver pipes. **NRS**
(B) Sprung trucks; gray pipes. T. Shepler Collection. **15 20 30**
(C) Rigid-frame trucks; finger tab couplers; gray pipes; came in set 14084 in 1962. J. Otterbin and J. Kimenhour comments. **15 20 30**

(0821-50) PIPE CAR: Yellow pipe load; otherwise identical to 0821; "-50" appears only on carton; catalogued in 1964 in set 14240; also catalogued 1965-66, the only years the yellow load was illustrated. **15 25 30**

(0821-100) PIPE CAR: Solid frame plastic trucks; otherwise identical to 0821; "-100" appears only on carton; catalogued in 1963 only in set 14193. **15 25 30**

0823 SOUTHERN PACIFIC TWIN MISSILE TRANSPORT: Red unpainted 50' flatcar; white lettering; "SOUTHERN PACIFIC" and "0823" on car side; two white missiles, like those on the O Gauge 45 Missile Launcher, mounted on black plastic frame; frame pressed into eight ¼" slots in car floor; two thin wire straps secure missiles to black frames; weighted car; sprung metal trucks; catalogued in 1960, separately and in set 5739, and in 1961, separately and in set 5758; often incomplete. **25 35 45**

0824200 NYC FLATCAR WITH TWO AUTOS: Painted black 40' car; white lettering; "NYC", "0824200", and "BLT. BY / LIONEL" on car side; separate brakewheels; two automobiles, like those on the 0814 Auto Loader, secured by rubber bands; no loading frame; automobile colors varied over the production period; catalogued separately in 1960 and available through 1961. **20 25 30**

0842 CULVERT PIPE CAR: 40' tank car frame with diamond markers and vertical brakewheel; white lettering; "TLCX" at one end, "0842" at other; three metal culvert pipes, like those used as O Gauge accessories; each pipe secured with an individual black rubber band; "LIONEL" on underframe; catalogued in 1960, separately and in set 5741, and in 1961, separately and in set 5757.

(A) Sprung metal trucks; 1960. **15 20 25**
(B) Solid metal truck side frames; plastic wheels; 1961. **15 20 25**

0845 FORT KNOX GOLD RESERVE TRANSPORT CAR: Clear plastic refrigerator car body; painted silver; portions of sides masked from paint and thus left clear to reveal gold bricks which are cast into the floor; black lettering; "0845" next to door; "FORT KNOX GOLD RESERVE" under windows; door modeled to represent bank vault door; 0357 car also has this type of door; weighted floor; "LIONEL" on underframe; solid frame talgo trucks; catalogued in 1962 in set 14084 and separately 1962-66; rare. **50 75 125**

(0860) PENNSYLVANIA DERRICK CAR: Painted semi-gloss gray; black lettering; "PENNSYLVANIA", "0860200", and "BLT BY / LIONEL" appear on car side; unpainted black plastic derrick with fine brass chain; two toolboxes and sidewalls painted gray; fragile separate casting of derrick breaks easily; catalogued in 1960, separately and in sets, and separately 1961-63. The car also came with tool boxes that were much darker gray than the gray body.

(A) Sprung trucks; 1960-62. **20 35 50**
(B) Solid frame trucks; 1963. **20 35 5**

0860200: See (0860)

(0861) LOG CAR: Unpainted black 40' hopper car frame; no lettering nor numbers on car; three darkly colored logs secured by two black rubber bands; approximately ⅜" in diameter, logs have a coat of glue and sawdust to simulate bark texture; sprung metal trucks; "LIONEL" on underframe; catalogued separately and in sets 1959-62; see also (0861-110). **10 15 20**

(0861-110) LOG CAR: Solid frame trucks; lightly colored logs; otherwise identical to 0861; catalogued 1963-66 separately and in various sets. **10 15 20**

0863 SOUTHERN PACIFIC FLATCAR WITH RAIL TRUCKS: Unpainted red 50' car; white lettering; "SOUTHERN PACIFIC" and

	Gd	Exc	Mt

"0863" are the only markings; three 1959-type freight car trucks mounted on unpainted black plastic frame like that used on the 0823 Missile Car; loading frame presses into holes in the car floor; separate brakewheel; weighted underframe; sprung trucks; "LIONEL" on underframe; catalogued in 1960, separately and in set 5749, and in 1961 in set 5762; the 1962 catalogue incorrectly illustrates this car with the Pennsylvania road name, which is spelled incorrectly to boot!

	25	35	40

0866-200 LIONEL LINES CIRCUS CAR: Unpainted white plastic 40' stock car; painted white operating doors; flat red roofwalk; red lettering; "LIONEL LINES" and "CIRCUS / CAR" on letterboards at left of door; "0866-200" and "BLT BY / LIONEL" at right; sprung trucks; detailed underframe with weight; very similar to O Gauge version; catalogued in set 5721 in 1959 and separately 1959-60; rare.

	20	30	45

0870 PENNSYLVANIA MAINTENANCE FLATCAR WITH GENERATOR: Painted, red body; white lettering; "PENNSYL-VANIA", "0870", and "BLT BY / LIONEL" appear on car side; gray, painted platform at one end; gray generator housing at other end; movable yellow work platform with fragile railings, as found on 0880 Maintenance Car; catalogued in set 5723 in 1959 and separately 1959-60.

	35	45	50

0872200 RAILWAY EXPRESS AGENCY REFRIGERATOR: Painted, deep green body; red Railway Express decal herald at right of door; gold lettering; "BLT BY / LIONEL" and "0872200" appear on car side; three heavy steps on each side; black plastic opening doors; produced from Lionel tooling; catalogued 1959-61.

	30	45	65

0873 RODEO CAR: Unpainted yellow 40' car body as used of 0370 with non-operating doors; two holes in each side of car; red lettering; "HORSE / TRANSPORT / CAR" at left of door; "0873" and "FAST EXPRESS" at right; no number boards; vertical shaft at center of car floor holds plastic arm, which extends the length of the car; a double horsehead casting is fastened to each end of the arm; the arm moves from side to side when the car rolls, thus the horses appear to sway in and out the window; detailed underframe; solid frame trucks; catalogued separately and in sets 1962-66.

(A) One brown horsehead and one white horsehead on either side.

	20	25	35

Seven of the 40-foot Lionel-manufactured gondolas offered from 1959 to 1963, including the very rare black 0862-200 with its red crates (the only ones I have ever seen); this car was part of an uncatalogued set. The other car on the second shelf and all below had the suffix number and load change from year to year as the car became cheaper. In many cases, the number was changed on the box only, while the car number remained unchanged.

	Gd	Exc	Mt		Gd	Exc	Mt

(B) Two brown horseheads on each side. J. Otterbin and J. Kimenhour comments.

20 25 35

(C) Lemon yellow plastic, unpainted; almost transparent. K. Fairchild Collection.

25 30 45

0875 SEABOARD FLATCAR WITH MISSILE: Painted black 40' car; white lettering; "SEABOARD", "0875", and "BLT BY / LIONEL" appear on car side; plastic missile with rubber tip, as found on O Gauge 6650 flatcar; "LIONEL" appears on weighted underframe; catalogued in 1959 separately and in sets 5719 and 5725; the catalogue illustration incorrectly shows that car with a brown or tuscan body; catalogued in 1960, separately and in set 5747, and in 1961, in set 5752.

(A) Red and white rocket; blue rubber tip; 1959-61.

15 25 35

(B) White rocket; blue rubber tip; not shown in catalogue illustration; 1961 only.

15 25 35

0889 ILLINOIS CENTRAL CRANE CAR: Unpainted black plastic frame, boom, and top access door; two metal hooks; one-piece housing and pulley assembly; components (nonoperating) attached to boom with metal pin; boom and access door raised and lowered by two wires; two metal cranks provided with car, but they do not operate the boom; flat orange cab with dark green lettering; "ILLINOIS CENTRAL" at rear of cab; "MWW 200" just ahead of cab door; "0889" on rear cab skirting; cab held to boom frame with three tabs that pass through the cab, one on either side and a third at the rear; cab and thin metal weight held to car frame with pressure nut; blackened six-wheel trucks, screw mounted to frame; "LIONEL" on truck frames; catalogued in 1961 separately and in set 5762; catalogue incorrectly shows a red crane; also catalogued in 1962, separately, and in 1963, separately and in sets 14193 and 14233.

35 55 75

GONDOLAS

The Lionel Corporation gondolas are among the most difficult to sort of Lionel HO models. The brown 0865 made in 1959 was the first and most attractive of these gondolas. In the following years, Lionel worked to produce models at lower and lower costs. Thus, by 1963 there were no longer loads in any of the gondolas, and all of these cars were simply molded in appropriate colors, as none were painted.

After 1963 the catalogue number and/or the suffix changed almost every year, although the car itself remained unchanged. For example, the blue 0865-400 of 1964 was catalogued and packaged with the suffix -425 in 1964 and -435 in 1965 and 1966. However, the car carried the number 0865-250 throughout this period. The red 0865-225 received similar treatment. The listing of gondolas is presented as clearly as possible. Cross-references are provided to assist the collector in identification of these cars. The scrap metal loads for those cars are extremely difficult to find in sealed envelopes.

0862: See 0862-200 and (0862-250).

0862-200 GONDOLA WITH RED CRATES: Uncatalogued, 1960-61; similar to 0862-250; black car; see also 0862-250.

(A) Loaded with red plastic wooden crates; "MACHINERY FOR THE LIONEL CORPORATION IRVINGTON, N.J." in white lettering on crates; these crates were also available at the same time in a three-car set headed by the 0058 Rock Island Husky; this set was catalogued by Kutler's Toy Store in the Germantown section of Philadelphia, Pennsylvania. K. Armenti, R. Kughn Collections.

NRS

(B) Loaded with scrap metal; G. Bunza, T. Shepler Collections.

15 25 35

(0862-250) MICHIGAN CENTRAL GONDOLA WITH SCRAP METAL: Flat black, painted body; white lettering; "MICHIGAN / CENTRAL", "MCRR", "0862200", and NYC System herald appear on car side; "BLT BY / LIONEL" also present; sold with a bag of scrap

Two of the last gondolas offered between 1963 and 1966, with the gray unpainted 0865-335 with metal slugs in a clear plastic bag; early loads were brown paper bags; 0865-435 was offered without a load. The second and third shelves show first the red 0836-60 and black 0836-1 painted Alaskan hoppers, followed by the same unpainted model offered in the late 1960s.

Seven operating cars offered by Lionel from 1960 to 1963 — all difficult to locate complete. The box on the top shelf contains the black plastic bridge vital to the operation of the Cop and Hobo Car, to the left. The third shelf shows two versions of the 0319, first carrying a helicopter with Lionel's name molded into its right side at the tail and with a sprung truck, while the -110 has solid trucks and an unmarked helicopter. The Giraffe Car is shown less its yellow plastic telltale, and at bottom, the only 0889 Crane Car with the Illinois Central road name.

	Gd	Exc	Mt

metal slugs as provided for O Gauge operating cranes; load much too heavy for the smaller cars; catalogued in 1959 separately and in set 5729; "0862-250" appears on carton; only 0862 portion of number used in catalogue; difficult to find with original slugs.

	12	20	25

(0865) MICHIGAN CENTRAL GONDOLA WITH CANISTERS: Painted, dark flat brown body; yellowish-gold lettering; NYC System herald at left; "MICHIGAN / CENTRAL" at center; "MCRR" and "0865200" with underscore at right; "BLT BY / LIONEL" also present; separate brakewheel; five unmarked red canisters; sprung metal trucks; first 0865-series gondola; catalogued in 1959 separately and in set 5727; catalogue incorrectly shows the Athearn car with canisters; scarce; see also 0865-400.

	25	35	40

0865200: See (0865)

0865225 MICHIGAN CENTRAL GONDOLA WITH SCRAP METAL: NYC System herald; "MICHIGAN / CENTRAL", "MCRR" and "0865225" on car side; "BLT BY / LIONEL" also present; separate brakewheel; metal slugs for load; sprung trucks.

(A) Unpainted gray plastic body; black lettering; catalogued 1960-62; illustrations incorrectly show the car as black.

	15	20	25

(B) Unpainted red plastic body; white lettering; catalogued in 1962 only in sets 14023 and 14084.

	10	15	20

0865250 MICHIGAN CENTRAL GONDOLA WITH CRATES: Flat red, painted, body; white lettering; NYC System herald; "MICHIGAN / CENTRAL", "MCRR", and "0865250" on car side; unpainted tan plastic crates; sprung trucks; catalogued in 1960, in sets 5735, 5743, and 5745, in 1961, separately and in sets 5751 and 5757, and in 1962, in sets 14003 and 14007; see also 0865-375 and 0865-400.

	10	15	20

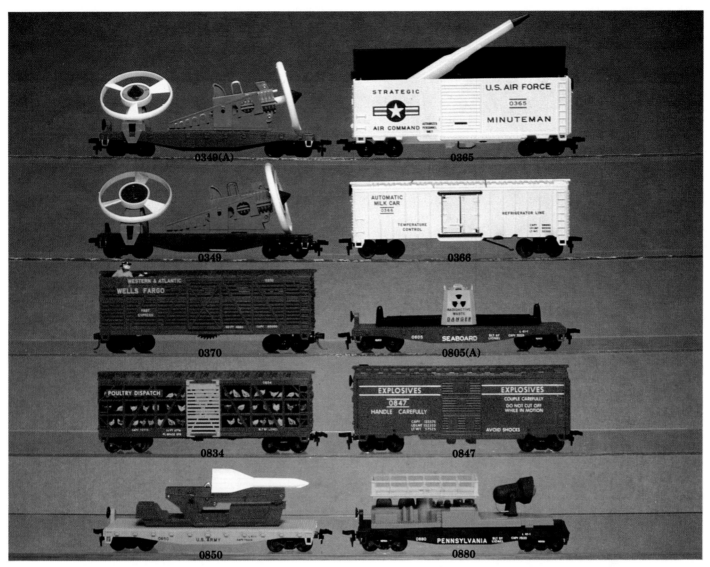

Operating cars offered between 1959 and 1966 — most are found without the operating loads. Note the rare maroon body on the 0349 Turbo Car on the second shelf, from the Ken Fairchild Collection, along with the smooth rocket of the 0365 Minuteman Car. The third shelf shows the common 0805(A) AEC car; it and the 0834 both use the black electrical pickup strip to light the cars. The 0880 Maintenance Car on the bottom is almost impossible to find with its yellow platform unbroken.

	Gd	Exc	Mt		Gd	Exc	Mt

(0865-335) MICHIGAN CENTRAL GONDOLA WITH SCRAP METAL: Solid frame trucks; otherwise identical to 0865225, including number on car side; catalogued in 1963. **10 15 20**

(0865-375) MICHIGAN CENTRAL GONDOLA: Solid frame trucks; no crates; otherwise identical to 0865250, including number on car side; catalogued in 1963-64. **10 15 20**

(0865-400) MICHIGAN CENTRAL GONDOLA: Unpainted blue plastic body; white Michigan Central lettering; "0865250" and "BLT BY / LIONEL" on car side; no load; no brakewheel; solid frame trucks. The plainest of the gondolas, this car has a confusing catalogue history. In 1964 it was catalogued as (0865-400) in sets and as separately (0865-435); in 1965-66 it was catalogued with the 1959 catalogue number of 0865 without a suffix. Note, however, that all of these cars carry the number 0865250 on the car side. **6 10 15**

(0865-435): See (863-400).

HOPPER CARS

08361 ALASKA RAILROAD: Painted flat black; orange lettering; "ALASKA / RAILROAD", "08361", "BLT BY / LIONEL" and the Alaskan boy appear on car side; made from Hobbyline dies; catalogued in 1959 separately and in set 5725; the car is shown incorrectly in both blue and yellow and black and white schemes; catalogued again in 1960 in set 5749 and separately 1960-63; see also (0836-60) and (0836-100).
(A) Painted shell. **20 25 30**
(B) Same as (A) with scrap metal. G. Bunza comment. **20 25 30**

(0836-60) ALASKA RAILROAD: Red body; "ALASKA / RAILROAD", white lettering; "08631", "BLT BY / LIONEL" and the Alaskan boy appear on car side; solid frame plastic trucks; catalogued in 1961 in set 5755; available as an uncatalogued item 1962-64; catalogued separately and in sets 1965-66; see also (0836-60) and (0836-100).

	Gd	Exc	Mt
(A) Painted red body; scarce.	15	25	30
(B) Unpainted red body.	10	15	20

(0836-100) ALASKA RAILROAD: Solid truck frames and 1963-type couplers; catalogued in 1963.
(A) Painted flat black; orange lettering; similar to 08361.

	15	20	30

(B) Unpainted red body; white lettering; similar to (0836-60)(B).

	10	15	20

(0836-110) ALASKA RAILROAD: Solid truck frames, 1963-type couplers, brakewheel, *painted* red body, white lettering similar to (0836-60), number stamped on late-style Hillside, New Jersey, box with fancy script; "The Leader in Model Railroading" in blue. G. Bunza comments.

(A) As described.	10	15	20
(B) Solid white "O" in "RAILROAD". G. Potts Collection.			NRS

08631: See (0836-60).

OPERATING ROLLING STOCK

0039 SOUTHERN TRACK CLEANING CAR: Unusual car type, longer than boxcars, higher cab than on steam locomotives; painted flat black plastic body; flat orange center cab; 1960-type motor drives two cleaning sponges; car unpropelled; sponges held on two vertical shafts driven by a brass worm gear; on/off switch on short end of car; white lettering; "TC-0039" and "SOUTHERN" on car side; cleaning fluid bottle, same as that used on O Gauge cleaning car, cradled in long end of car; buffing pad under car; car sold with two extra sponges and one wiper pad; catalogued separately in 1961-62 only; rarely found in mint condition or complete with attachments. **35 50 75**

Note: This car was manufactured with both black and cream-colored spindle and plate assembly to hold the sponge pads. G. Juhasz comment.

0300 OPERATING LUMBER CAR: Two-piece body; frame and operating mechanism constructed of black metal and plastic; red plastic superstructure; two stakes cast onto tilting gate; three fixed stakes hold logs, which are wooden 1/2" dowels with sawdust glued to them, giving them a rough appearance; white lettering; "TLCX" and "0300"; same tripping mechanism as used with 0900 unloading ramp; ramp sold separately; log tray and logs sold with car; logs appear in various shades (mahogany and walnut stain); catalogued in 1960 in sets 5743, 5749, and 5771, and separately 1960-63; very common. **20 25 40**

0301 PENNSYLVANIA OPERATING COAL CAR: Black frame and mechanism as found on 0300; light gray unpainted superstructure; black lettering; keystone herald, "0301", and "PENNSYLVANIA" on side; sold with brown unloading bin and clear plastic bag of coal; catalogued in 1960 in four sets, in at least one set 1961-63 and separately 1960-66; very common, but may be incomplete. **20 25 40**

0319 SOUTHERN PACIFIC OPERATING HELICOPTER CAR: Light blue-painted 50' flatcar; white lettering; "SOUTHERN PACIFIC" and "0319" on car side; red plastic helicopter body; black blade and landing gear; clear nose; helicopter same as that sold on O Gauge 3619 car; spring-wound assembly releases helicopter when car is backed over a trip fastened to the track; car derails when operated if springs wound too tightly; sprung trucks; catalogued in 1960 separately and in sets 5737, 5745, and 5747; shown in 1960 with a large gray helicopter, unlike that actually produced; catalogued in set 5753 in 1962 and illustrated more accurately; difficult to find in good condition. Car included adjustable metal track trip for operation.

	Gd	Exc	Mt
(A) Early sprung truck type car, "Built by Lionel" on right rear tail of helicopter body.	20	30	40
(B) Later solid frame truck type car, no lettering on helicopter body. "0319-110" on carton.	30	35	45

0319-110: See 0319

0333 SOUTHERN PACIFIC OPERATING SATELLITE LAUNCHING CAR: Blue 50' flatcar; white lettering; "SOUTHERN PACIFIC" and catalogue number appear on car side; gray plastic control panel and yellow radar screen at one end; black plastic satellite at other end; chrome top on satellite; both satellite wings trimmed with white checkerboard on top; twelve circular holes in its base; same screen and satellite also used on O Gauge 3519 car; catalogued in 1961 separately and in sets 5754 and 5758; catalogued separately 1962-66; very rare complete with its metal track trip.

(A) Sprung trucks; 1961-62.	30	50	60
(B) Solid truck frames; 1963-66.	30	50	60

0337 LIONEL LINES CIRCUS CAR OPERATING GIRAFFE CAR: Modified 40' stock car body; unpainted white plastic; sliding doors; red lettering; "LIONEL LINES" and "CIRCUS / CAR" on letter boards at left of door; "0337" on car body at right; long yellow shaft with giraffe head on top fastened to metal floor; metal shoe with magnet suspended from floor; when car passes beneath telltale, giraffe ducks its head into car; catalogued in 1961 separately, in set 5751, and in the "Valise Pack" 5767.

(A) Poorly-matched painted white doors; common variation.

	25	30	45

(B) Unpainted white plastic doors; scarce.			NRS

0349 OPERATING TURBO MISSILE CAR: 40' flatcar body; no lettering; unpainted blue catapult and reserve housing, each holding one missile, same as those used on O Gauge missile car; unpainted white plastic missiles with red center, also the same as found on O Gauge cars; catapult loaded by inserting missile and turning same to lock in place; fired manually; black undercarriage marked "LIONEL"; difficult to find with missiles unbroken; catalogued in 1962 separately and in sets 14043 and 14098; catalogued only separately 1963-66.

(A) Unpainted red flatcar body.	35	45	60
(B) Maroon flatcar body; rare. K. Fairchild Collection.			
	40	55	75

0357 COP AND HOBO CAR: House-type car, similar in construction to the Railway Express refrigerator; nonopening door; unpainted light blue plastic; white lettering; "LIONEL LINES" and "0357" at left of door; "HYDRAULIC / PLATFORM / MAINTENANCE / CAR" at right; gray plastic platform on rooftop; cop and hobo figures are transferred from the top of the car to the black plastic trestle bridge each time the car passes under the bridge; catalogued 1962-66; incorrectly illustrated with a stock car body every year except 1966; usually found without bridge or figures. **25 40 70**

0365 U.S. AIR FORCE MINUTEMAN LAUNCHING CAR: Unpainted white plastic modified Hobbyline boxcar body; separate, unpainted blue roof with two arms that secure the roof and allow it to move when the launching mechanism is tripped; blue and red; "STRATEGIC / AIR COMMAND" and Air Force insignia at left of door; "U.S. AIR FORCE / MINUTEMAN" and red "0365" at right; spring-loaded mechanism with four metal geared wheels and metal frame; unpainted white plastic rocket, approximately 3 1/2" long, with blue rubber tip; two 1/16" x 1/2" fins cast into rocket body; no lettering; catalogued in 1962 separately and in sets 14033, 14064, and 14098; catalogued in 1963 separately and in set 14193; offered only separately 1964-66; rare. Operated from same metal track trip as many other operating cars. **35 45 60**

	Gd	Exc	Mt		Gd	Exc	Mt

0366 AUTOMATIC MILK CAR: White operating refrigerator car; black lettering; "AUTOMATIC / MILK CAR" and "0366" at left; "REFRIGERATOR LINE" and dimensional data at right; the eight metal milk cans are loaded through a door located at the center of the roof; cans are pushed through spring-loaded plug doors onto plastic loading dock and held to platform with a magnet installed in platform by the customer; white rubber man inside; eight steel cans packaged in brown paper envelope; catalogued 1961-66; rarely found complete.

(A) Painted body; sprung trucks; 1961-62.   **25   35   50**

(B) Unpainted body; solid frame trucks; 1963-66.

                                      20   30   35

0370 WESTERN & ATLANTIC OPERATING SHERIFF AND OUTLAW CAR: Unpainted red plastic stock car body; yellow lettering; "WESTERN & ATLANTIC", " WELLS FARGO", and "FAST / EXPRESS" on two letterboards at left of door; "0370" near roof line at right; catalogued in 1962 in set 14084 and separately 1962-66.

(A) Operating version; two square holes diagonally opposed at opposite ends of roof; geared mechanism, plastic with metal arms, raise Sheriff then Outlaw so that they can exchange fire; both figures painted, Sheriff yellow and Outlaw blue; metal floor; sprung trucks; 1962.

                                      20   25   40

(B) Similar to (A), except solid frame trucks; 1963-66.

                                      20   25   40

(C) Nonoperating version made for special Sears train sets in the early 1960s; no holes in roof; no figures nor mechanism; metal floor; solid frame trucks; rare.   **NRS**

0805 SEABOARD AEC FLATCAR: Painted red 40' car; white lettering; "SEABOARD", "0805", and "BLT BY / LIONEL" appear on car side; light gray canister mounted on black base; power feed same as that on 0834 Poultry Car; "RADIOACTIVE / WASTE / DANGER" in red lettering on canister; blinking red light under canister; plastic truck frames; metal wheels; electrical collector-type trucks; catalogued every year 1959-66 in sets and/or separately.

(A) Early couplers without manual uncoupling pin; 1959-62.

                                      10   15   25

(B) 1963-type couplers with manual uncoupling pin; partial copper wheel for blinker; stake holes along each side; no lettering on canister; 1963-66. J. Otterbin and J. Kimenhour comments. **8   10   20**

Note: This car has also been reported to have been seen in a set box with a punched liner to fit the car. The car held two waste containers. Verification requested.

(C) Similar to (B); partial steel wheel for blinker; two stake holes at center of car.   **8   10   20**

(D) Same as (A) with "0805200" on car.   **NRS**

(E) Same as (A) with much deeper red color of body. Original box, numbered "0805-1". G. Juhasz comments on (D) and (E).   **NRS**

0805200: See 0805

0834 POULTRY CAR: Red 40' modified stock car body; white lettering; "POULTRY DISPATCH" at left; "0834" and "BLT BY / LIONEL" at right of door; open side panels with plastic inserts; chickens painted on side panels; illuminated; chickens appear to fly when car moves; detailed underframe; sprung trucks with current collection; catalogued in 1959 in sets 5717, 5725, and 5733, and separately 1959-60.

Top: The Rocket Fuel and the unpainted cheapened 0815-85. Middle: The rare Sun Oil car and the 0815-75 that carries the suffix of -200. Last is the cheapened version of the Rocket Fuel Car of 1962. All are difficult to find — especially the Sun Oil car, which does not carry a Lionel catalogue number of any kind.

	Gd	Exc	Mt

(A) Painted car body and door; black door painted gray; 1959. T. Shepler Collection. **NRS**

(B) Unpainted car body; black door painted gray; 1960.

	30	40	50

0847 EXPLODING TARGET RANGE CAR: Four-piece body assembly; floor and ends molded together; separate roof; two separate sides; red unpainted plastic body; white lettering; round "DANGER" sign and "0847" at one side of door; "EXPLOSIVES" on other side; internal spring mechanism set like an old mousetrap — making reassembly of car very tricky; car "exploded" when struck by missile or other object; locking mechanism built into floor can be set so that car will not fly apart when used as a piece of non-operating rolling stock; sprung trucks; catalogued separately and in sets 1960-62; very common; see also 0847(-100).

	5	10	15

0847(-100) EXPLODING TARGET RANGE CAR: Similar to 0847, except solid frame trucks are present on this car; otherwise identical to 0847; "-100" suffix appears on carton only; catalogued 1963-65.

	5	10	15

0850 U.S. ARMY MISSILE LAUNCHING FLATCAR: Light gray unpainted 40-foot flatcar; unpainted red firing platform; black lettering; "U.S. ARMY" and "0850" appear on side; platform pivots about single rivet fastened through car body; firing portion of platform is spring loaded and rises 2" in height; two red plastic firing arms extend from sides; rockets same as that loaded on 0823 flatcar; separate brakewheel; catalogued in sets 1960-63 and separately 1960-65; red actuator arms are often broken; see also 0850-110.

(A) Sprung trucks; 1960-62.

	15	20	30

(B) Solid frame trucks; 1963-65.

	15	20	30

0850(-110) U.S. ARMY MISSILE LAUNCHING FLATCAR: Identical to 0850(B); "-110" appears on carton only; 1966. **NRS**

0880 PENNSYLVANIA OPERATING MAINTENANCE CAR WITH LIGHT: Black, painted 40' flatcar; gray and yellow work platform as found on 0870; searchlight located in place of 0870's generator; white lettering; "PENNSYLVANIA", "BLT BY / LIONEL", and "0880" appear on car side; metal searchlight as found on the O Gauge four-light tower and 410 Blinking Billboard; unlike O Gauge car, does not have on/off switch; light remains on as long as track is powered; catalogued 1959-61 separately and in sets.

	30	35	50

TANK CARS

0815(-50) ROCKET FUEL: Unpainted black frame; flat white, tank body; red lettering; "0815" appears above the wire handrails; no red lines around catalogue number, as found on 0816; "-50" suffix does not appear on car; "ROCKET FUEL", "LIQUIFIED CONTENTS / HYDROGEN (H$_2$) / SUPER COOLED", and "DANGER / HIGHLY EXPLOSIVE" appear below the handrails; black plastic platform around single dome; metal ladder extends from platform to frame on each side and secures tank body to frame; "The Lionel Corporation / Made in New York, N.Y. / U.S. of America, and "USA" appear on underframe; solid frame trucks; separate brakewheel; catalogued in 1963, in sets 14143 and 14230, and in 1964, in set 14300; the illustration of set 14300 incorrectly shows the orange Lionel Lines tank car; catalogued in 1966 in set 14300.

(A) Painted tank.

	20	25	35

(B) Unpainted tank.

	20	30	40

(C) Same as (B), but with red lines around "0815".

	20	30	40

0815(-60) ROCKET FUEL: Same description as 0815(-50), but with "0815-60" rubber-stamped on late Hillside, New Jersey- style box. G. Bunza Collection. **NRS**

(0815-75) LIONEL LINES: Unpainted black frame; flat orange, painted body; black band under platform; body secured to frame with metal ladders from platform; black lettering; "LIONEL LINES", "0815-200", and the Lionel logo appear on car side; separate brakewheel; catalogued in 1963 in sets 14153, 14183, and 14233; the "-75" appears in the illustrations, but not on the actual car; catalogued in set 14300 in 1965-66, but listed with the Rocket Fuel tank car number; difficult to find with unbroken platform; see also (0815-85).

	25	35	40

(0815-85) LIONEL LINES: Unpainted black frame; no wire handrails nor ladders; dull unpainted orange body; thin black lettering; "LIONEL LINES", "0815-200", and Lionel logo appear on car side; red triangular placards on frame; solid truck frames; finger tab couplers; catalogued separately in 1963 only; see also (0815-75).

(A) With platform. T. Shepler Collection.

	20	30	40

(B) Without platforms, handrails, or placards.

	20	30	40

(C) No platform, with wire handrails and red placards. G. Bunza comment.

	20	30	50

(0815-110) SUN OIL CO.: Unpainted black frame; body secured to frame with metal ladders from platform; wire handrails present; semi-gloss black, painted body; white lettering; "SUNOCO" and "N.A.T.X. 25064" appear on car side; no Lionel number; separate brakewheel; "LIONEL", "N.Y. N.Y.", and "USA" appear on car frame; solid frame trucks; uncatalogued; this car came in set 14310 in place of a Rocket Fuel

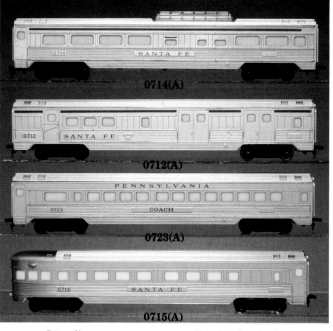

0714(A)

0712(A)

0723(A)

0715(A)

Lionel's passenger cars were offered in four body styles, as shown — dome, baggage, Pullman, and observation — with only the Pennsylvania and Santa Fe road names being used. All the cars were sold both lighted and unlighted, while the Santa Fe cars can be found with and without the red stripes at the roof line. The PRR cars can be found with silver or tuscan roof, the latter being the hardest to locate. Note that the last car has tuscan lettering, not the bright red used on most of the SF cars.

	Gd	Exc	Mt

tank listed and illustrated on the set box; car in sealed set held in the T. Armenti, G. Horan, and R. Kughn Collections; very rare.

	35	60	125

0815-200 LIONEL LINES: See (0815-75) and (0815-85) for description. Available in 1959 in set 5733. K. Fairchild comment.

0816 ROCKET FUEL: Unpainted black plastic frame; flat white, painted frame; red lettering; "0816", with red border, above handrails; "ROCKET FUEL", "LIQUIFIED CONTENTS / HYDROGEN (H$_2$) / SUPER COOLED", and "DANGER / HIGHLY EXPLOSIVE" below handrails; red outline of rocket; sprung trucks; catalogued separately in 1962; see also 0816-50.

	15	25	40

0816(-50) ROCKET FUEL: Solid frame trucks; otherwise identical to 0816; "-50" does not appear on car side; catalogued separately 1963-66.

	15	25	40

25064: See (0815-110).

PASSENGER CARS BUILT BY LIONEL, 1961–1966

The cars produced with new Lionel tooling are models of streamlined cars with fluted sides and roofs made by the Budd Company of Philadelphia. All of the cars have heavy plastic shells. There are two main castings: one with the sides, ends, and floor, the other with roof and windows. The illuminated cars have four-wheel metal trucks which are insulated on opposite sides. The light bulbs are secured to a copper strip that is fastened to the car floor, and current flows from the trucks to the copper strip through the fluted metal truck pin. A third pin at the center of the car also fastens the strip in place. Each car side has a smooth surface around and immediately above the windows; there are three smooth number boards in the fluted area. These were used for any striping or lettering that appeared on the cars. There are only two road names in the series, Santa Fe and Pennsylvania. These lighted cars are readily identified by locating the central hole for the pin that secures the lighting strip. All of these cars are scarce — the Penn road name leads the list, followed by the SF without stripe or light. K. Fairchild comment.

0712 SANTA FE BAGGAGE CAR: Semi-gloss silver finish; red lettering; catalogue number and road name appear on two or three of the molded letterboards; third board is always blank; frosted windows; catalogued in 1961 in set 5759, in 1962 in set 14108, in 1963 in set 14173; no baggage cars were made available after 1964.

(A) Heat-stamped red stripe above windows; illuminated.

	20	30	45

(B) Similar to (A), no lights.

	20	25	35

(C) No stripe; no lights.

	25	35	45

0713 SANTA FE PULLMAN: Semi-gloss silver finish; red lettering; catalogue number and road name on car side; road name on center panel;

The 0414 eighteen-piece village set, catalogued in 1959 only, and the 0418 seven-piece industrial set, catalogued in 1960. Both are spinoffs of the Plasticville line by Bachmann Brothers of Philadelphia, as are all of the Plasticville items pictured.

	Gd	Exc	Mt

frosted windows; catalogued in the same sets as noted for 0712; also available 1963-64. See also (0733), which has "0713" on the car side.

(A) Heat-stamped red stripe above windows; illuminated.

	20	35	50
(B) Similar to (A), no lights.	15	30	40
(C) No stripe; no lights.	25	35	45

0714 SANTA FE VISTA DOME: Semi-gloss silver finish; red lettering; clear plastic dome; dozen red passenger seats visible through dome; catalogued with other striped cars in same sets; discontinued in 1964; much more difficult to find than other Santa Fe cars.

(A) Heat-stamped red stripe above windows; illuminated.

	25	35	50
(B) Similar to (A), no lights.	20	30	40
(C) No stripe; no lights.	25	35	45

0715 SANTA FE OBSERVATION: Semi-gloss silver finish; red lettering; catalogued like the foregoing Santa Fe cars; more easily found than the 0712 or 0714. See also (0735), which has "0715" on the car side.

(A) Heat-stamped red stripe above windows; illuminated.

	25	30	40
(B) Similar to (A), no lights.	20	30	35
(C) No stripe; no lights.	25	35	45

0723 PENNSYLVANIA PULLMAN CAR: Tuscan lettering; no lighting; four-wheel metal trucks; catalogued in 1963 in set 44163, and again in 1964-65.

(A) Silver body; tuscan roof; clear window insert; 1964; rare.

	40	50	75
(B) Silver body and roof; frosted window insert; 1965-66.			
	25	35	45

0725 PENNSYLVANIA OBSERVATION CAR: Tuscan lettering; no lighting; four-wheel metal trucks; catalogued in 1963 in set 44163, and again in 1964-65.

(A) Silver body; tuscan roof; clear window insert; 1964; rare.

	35	50	70
(B) Silver body and roof; frosted window insert; 1965-66.			
	20	30	45

(0733) SANTA FE PULLMAN: Painted silver; tuscan lettering; car numbered "0713", although catalogue number differs due to change in color of lettering; no stripe; no lights; four-wheel metal trucks; catalogued in 1964 in set 14290, which had two Pullmans because the vista dome and baggage were unavailable, and in different sets 1965-66; scarce. **30 40 50**

0735 SANTA FE OBSERVATION CAR: Similar to (0733); car numbered "0715", rather than "0735"; catalogued like (0733); scarce. **30 40 50**

ACCESSORIES

All of the HO accessories offered by Lionel were direct descendants of the O Gauge line that proved so successful for Lionel. It should come as no surprise that they would try to duplicate the same models in the HO line.

Many of the componenets found on the HO models will also be found on the O Gauge counterpart. Example: the whistle or horn found in the HO engine house are the same as used in the O Gauge steam locomotives and diesel units with sound. The 0145 Gateman and the 0197 Radar Tower were simply made smaller, while the 0140 Operating Banjo Signal was almost an exact copy. The 0282 Illinois Central Gantry Crane did differ from its O Gauge brother in that it was manually operated.

	Gd	Exc	Mt

All were manufactured by Lionel and can be quite difficult to locate, especially the engine house with sound. Many of these were bought up by O Gauge people for the whistle or horn units inside, and were used to repair the larger steam tenders and diesel units with the horn.

The collector will find that a challenge awaits those interested in HO accessories. All those photographed for this chapter are from the Ken Fairchild Collection.

0110 GRADUATED TRESTLE SET: Unpainted gray plastic; four piers and twenty-two risers; twenty-four metal track clips; catalogued 1958-66; common. **5 15 20**

0111 TRESTLE SET: Unpainted gray plastic; twelve "A" piers as used in the 0110 set; twenty-four metal track clips; catalogued 1960-66; more difficult to find complete. **3 5 20**

0114 ENGINE HOUSE WITH HORN: Light gray sheet metal base with horn unit as found in O27 diesels riveted in place; heavy plastic building; walls painted red; unpainted tan corners and roof; two clear plastic windows in each side wall; four clear plastic sky lights in roof; two door openings in each end of building; building fastened to floor with two screws, which pass through roof; "LIONEL" and "0114" stamped on metal frame; requires "D" size battery; catalogued 1958-60.

	30	50	75

0115 ENGINE HOUSE: Kit version of 0114, except no horn unit; "LIONEL" and "0115" stamped on metal floor; colors as described for 0114; catalogued 1961-63. R. Kughn Collection; scarce.

	20	25	60

0117 ENGINE HOUSE: Assembled version of 0115, without horn; gray, painted walls; unpainted tan corners and roof; catalogued in 1959-60; scarce. **20 25 60**

0118 ENGINE HOUSE WITH WHISTLE: Sheet metal base with plastic whistle housing, as used in O27 steam locomotive tenders, screwed in place; gray, painted walls; unpainted tan corners and roof; "LIONEL" and "0118" stamped on base; catalogued in 1958-62; some boxes contained Ray-O-Vac batteries. **30 40 70**

0119 TUNNEL: Painted cardstock; 10" high, 12" long; painted concrete tunnel portals; extremely difficult to find, especially in good condition, but generally unwanted by collectors; catalogued in 1959-66. **5 8 25**

0140 OPERATING BANJO SIGNAL: Unpainted black plastic; lighted; 1"-diameter metal tube connects base to upper signal housing; electrical connections concealed in base; "LIONEL" on base; vibrating mechanism which activates the swinging warning sign, which says "STOP", enclosed in a small metal housing — often missing; "RAILROAD / CROSSING" boards at top; "STOP / WHEN / SWINGING" sign on post; packaged with instruction sheet and an operating track section; copied from the O Gauge line; catalogued in 1962-66; rarely found in excellent condition. **20 45 65**

0145 AUTOMATIC GATEMAN: Silver plastic building; red roof, door, windows, and road crossing sign; frosted plastic window inserts; small blue rubber figure with lantern; nonoperating lantern molded with figure, but painted red; unpainted tan plastic base; operates with track pressure switch included in original packages; house illuminated; electrical contacts on concealed sheet metal base; "LIONEL" and "0145" stamped on metal base; copied from O Gauge line; catalogued 1959-66.

	25	30	50

0197 RADAR ANTENNA: Plastic; 7½" tall; gray, painted base; unpainted black plastic superstructure and red plastic top; two-piece silver and black radar screen with separate base (the same screen used

	Gd	Exc	Mt

on the O Gauge 3540 operating radar car), which fits over the coil mechanism that drives the screen with a rubber washer; central metal rod carries current to the driving coil mounted at its top; metal ladder serves as a ground; originally packaged with two wires, instruction sheet, and black whip antenna, which fits into one corner of the upper red platform; no on/off switch included, but unit which uses AC may be used with 364C control button; "LIONEL" and "0197" stamped on base; always packaged in orange window box; copied from O Gauge line; catalogued in 1958-61. **25 30 45**

200: See (0282)

0214 GIRDER BRIDGE: Painted flat black; sheet metal base with plastic sides riveted in place; no lettering; "LIONEL" and "0214" stamped on metal frame and inside each side; packaged in an orange and white solid carton with a picture of the bridge on its top; 1½" wide, 9" long, 1¼" high; common. **8 12 20**

0221 TRUSS BRIDGE AND TRESTLES: Unpainted gray plastic bridge; includes trestles from 0110 graduated set and 3" bridge piers; catalogued in 1961 only. **5 10 15**

0222 DECK BRIDGE AND TRESTLES: Unpainted gray plastic bridge; includes trestles from 0110 and 3" bridge piers; catalogued in 1961 only. **5 10 15**

0224 GIRDER BRIDGE AND TRESTLES: Painted black bridge (0214); includes trestles from 0110 and 3" bridge piers; catalogued in 1961 only. **5 10 15**

(0282) GANTRY CRANE: Plastic superstructure and base from Radar Tower and Light Beacon; top platform unpainted black plastic; black plastic boom with two wire guides and two metal hooks; two plastic spools hidden inside cab, one to raise and lower the boom, the other to operate the larger hook; manually operated with two metal cranks; flat orange, painted cab with light green lettering; "ILLINOIS CENTRAL" logo and "MWW 200" on cab; catalogue number 0282 on skirting below cab floor; catalogued in 1961-63; shell is the same as that used on 0889 Crane, with number changed; rare. **30 50 75**

0310 BILLBOARD SET Five dark green plastic frames; five printed color posters, each with the name of a prominent advertiser; the HO posters do not resemble those in the O Gauge line; the HO posters have a white background without the green border used on the O Gauge posters; the following poster names have been identified: 1959 "Join the Navy", Underwood Typewriters, Navy — Space/Age, Chevrolet Used Cars and Trucks, Cities Service Eager Beaver, Airex Reels, Target Range, Join the Navy, Juicyfruit, Lionel HO, Lionel Spear, Navy "Stay in School", Cities Service, Big Gallon, Swifts Franks, Finish Line, Lionel Science Series, and Lionel Porter; catalogued in 1959-66. Inserts from Ken Fairchild Collection. **3 5 10**

0470 I.R.B.M. MISSILE LAUNCH PLATFORM: Unpainted 11" x 12" tan plastic base, similar to a turntable pit; manually-operated blue and black rocket launcher mounted within circle; red and white rocket with blue rubber tip; Quonset hut molded into base at one corner; yellow horn and two-sided antenna dish on roof of hut; red 0847 Explosive Boxcar included in separate carton; rocket and platform same as those used on O Gauge Satellite Car; set packed in solid orange carton with black lettering; catalogued in 1960 and 1962; available uncatalogued in 1961; difficult to find complete set. **25 35 50**

0480 MISSILE FIRING RANGE: Same type of unpainted tan base as that on 0470, but without round bit; two-section base; one section holds Lychen trees included with set; larger section bears gray firing platform; four white missiles; blue rubber figure; firing platform, missiles and figure identical to those on O Gauge 6544 Missile Car; catalogued in 1962-63; difficult to find complete. **30 50 90**

Top: 0102 fixed voltage unit that could be used with several of the smaller 0181 cab controllers and larger 0104 2½-amp multivolt controller, large enough to control two individual trains plus AC accessories. Middle: 0100, also a 2½ amp unit, which included a circuit breaker and reversing switch. Bottom: 0150 rectifier, used to convert AC to DC power; 0103, one of the smallest power packs offered, used in many sets from 1960 until end of production; 0181 unit, for use with any DC power pack to control speed and direction; 0101, 1¼-amp DC AC power unit to control both speed and direction.

	Gd	Exc	Mt

0494 ROTATING BEACON: 7" tall; base 3" square; unpainted black plastic tower housing; one red and one green plastic lens; red top and railing; metal ladder and center pole supply current to bulb at top and secure tower to base; brown unpainted base with four rubber pads; "LIONEL" and catalogue number on base; driven with rubber finger washer as used in O Gauge models; 14-16 volt AC operation; catalogued 1959-63; difficult to find unbroken. **20 30 50**

Track Inventory

The following list was compiled by Dr. Geoffrey Bunza and includes some comments by George Horan.

0900 REMOTE TRACK: Used with all remote-controlled operating cars from 1960 to 1966; 9"-section of track with ramp, directions for use and 0190 control button; maroon plastic housing detailed like wooden boards; black plastic bottom frame; metal arm extends towards track and trips car mechanism; operates with a 14-16 volt AC power pack.

0903 STRAIGHT TRACK, 3"
0905 STRAIGHT TRACK, 1½"
0906 STRAIGHT TRACK, 6"
0909 STRAIGHT TRACK, 9"
0919 UNCOUPLER RERAILER
0921 PAIR REMOTE SWITCHES
0922 REMOTE CONTROL SWITCH, RIGHT
0923 REMOTE CONTROL SWITCH, LEFT
0925 STRAIGHT TERMINAL TRACK, 9"
0929 UNCOUPLING TRACK, 9"
0930 30-DEGREE CROSSING
0939 UNCOUPLER
0941 PAIR MANUAL SWITCHES
0942 MANUAL SWITCH, RIGHT
0943 MANUAL SWITCH, LEFT
0950 RERAILER

Left: 0421 farm set that included a Cape Cod house in its twenty-four pieces. Top right: The smaller 0417 twenty-one-piece set. Below: 0415 Cape Cod set, with nineteen pieces.

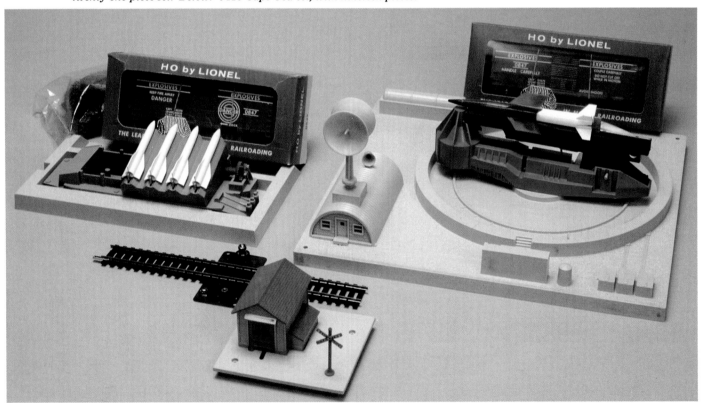

Three of the larger accessories, the top two being manually operated and the gateman controlled by the same 0145-200 pressure track section as operated the banjo signal. Top left: 0480 missile range with 0847 Exploding Boxcar, lychen trees, and the four 2¼-inch white rockets. Note red wheel at right of firing platform that was triggered to fire missiles. To the right: 0470 IRBM missile launch, complete with its missile and the same 0847 Exploding Boxcar as used on the 0480. Also shown is the 0145 Automatic Gateman, with the 0145-200 pressure track section; it is difficult to find complete with its removable roof and crossing signal and is one of the few accessories to have a metal base.

Left: The 0416 rail station set that included paint and a brush to finish the figures that came with the twenty-piece set. *Middle:* 0420 railroad set, similar to the 0416. *Right:* The 0426, including crossing gate, signal, figures, barrels, and crates.

Left to right: The 0411 figure set, including brush and paint; 0419 rail junction set with coal tower, freight shed, and switch tower; 0425 set with twenty-four figures, paint, and brush.

0960 BUMPER (ATLAS) Available in 1957, the bumper was an Atlas-made item catalogued in 1957-59. The Lionel-made bumper was catalogued new in 1962-63.
0961 ILLUMINATED BUMPER Snap-on, with electrical pickup in rear legs. Only known to exist in black unpainted Lionel-made plastic. Catalogued new in 1962-63.
0962 NON-ILLUMINATED BUMPER Unlighted snap-on. Lionel production; catalogued same as 0961.
0975 CURVED 18"-RADIUS TERMINAL TRACK
0982 CURVED 22"-RADIUS, 8½"
0983 CURVED 18"-RADIUS, 3"
0984 CURVED 18"-RADIUS, 4½"
0985 CURVED 15"-RADIUS, 9"
0986 CURVED 15"-RADIUS, 4½"
0989 CURVED 18"-RADIUS, 9"
0990 90-DEGREE CROSSING
0145-200 PRESSURE TRACK SWITCH
0771 FREIGHT CAR TRUCKS
0771-100 MAGNETIC BAR AND TEN COUPLER MAGNETS
390C SWITCH
5602 RAILROAD AND ROADWAY 90-DEGREE CROSSING

Power Packs

Lionel offered an array of power packs in their HO lines. The smaller units came with sets, while larger multipacks, rectifiers, and circuit breakers were offered for separate sale. See the photograph on page 85 and caption; also available but not shown were:

- 91 Circuit Breaker
- 1144 Multivolt AC power unit for use with switches and accessories
- 0103-800 Milliamp Power Pack

Scenic Accessories

All of the buildings, telephone poles, and figures were made by Plasticville and sold both in the Lionel and Plasticville catalogues. The Lionel accessories were packaged in the distinctive orange and white boxes, but the parts contain no Lionel identification. Once unpacked, the accessories are indistinguishable from regular Plasticville items, although colors occasionally varied between the two lines. Only an item found in an unopened Lionel carton can be identified as a Lionel product.

First catalogued in 1959, the scenic accessories were offered through 1962. Some items appeared in only one catalogue, although most were available for at least two years. Only the figures and billboard sets were catalogued in 1963. By 1964 Lionel had discontinued the figures, and only the 0310 Billboard set remained. Each set came with an illustrated instruction sheet, and the later sets that required painting came with paints and a separate sheet with painting instructions. With the exception of coloration, the catalogue pictures are fairly accurate in showing the actual contents of each accessories package. Most of the items remain available in the current Plasticville line, although, as we noted, the colors vary.

Catalogued from 1959 through 1962, the following items are thought to be products of Life-Like Products in Baltimore, Maryland. However, this has not been confirmed. The items tend to be of little interest to collectors.
0430 TREES
0431 LANDSCAPE SET
0432 TREE ASSORTMENT
0433 SCENERY SET

Gd Exc Mt

Listings of Scenic Accessories

0410 RANCH HOUSE SET: Eight-piece set; aqua blue walls; white roof and trim; two telephone poles; five pine trees with brown plastic trunks; six separate green pieces stack on each trunk; trees are scarce; catalogued 1959; available uncatalogued in 1960-61.
8 12 15

0411 FIGURE SET: Sixteen-piece set; twelve unpainted plastic figures, with paint set and brush; unpainted plastic watchman's shanty with gray walls and base, and light brown roof and trim; small jar of styrene cement with a caution for indoor use included with paint set; figures also available in other sets; difficult to find in Lionel packaging; catalogued in 1959 only.
8 12 15

0412 FARM SET: Eighteen-piece set; barn, silo, and Cape Cod farmhouse; all buildings have white walls, red roofs, and red trim; also includes dog, two cows, and thirteen chickens; all figures unpainted brown plastic; catalogued in 1959 only.
10 15 20

0413 RAILROAD STRUCTURE SET: Seven-piece set, unpainted plastic.
(A) Gray water tower with brown roof and trim; gray switch tower also with brown roof and trim; gray freight shed with brown roof and ends; four brown telephone poles; catalogued in 1959. 10 20 25
(B) Brown water tower with gray roof and trim; brown switch tower with gray roof and trim; brown freight shed with gray roof and ends; four gray telephone poles; uncatalogued; 1960. 10 15 20

0414 VILLAGE SET: Thirty-seven-piece set, unpainted plastic; four telephone poles; four pine trees; twenty-four figures; a white theater with gray roof and trim; white firehouse with red roof and trim; paints and brush included for decoration of figures; difficult to find complete set; catalogued in 1959 only. 15 20 25

0415 CAPE COD SET: Nineteen-piece set; house with white walls, brown roof, six green awnings, gray windows and doors; gray back porch with green roof; two white lounge chairs and table formed with porch; two telephone poles; two pine trees with brown trunks; six green foliage pieces for each tree; twelve sections of white picket fence and gate; difficult to find complete; catalogue incorrectly illustrated house with yellow or tan walls; these colors were not made for Lionel; catalogued in 1960-61. 5 10 15

0416 STATION SET: Twenty-piece set, unpainted plastic; white suburban station with brown roof and gray loading platform; gray windows and brown doors in station; Plasticville name boards on rooftop; two brown telephone poles; one black block signal; white crossing signal; twelve figures; paint set and brush included for figures; catalogued in 1960 only. 10 15 20

0417 FARM SET: Burgundy barn walls; gray barn and silo roofs; white house walls; brown roof and green awnings on house; gray porch with a table and two lounge chairs; green porch roof; two solid plastic pine trees; six chickens, a horse, three cows, two pigs, a sheep and lamb, and one dog included; female figure and two pieces of green foliage also included; neither porch nor trees mentioned in catalogue; catalogued in 1960 only. 5 10 15

0418 INDUSTRIAL SET: Seven-piece set; white gas station with red roof and trim; two sets of gas pumps and two racks of oil cans; red automobile; tan factory with light gray roof and dark gray loading docks; gray factory doors and windows; matching water tower on factory roof; two brown telephone poles; catalogued in 1960. 10 15 25

0419 RAIL JUNCTION SET: Similar to 0413; gray coaling station with brown roofs and trim replaces water tank; six telephone poles; block

The 0422 freight set, with its twenty-six pieces including figures and telephone poles, and the 0413 railroad structure set (this one catalogued in 1959; in 1960 its roof and wall colors were reversed).

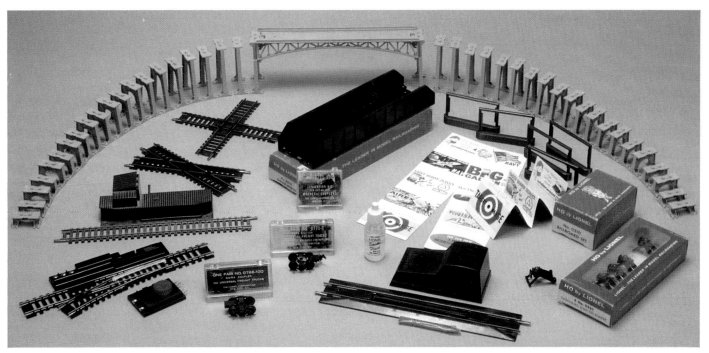

Shown across the top is the common 0110 graduated trestle set in gray (I have information it was also available as 0110-18 with trees and a black unpainted bridge; verification requested). From lower left corner, clockwise: The 0923 remote switch, 0900 remote platform for operating cars, 0930-300 crossing, 0990-900 crossing, 0214 girder bridge, 0310 billboard set with different insets, 0147 horn controller for use with 0535W SF Alco B unit, six 0961 illuminated bumpers, 0919 combo rerailers, uncoupler track section and tube of lubricant, bottle liquid smoke, and two packages of couplers.

Left to right: 0197 radar antenna; 0282 Gantry crane, which was manually operated (note the metal crank hole in side of cab); 0494 rotating beacon. All were manufactured by Lionel with all three using the same base, tower, sides, and top. The crane platform is black, while the other two are red. All are difficult to locate unbroken. At bottom, the 0140 banjo signal, still one of the hardest accessories to find, shown here with the 0145-200 track section that made the signal operational as the weight of a train passed over it.

	Gd	Exc	Mt

signal; crossing signal; three figures; several barrels and crates; catalogued in 1960 only; difficult to find complete.

	10	15	20

0420 RAILROAD SET: Similar to 0416; white station with brown roof and trim; four telephone poles; four pine trees; six separate foliage pieces for each tree; figures, paint set, block signal, and crossing signal included, though not listed in catalogue; catalogued in 1961; difficult to find complete.

	10	15	20

0421 FARM SET: Twenty-four-piece set; barn; farmhouse; white dog house, hen house, and garage with red roofs; red corn crib with white roof; sixteen unpainted figures; catalogued in 1961- 62; difficult to find complete.

(A) Burgundy barn with gray roof; white house with brown roof and trim; 1961.

	10	15	25

(B) White barn with red roof; matching house; 1962.

	10	15	25

0422 FREIGHT SET: Twenty-six-piece set; gray water tower, coaling station, switch tower, and freight station with brown roofs; set included new railroad work car built to resemble bunk car without wheels; work car has brown sides and a gray roof, rather than all-red color shown in catalogue; six telephone poles; four figures; several barrels and crates; one of the biggest catalogued sets; also most expensive, set sold for $5; catalogued in 1961-62.

	5	10	15

0425 FIGURE SETS: Twenty-four figures and crossing gate; paint, thinner, and brush included; catalogued in 1962-63.

	12	15	20

0426 RAILROAD STATION SET: White suburban station with brown roof; platform added to station; four telephone poles; crossing

The four known engine houses offered by Lionel, 1958-1963. Top: The very plain-looking 0115, as unassembled kit; no sound components; 0117 assembled house, also without sound, and with painted walls as shown. Bottom: 014 with horn that required a D battery; the 0118 engine house with whistle unit seen through side windows (whistle and horn were the same ones used in the O Gauge locomotives). All four models have metal floors with catalogue number along with clear windows and skylights; note dark brown walls of 0118 unit.

gate; block signal; crossing signal; unpainted black plastic signal bridge; four figures; barrels, crates, and bench; catalogued in 1962 only.

	10	15	20

NOTES

1. Phone interview with L. Dean, July 1984.
2. T. McComas and J. Tuohy, *A Collector's Guide and History, Vol III: Standard Gauge,* TM Productions, 1978.
3. Ibid., p. 107.
4. Survey information adapted from *Railroad Model Craftsman*, May 1961, pp. 31-32.
5. *Railroad Model Craftsman*, May 1962, p. 18.
6. Comment by Jack Fulton; verified by V. Rosa; March 4, 1984.
7. Ibid.

CHAPTER VI
Catalogued and Uncatalogued Sets

CATALOGUED SETS

The following listings indicate for each set the catalogue number, the road name, the locomotive(s), the number of cars, and the year in which the set was sold or catalogued. Values are given in this book only if six or more sales reports for a particular set were available for examination. As a rule of thumb, use today's quoted value for each piece in the set plus a premium for the carton.

Passenger Sets

5714 NEW HAVEN: 1958. 0533 F-7 A powered, 0553 A powered, four cars.
5732 THE TEXAS SPECIAL: 1959. Two 0566 Alco A powered, 0576 dummy, four cars.
5742 PENNSYLVANIA: 1960. 0581 rectifier, three cars.
5756 SOUTHERN PACIFIC: 1961. 0635LT Pacific locomotive and tender, three cars.
5759 SANTA FE: 1961. 0565 Alco A powered, 0595 A dummy, four cars.
5770 THE TEXAS SPECIAL: 1960. Two 0566 Alco A powered, 0576 B dummy, four cars.
14054 THE TEXAS SPECIAL: 1962. 0566 Alco A powered, four cars.
(A) As catalogued with a baggage car, two dome cars, and an observation car.
(B) Three dome cars and an observation; cardboard insert die-0cut for three dome cars; no short opening for baggage car. D. MacNary Collection; J. Fulton comment.
14108 SANTA FE: 1962. 0535 Alco A powered, 0535W B dummy with horn, four cars.
14163 PENNSYLVANIA: 1963. 0571P Alco A powered, three cars.
14173 SANTA FE: 1963. 0555P Alco A powered, 0595 Alco A powered, four cars.
14290 SANTA FE: 1964. 0555P Alco A powered, three cars.
14320 SANTA FE:
(A) 0555P Alco A powered, 0575 B dummy; three cars; 1965.
(B) 0556 Alco A powered; three cars; 1966.

Freight Sets

Note: "FM" stands for the Fairbanks-Morse diesel.

1957

5700 (UNLETTERED): 0600 switcher, three cars.
5701 ILLINOIS CENTRAL: 0505 FM A powered, five cars.

5702 WABASH: 0502 FM A powered, 0522 B dummy, five cars.
5703 WESTERN PACIFIC: 0503 FM A powered, 0523 B dummy, and 0513 A dummy, five cars.
5704 (UNLETTERED): 0610 Consolidation, six cars.

1958

5705 NAVY YARD: 0570 Husky-type, four cars.
5707 WABASH: 0580 GP-9, four cars.
5709 THE MILWAUKEE ROAD: 0531 F-7 A, five cars.
5711 VIRGINIAN 0590 rectifier, six cars.
5713 BALTIMORE AND OHIO: 0532 F-7 A powered, 0542 B dummy, five cars.
5715 RIO GRANDE: Two 0530 F-7 A powered, five cars.
5717 BOSTON AND MAINE: 0615LT Pacific locomotive and tender, which was never made; six cars; not manufactured.

1959

5717 SOUTHERN PACIFIC: 0625LT Pacific, six cars.
5719 AEC: 0056 Husky, three cars.
5721 THE TEXAS SPECIAL: 0566 Alco A unit, four cars.
5723 (UNLETTERED): 0605 steam switcher, four cars.
5725 NEW HAVEN: 0591 rectifier, five cars.
5727 NEW YORK CENTRAL: 0596 GP-9, five cars.

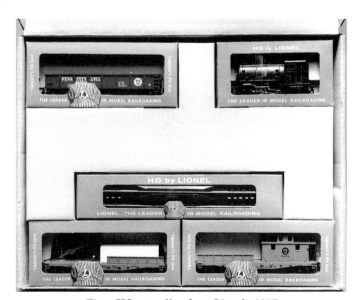

First HO set offered as Lionel, 1957
Rivarossi No. 5700

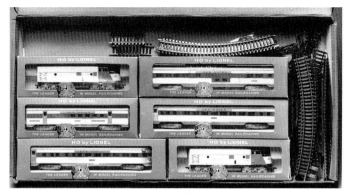

An early Athearn set, No. 5714

5729 ALASKAN RAILROAD: 0567 Alco A powered, 0577 B dummy, five cars.
5731 SOUTHERN PACIFIC: 0625LT Pacific locomotive and tender, five cars.
5733 SANTA FE: Two 0565 Alco A powered, 0575 B dummy, 0595 A dummy, seven cars.

1960

5735 ROCK ISLAND: 0058 Husky, three cars.
5737 (UNLETTERED): 0605 steam switcher, four cars.
5739 CHESAPEAKE AND OHIO: 0564 Alco A, four cars.
5741 PENNSYLVANIA: 0602LT steam locomotive and tender, four cars.
5743 NORTHERN PACIFIC: 0597 GP-9, five cars.
5745 SOUTHERN PACIFIC: 0625LT Pacific locomotive and tender, five cars.
5747 SANTA FE: 0565 Alco A powered, 0575 B dummy, five cars.
5749 PENNSYLVANIA: 0602LT steam locomotive and tender, six cars.
5771 SOUTHERN PACIFIC: 0625LT Pacific locomotive and tender, six cars.

1961

5750 M & StL: 0055 Husky, three cars.
5751 (ERIE): 0545 GE switcher, three cars.
5752 (UNLETTERED): 0642LT steam locomotive and tender, four cars.
5753 CHESAPEAKE AND OHIO: 0564 Alco A, four cars.
5754 SOUTHERN PACIFIC: 0625LT Pacific locomotive and tender, five cars.
5755 NEW YORK CENTRAL: 0598 GP-7, five cars.
5757 SOUTHERN PACIFIC: 0635LT Pacific locomotive and tender, five cars.
5758 SANTA FE: 0565 Alco A powered, 0575 B dummy, six cars.
5762 SOUTHERN PACIFIC: 0635LT Pacific locomotive and tender, seven cars.
5767 (UNLETTERED): 0642LT steam locomotive and tender, three cars.

1962

14003 M & StL: 0055 Husky, three cars.
14013 (ERIE): 0545 GE switcher, three cars.
14023 (UNLETTERED): 0642LT steam locomotive and tender, four cars.
14033 UNION PACIFIC: 0568 Alco A, four cars.

14043 SOUTHERN PACIFIC: 0635LT Pacific locomotive and tender, four cars.
14064 NORTHERN PACIFIC: 0597 GP-9, five cars.
14074 SOUTHERN PACIFIC: 0645LTS Pacific locomotive and tender, four cars.
14084 SANTA FE: 0535 Alco A powered, 0535W B dummy, five cars. J. Otterbin, J. Kimenhour Collections.
14087 SANTA FE: 0535 Alco A powered, 0536W B dummy, five cars.
14098 SOUTHERN PACIFIC: 0645LTS Pacific locomotive and tender, five cars.

1963

14133 (UNLETTERED): 0643LT steam locomotive and tender, three cars.
14143 SANTA FE: 0594P GP-9 (incorrectly catalogued as GP-7), five cars.
14153 SOUTHERN PACIFIC: 0626LT Pacific locomotive and tender, six cars.
14183 SOUTHERN PACIFIC: 0636LTS Pacific locomotive and tender, eight cars.
14193 NORTHERN PACIFIC: 0593 GP-9 powered, 0593T dummy, seven cars. This particular nine-car set was issued with the Northern Pacific Geep stamped with the 0597 number on one side, with the 0593 on the other. It is a true factory error. Collections of F. Coppola, Matt Padgett, Ken Fairchild, and Richard Kughn. Verified by George Horan.
14203 SANTA FE: 0536P Alco A powered, 0535W B dummy, 0595 A dummy, seven cars.
14233 SOUTHERN PACIFIC: 0646LTS Pacific locomotive and tender, eight cars.

1964–1966

14240 M & StL: 0055 Husky, three cars, 1964-66.
14250 M & StL: 0055 Husky, three cars, 1964-66. Same as 14240, less terminal track.
14260 SANTA FE:
(A) 0594P GP-9, four cars, 1964-65.
(B) 0592 GP-9, four cars, 1966.
14270 SOUTHERN PACIFIC: 0626LT Pacific locomotive and tender, four cars, 1964.
14280 SOUTHERN PACIFIC: 0636LTS Pacific locomotive and tender, six cars, 1964-66.
14300 SOUTHERN PACIFIC:
(A) 0646LTS Pacific locomotive and tender, seven cars, 1964-65.
(B) 0647LTS Pacific locomotive and tender, six cars, 1966.
14310 SANTA FE: 0536 Alco A powered, 0535W B dummy with horn, 0595 A dummy, seven cars, 1964-66.
17190 M & StL: 0055 switcher, three cars; combination HO raceway and train outfit. Shown on last page of 1965 consumer catalogue. G. Bunza comment.

UNCATALOGUED SETS

Lionel catalogued many train sets between 1957 and 1966, but there are many sets that were not catalogued. The authors invite collectors to send to George Horan c/o Greenberg Publishing Company details of any not listed below, including set number and set name (if any), locomotives, and rolling stock found in set, and a description of the packaging and enclosed literature.

The following uncatalogued sets appeared in Polk's Model-Craft Hobbies catalogue in 1961, 1962, and 1963 as special dealer sets. They are listed by catalogue numbers within year spans. Not enough sales have been reported to average out a price on these sets. **Note:** All locomotives in all sets are lighted.

Sets prefixed by "(A)" were catalogued but in the advance dealer catalogue only. Lionel's advance catalogues have over the year shown pieces that were not made and sets that were not available. The HO line was no exception. For example, in the 1959 advance catalogue, page 37, two Athearn sets are shown with the D-260 Two Tier Circular Display and five sets with the D-227 HO Step Display; five were Rivarossi sets that had not been available since 1957. And page 40 shows the 0808 Flatcar with Tractor and the 0880 Maintenance Car with Light. Although both cars were made, the finished products were quite different from those illustrated. On page 41, Lionel illustrated an 0870 Maintenance Car with Generator, shown with three men and a ladder, but the finished product lacked the men and the ladder. The 0806 Flatcar with Helicopter had an unusual feature for a Lionel helicopter: a three-blade main rotor and four landing wheels that were never used on a production run.

Note the 1500-series set numbers used in 1962. A notation accompanying their introduction to the dealers that year stated the sets would not appear in the consumer catalogue and were for dealer break-ups or promotion as they saw fit. Some sets contained track and transformer while others did not. The cartons examined by George Horan have the white paper sticker glued over the regular catalogue number, with the new 1500 number stamped in black on the sticker.

There is no way of knowing just how many of these sets were sold as sets, but we know there were some. All the sets contained regular line items with no special items made just for these sets. For this reason no value can be given except for the price shown for that year. By 1965 these special sets had disappeared from Polk's catalogue, with the 1965 cover showing a picture of radio and TV personality Arthur Godfrey, who appeared as product spokesman in an article headlined "Lionel Levels with the Trade: An advertisement in which we admit past mistakes, tell you where we stand today, and offer you an interesting proposition for the future." Even with the use of celebrities, Lionel disappeared from HO the following year.

1960

(A) 5760 SENTINEL: Ca. 1960. 0057 Union Pacific Husky locomotive, 0847 Exploding Boxcar, 0850 U.S. Missile Launching Car, 0805 AEC Car, 0817-325 Union Pacific caboose. Reported by J. Fulton, J. Otterbein, and J. Kimenhour.

(A) 5761 THE WORK HAWK: 1960. 0605 black steam switcher (no road name), 0319 Southern Pacific operating helicopter car, 0301 operating Pennsylvania coal dump car, 0842 culvert car with three pipes, 0841 painted red caboose without a road name; no track or transformer. K. Armenti Collection. Verified by G. Horan.

1961

(A) 5763 THE MARKSMAN: 1961. 0058 Rock Island Husky, 0847 exploding boxcar, 0809 cylinder transport, 0850 U.S. rocket launcher car, 0841 unmarked caboose; no track or transformer. White paper sticker on carton end. G. Horan Collection.

(A) 5764 THE EXPLORER: 1961. 0605 steam locomotive, 0805 radioactive waste car, 0337 giraffe car, 0319 operating helicopter car, 0841 unmarked caboose; included instruction book, track, and transformer.

(A) 5765 THE INDUSTRIALIST: 1961. 0602 Pennsylvania with tender, 0301 operating coal car, 0300 operating log car, 0366 operating milk car, 0817-150 ATSF caboose, 0919 operating milk platform, one sheet of fine billboards; no track or transformer. P. Besser, D. M. Harkcom Collections.

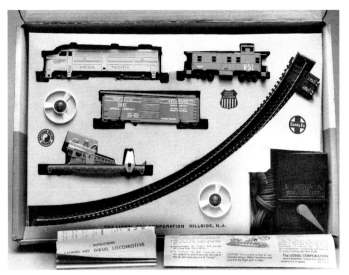

1963 uncatalogued set No. 14123

(A) 5766 THE TITAN: 1961. 0581 Pennsylvania rectifier, 0850 U.S. Army missile car, 0333 satellite car, 0860-200 Pennsylvania derrick car, 0847 exploding boxcar, 0841 unmarked caboose; no track or transformer.

10100 SEARS SPECIAL #48-3214: Flat orange and white set box with silhouette of Pacific logo on lid. Punched liner to accept 0545, cylinder flatcar, Mercury capsule car, torbo flatcar, 0841 red caboose, and six sections of double 18"-radius track, transformer, and instruction booklet. Richard Kughn Collection.

1962

14054 THE TEXAS SPECIAL PASSENGER SET: 1962. Square orange master carton, 9" x 10½" x 7", with white label glued over original number, contains Alco 0566 power and 0586 dummy plus 704 baggage, two 706 dome cars, 707 observation plus twelve sections of 18"-radius track, booklet, and transformer; all items packed in individual boxes. Richard Kughn Collection.

(A) 15503 THE SPACE EXPLORER: 1962. 0059 white Minuteman husky, 0349 operating turbo missile firing car, 0847 exploding boxcar, 0813 Mercury capsule car, 0841-125 AEC caboose, 0103 transformer, four sections of track (straight and curved). F. Coppola Collection. Original price: $35.75

(A) 15513 THE OVERLANDER: 1962. 0642 2-4-2 black steam switcher (no road name) with slope-back tender, 0337 white operating giraffe car, 0861 timber transport car (no road name), 0873 yellow horse transport (rodeo car), 0841 red-painted caboose (no road name), 0101 transformer, four sections of straight track and eight sections curved. B. Robbinson, W. Tucker Collections. Original price: $45.30

(A) 15528 THE METEOR: 1962. 0565 Santa Fe power A unit, 0595 Santa Fe dummy A unit, 0365 Minutemen missile launching car, 0349 turbo missile firing car, 0470 missile launching platform with 0847 exploding boxcar, 0816 rocket fuel tank car, 0823 twin missile carrying car; 0103 transformer and track included. Original price: $66.

(A) 15708 THE CELESTIAL: 1962. 0605 0-4-0 steam switcher (no tender, no road name), 0349 turbo missile firing car, 0319 operating Southern Pacific helicopter car, 0333 operating Southern Pacific satellite car, 0827 illuminated Safety First red caboose; no track or transformer. F. Coppola Collection. Original price: $39.75

The Athearn Pacific catalogued in set No. 5717 as the 0615LT in 1958. Many bugs forced Athearn to cancel production of the locomotive. Added to the Athearn HO line in 1960 with gear drive, it is one of the rarest Athearn-made locomotives. Ken Fairchild Collection.

(A) 15718 THE SHARPSHOOTER: 1962. 0598 New York Central GP- 7, 0365 Minuteman missile launching boxcar, 0816 rocket fuel tank car, 0847 exploding boxcar, 0819-275 C and O work caboose; no track or transformer. K. Armenti, G. Horan Collections. Original price: $36.75

(A) 15728 THE JOURNEYMAN: 1962. 0625 4-6-2 Pacific with short tender lettered for the Southern Pacific, 0708 black and tuscan Pennsylvania baggage car, 0709 black and tuscan Pennsylvania vista dome car, 0710 black and tuscan Pennsylvania observation car, 0118 gray and tan English house with whistle; no track or transformer. Set boxed in brown shipping carton only with individual orange cartons. Original price: $42.75

1963

(A) 14113 THE HERCULES: 1963. 0055 M & StL red Husky, 0861 timber transporter (no road name), 0865-350 blue unpainted gondola without load (the car is stamped 0865-250), 0837 M & StL red caboose; two sections of straight track and eight sections curved, with 0103 transformer. G. Horan Collection. No price given.

(A) 14123 THE SPACE PROBER: 1963. 0569 Union Pacific power Alco A unit, 0349 turbo missile firing car, 0847 exploding boxcar,

0841-125 AEC white caboose; 0103 transformer and eight sections of track, curved and straight. B. Robbinson, W. Tucker Collections. No price given.

(A) 14213 THE ATLAS: 1963. Has same components as set 14113, less track and transformer. No price given.

(A) 14223 THE SATURN: Same components as set 14123, less track and transformer. W. Tucker Collection.

COMMENT ON PROMOTIONAL SETS

Lionel dealers sold promotional sets, which they were responsible for advertising. The sets were all packaged in regular Lionel display cartons with fold back-type tops. The set number and name usually appeared on white or yellow paper stickers glued over the original set number, although a few of these sets came with the number stamped right on the carton. These sets command a premium price today.

CHAPTER VII
Catalogues and Paper Items

By I. D. Smith
With the assistance of Robert J. Osterhoff

1957

	Gd	VG	Exc	Mt

ADVANCE CATALOGUE: 11" x 8¼", 54 pages, red and black covers, black and white coated stock.   **5**   **10**   **15**   **20**

AND NOW HO — BY LIONEL: 10¾" x 7⅝", "For the Discriminating Hobbyist . . .", supplement to Advance Catalogue, four-page color folder, may have been distributed separately and/or in consumer catalogue in addition to Advance Catalogue.
   .25   **.50**   **1**   **2**

CATALOGUE: 11¼" x 7½", 52 pages, full color, coated stock, cover has "New Super 'O' Track".   **1**   **2**   **3**   **7**

ACCESSORY CATALOGUE: With Service Station Directory for 1957-58, 10" x 7½", 32 pages, red and black covers, black and white pulp paper.   **.25**   **.50**   **1**   **2**

HOW TO OPERATE LIONEL TRAINS AND ACCESSORIES: 8½" x 5½", 64 black and white pages plus red and black wraparound cover, pulp paper.   **.25**   **.50**   **1**   **2**

BANNER: HO BY LIONEL THE LEADER IN MODEL RAIL-ROADING: 21³⁄₁₆" x 6½", yellow paper printed with black and red ink. Graham Collection.   **.50**   **1**   **2**   **3**

1958

ADVANCE CATALOGUE: 10⅞" x 8¼", 64 pages, red and black cover, NH and M & StL trains passing missile launching site, black and white, HO scale section (pages 50-55) has burgundy marker with gold-stamped "HO".   **5**   **10**   **15**   **20**

CATALOGUE: 11¼" x 7⅝", 56 pages, cover like Advance Catalogue but in full color on coated stock.
   2   **4**   **6**   **8**

ACCESSORY CATALOGUE: With Service Station Directory, 11⅛" x 8", 32 pages, red and black cover, black and white, pulp paper. Titled "Lionel 1958 Accessory Catalogue"; contains individual items only. Cover picture is similar to regular catalogue, inside front cover copyrighted 1958. Weber Collection.   **.50**   **1**   **2**   **3**

ADVANCE HO CATALOGUE: 10⅞" x 8⅛", eight pages, black and white, cover has red background and illustration of HO display, rear cover shows dealer displays "For Your HO Department".
   .50   **1**   **2**   **3**

HO CATALOGUE:
(A) 8⅛" x 10⅞", six-page fold-out, full color, coated stock.
   .50   **1**   **2**   **3**

	Gd	VG	Exc	Mt

(B) 8¼" x 11¼", eight pages, full color, coated stock.
   .50   **1**   **2**   **3**

(C) 8" x 11", six-page fold-out, full color, coated stock, copyright 1958 by The Lionel Corporation. Published in *Railroad Model Craftsman* magazine, October 1958, as unnumbered pages 35 through 40, in October 1958 issue of *Model Railroader*, and in Fall 1958 issue of *Model Trains* magazine.   **1**   **2**   **3**   **4**

PRIVATE CATALOGUE: "Lionel 1958", large eight-page illustrated edition, as issued by Ray's Bike & Key Shop, Geneva, New York. Features 2018 locomotive with tender on cover, in red and black on newsprint paper. Osterhoff Collection.   **NRS**

1959

ADVANCE CATALOGUE: 8½" x 10⅞", 44 pages, full color, black and white, fold-out pages, coated stock, cover lettered "Lionel 1959", illustration shows 1872 General and 44 missile launcher.
   3   **7**   **12**   **18**

CATALOGUE: 11" x 8½", 56 pages, full color, coated stock, cover illustration shows 736, 1872 General, and 44 U.S. Army; HO featured on pages 48-55.
(A) U.S. Edition, with prices.   **3**   **5**   **9**   **12**
(B) Canadian Edition, without prices; two-page insert, "Lionel Trains Canadian Price List 1959". Osterhoff Collection.   **NRS**

ACCESSORY CATALOGUE: 11" high x 8" wide, red and black front cover with 1872 and 44 locomotives, black ink only on pulp interior pages, 36 pages. Schreiner Collection.   **.75**   **1.50**   **2**   **3**

HO CATALOGUE: 8⅛" x 11", eight pages, full color, coated stock, copyright 1959 by The Lionel Corporation, published in *Railroad Model Craftsman* magazine, October 1959, as unnumbered pages 35 through 42, and in Fall 1959 issue of *Model Trains* magazine.
   1   **2**   **3**   **4**

PRIVATE CATALOGUE: "Lionel 1959 Trains and Accessories", published by Distributors' Promotions, Inc., Philadelphia. Red and black on white cover, 20 pages. Osterhoff Collection.   **NRS**

WINDOW POSTER: 22" x 9", "HO by Lionel", full color, illustrating HO motor and truck. Included in 1959 dealer promotional kit. Osterhoff Collection.   **2**   **4**   **6**   **8**

WINDOW POSTER: 22" x 9", "HO by Lionel", full color, illustrating HO engines, set. Included in 1959 dealer promotional kit. Osterhoff Collection.   **2**   **4**   **6**   **8**

1960

ADVANCE CATALOGUE: 8½" x 11", 60 pages, color cover, black and white, red and white back cover with promotional slogan, coated

	Gd	VG	Exc	Mt

stock, cover illustration shows father and son viewing twin railroad layout.

(A) "Lionel 1960" cover, dark brown heading.

	3	5	7	12

(B) "Lionel 1960" cover, red-orange heading. Osterhoff Collection.

				NRS

CATALOGUE: 11" x 8⅜", 56 pages, full color, coated stock, cover illustration shows family viewing close-up section of twin railroad layout; HO section on pages 44-54.

	3	5	9	12

ACCESSORY CATALOGUE: With Service Station listing, 8⅝" x 11", 40 pages, color cover, black and white pulp paper.

	1	2	3	4

HOW TO OPERATE LIONEL TRAINS AND ACCESSORIES

(A) 8½" x 5⅜", 64 black and white pages on coated stock, heavy paper wraparound cover in black and white with red background, Form 926-60.

	1	2	3	4

(B) Cover shows black and white photo of N & W Y6b, left and rear side with orange-red right half with black and white lettering, 62 pages, copyrighted 1960 inside rear cover. Smith and Weber Collections.

	1	2	3	4

LIONEL TRACK LAYOUTS FOR "O27", SUPER "O" AND HO GAUGES, START BUILDING YOURS TODAY!: 8⅜" x 11", four pages, not numbered.

(A) Price 10 cents on front, page 2 has "1–115" on lower right, heavy white paper, black and gray. "Address inquiries to: Lionel Service, Dept 74-E, Hoffman Place, Hillside, NJ 07205" on back page. Smith Collection.

	.25	.50	.75	1

(B) Similiar to (A), but no price, no number, coated paper stock. On bottom last three pages concerning inquires, "simply write to: Engineer Bill c/o The Lionel Corp., 15 East 26th St., New York, 10 NY". Smith Collection.

	.25	.50	.75	1

HO CATALOGUE: 8½" x 10⅞", 12 pages, full color, coated stock, cover reads, "Operating Cars — 1960's Most Exciting HO News".

	1	2	3	4

HOW TO OPERATE LIONEL HO TRAINS: 8½" x 5½", 24 pages plus red and black covers.

	.50	1	2	3

WINDOW STREAMER: "See . . . Get . . . Brand New Operating Cars — Lionel HO", 22" x 8½", black and red on white glossy paper. Included in 1960 dealer promotional kit. Osterhoff Collection.

	2	4	6	8

STORE POSTER: "Vital Small Parts" and "Control and Operating Accessories for HO by Lionel", 20" x 14", black on white paper. Included in 1960 dealer promotional kit. Osterhoff Collection.

	1	2	3	4

1961

ADVANCE CATALOGUE: 8½" x 11", 76 pages, John Bruce Medaris on color cover, black and white coated stock.

(A) Pages numbered, page 3 begins "Cleared For Immediate Release".

	3	5	7	10

(B) Pages not numbered, page 3 begins with letter dated "1 Aug '60" from Medaris; pre-1961 Toy Show edition. Osterhoff Collection.

	5	8	12	16

CATALOGUE: HO section on pages 60-70.

(A) 8½" x 11", 56 pages, layout and science sets on cover, red, and black covers, inside black and white pulp paper, "Honorary Stockholder" on rear cover.

	.50	1	2	3

(B) 8½" x 11", 72 pages, cover same as (A), but catalogue differs, full-color coated stock, HO raceways on rear cover.

	1	2	4	6

(C) 8½" x 11", 72 pages, HO raceways on rear cover, but Canadian Edition. No prices published in catalogues, but does include a separate four-page flyer "Canadian Price List 1961". Osterhoff Collection.

	–	–	–	15

DEALER WINDOW POSTER: 21½" x 9", "HO By Lionel — The Leader in Model Railroading". Black and red on yellow rag paper. Included in 1961 dealer promotion kit. Osterhoff Collection.

	2	4	6	8

LIONEL TRACK LAYOUTS FOR "O27", SUPER "O" AND HO GAUGES, START BUILDING YOURS TODAY!: 8⅜" x 11", four pages, not numbered. Included in 1961 dealer promotion kit. Osterhoff Collection.

	1	2	3	4

1962

CATALOGUE: 8½" x 11", 100 pages, cover lettered "Lionel 1962".

	1	2	4	6

ADVANCE CATALOGUE: "Lionel Trains and Accessories — The Leader in Model RR 1962" 64 pages, four-color cover, black and white inside, includes displays and HO. 8½" x 11" vertical.

(A) First Edition Pre-Toy Show; bright blue cover, back page "Three Powerful New Lionel Lines". Osterhoff Collection. **NRS**

(B) Second Edition; dull blue cover, back page "Four Powerful New Lionel Lines". Osterhoff Collection. **NRS**

ACCESSORY CATALOGUE: 8⅜" x 10⅞".

(A) 62 pages, full-color cover, first two and last two pages are coated stock, rest is black and white pulp. Ocilka Collection. **NRS**

(B) 40 pages, red and black cover, black and white, pulp paper.

	1	2	3	4

CONTROL AND OPERATING ACCESSORIES FOR HO BY LIONEL: Sales sheet, printed one side only, 20" x 14", black on white paper, lists No. 928 Maintenance Kit at $2.50. Included in 1962 dealer promotion kit. Osterhoff Collection.

	1	2	3	4

LIONEL TRACK LAYOUTS FOR "O27", SUPER "O" AND HO GAUGES, START BUILDING YOURS TODAY!: 8⅜" x 11", four pages not numbered. Included in 1962 dealer promotion kit. Osterhoff Collection.

	1	2	3	4

ADVERTISING PROOF SHEETS: 11" x 17", black on white high-gloss paper, complete set of ad mats for all products. Printed one side only.

(A) "O" and "O27" trains, eight pages. Osterhoff Collection.

	–	–	–	35

(B) "HO" trains, six pages. Osterhoff Collection. **NRS**

(C) Lionel-Tri-Ang Scalextric, two pages. Osterhoff Collection.

	–	–	–	10

(D) Lionel-Spear Line, two pages. Osterhoff Collection.

	–	–	–	10

(E) Lionel's New Line of Science Sets, seven pages. Osterhoff Collection.

	–	–	–	22

1963

CATALOGUE: 8⅜" x 10⅞", 56 pages, color cover, red and black interior coated stock.

	1	2	4	6

ADVANCE CATALOGUE: "Lionel 1963", 8½" x 11", 80 pages; yellow, black, and white cover; interior black and white; includes trains, Lionel-Porter, and racing sets, etc. Smith and Zydlo Collections. **NRS**

	Gd	VG	Exc	Mt

ACCESSORY CATALOGUE: With Service Station listing, 8⅜" x 10⅞", 40 pages, blue and black cover, interior black and white pulp paper.   .50   1   2   3

1964

CATALOGUE: 8⅜" x 10⅞", 24 pages, black and blue.
(A) Pulp paper, page 13 lists 6402 flatcar at $2.50.
                  1   2   4   5
(B) Same as (A), but 6402 is incorrectly listed at $3.95.
                  1   2   4   5
(C) Same as (A), but coated stock.   1   2   5   7
(D) Same as (B), but coated stock.   1   2   5   7

1965

CATALOGUE: 8½" x 10⅞", 40 pages, multicolor printing and backgrounds.
(A) Pulp paper.   1   2   4   5
(B) Coated stock.   1   2   5   7
(C) Same as (A), 6119 and 6401 (errata).
                  1   2   4   5

	Gd	VG	Exc	Mt

(D) Same as (B), 6119 and 6401 (errata).   1   2   5   7

HOW TO OPERATE LIONEL TRAINS: 8½" x 11", 32 pages, black and white plus yellow wraparound cover, uncoated paper.
                  .50   1   2   3

1966

ADVANCE CATALOGUE: 19⅞" x 8½", 40 pages, full-color coated stock front and back cover, but unlike the consumer edition, front color is deep blue rather than purple. Page 2 printed "Advance Catalog" and all inside pages are black and white. Osterhoff Collection.   **NRS**

CATALOGUE: 10⅞" x 8⅜", 40 pages, full-color coated stock, cover illustration shows father and son watching trains rush past.
(A) Set illustrations on pages 8 and 10.
                  .50   1   2   3
(B) No illustrations as in (A).   .50   1   2   3

Note: There are other references to Lionel HO published by Lionel beyond the 1966 time frame. For example, the Lionel 1970 Numerical Parts List contains a detailed HO parts list on pages 94 to 115. Spanning several years is, of course, the *Lionel Service Manual*; HO selections appear on pages 116–140.

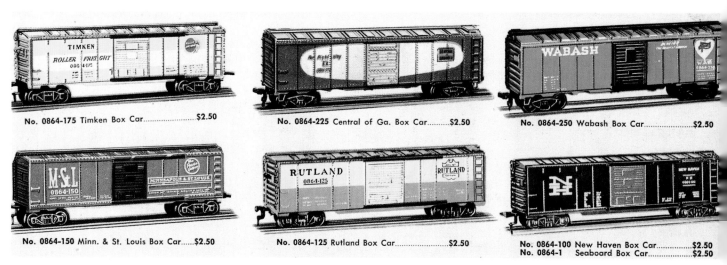

No. 0864-175 Timken Box Car..............$2.50

No. 0864-225 Central of Ga. Box Car.........$2.50

No. 0864-250 Wabash Box Car..............$2.50

No. 0864-150 Minn. & St. Louis Box Car.....$2.50

No. 0864-125 Rutland Box Car.............$2.50

No. 0864-100 New Haven Box Car..............$2.50
No. 0864-1 Seaboard Box Car..............$2.50

Part of a page from a 1958 Lionel catalogue. The two on the bottom right are Rivarossi manufacture, the others are Athearn.

A FIRST IN HO...
BRAND NEW
ACTION-PACKED

OPERATING CARS

Helicopter takes off

0319 SOUTHERN PACIFIC

NEW! No. 0319 Operating Helicopter Launching Car—
"Whirlybird" soars into the air when released by a track-side actuator. $7.95

EXPLOSIVES
0847
DANGER
KEEP FIRE AWAY

EXPLOSIVES
DANGER

Car "explodes" when hit

NEW! No. 0847 Exploding Target Car
—Car "explodes" when hit by missile from Missile Launching Car. Car reassembles easily. $4.95

Missile is fired at Target Car

0850 SOUTHERN PACIFIC

NEW! No. 0850 Missile Launching Car—Set angle of launching pad, press firing pin and missile blasts off toward the Exploding Target Car. $5.95

Logs roll into bin

NEW! No. 0300 Operating Lumber Car—Carrying frame tilts by remote control and logs roll off into bin. Car, logs, bin included. $4.95

Cargo dumps into bin

TO OPERATE No. 0300 AND No. 0301—No. 0900 REMOTE CONTROL OPERATING PLATFORM IS REQUIRED.

NEW! No. 0301 Operating Dump Car—As carrying body tilts, cargo is dumped into receiving bin by remote control. Car, cargo, bin included. $4.95

From a page in the 1960 Lionel catalogue, proudly announcing the line of HO cars that offer play value.

CHAPTER VIII
Oddballs and Forgeries

By George Horan

It was April 1986, at the York, Pennsylvania, TCA train meet. The occasion shall remain firmly implanted in my mind for many years to come. I had completed my mission: *Greenberg's Guide to Lionel HO Trains* was on the market. With the help of my coauthor Vince Rosa I felt we had done a good job for the collector of Lionel HO.

In the last six years, I have met and received numerous letters and phone calls, both pro and con, on the published information — they came from collectors all over and outside of the United States and included calls from West Germany, Switzerland, and Canada. Almost all of the calls and letters offered oddball pieces of one sort or another to be included in a second edition. Of course I took these new friends up on their offers, and those items will be covered here.

The second part of this chapter, "Forgeries," was the most difficult to write. I had to admit that we in the HO collecting field also had our share of the "anything-for-a-buck" guys. They are making their presence felt!

I personally have purchased only a few of the items pictured — all found at local meets in southern or northern New Jersey, New York, and Pennsylvania; others came from Texas and California. Two of these cars were priced at $75 each. After spending an hour assuring the seller that being in a Lionel box did not make it a true Lionel item, and also assuring myself that he had not made them up himself, I purchased the two pieces for $30 — still more than they were worth — in order to have them pictured. in the book.

Other pieces shown were purchased at a large meet in Philadelphia, Pennsylvania, by friends who had purchased many Lionel pieces for me when I was not present at that same meet. They were purchased because they carried that little circle with the letter L in it that I had, many times over the last ten years, asked them all to watch for. I reimbursed my friends and felt they had spent in good faith for my benefit. Three phone calls to the Meet Host failed to get a table number or name for the dealer, since I could not positively identify his location. The hosts of major meets I have attended have all promised, since this problem has come to light, that they will use meet floor plans to identify a dealer by name if it is proved that a piece is knowingly sold at their meet and is a forgery.

Since these were Athearn-stamped items sold as Lionel, I feel sure that this was just the beginning of the forgery problem we must all now watch for. I would remind the anything-for-a-buck guys that to reproduce the Lionel trademark most certainly is against the law. If a name can be put with this type of practice, I would be the first to call Mr. Richard Kughn, who now owns the trademark, with that name. I am sure legal steps would be taken to stop such practice. As far as is known there are two types of logos being used: the ⅛- and 1/16-inch sizes. (Closeup photos will be included in this chapter.) With all the letters and phone calls these last six years, I still have not found one collector who has ever seen a Gulf tank car of Athearn production with the Lionel logo on its side.

A half dozen pieces with phony Lionel logos were received for examination by your author but are not pictured because of insufficient information and the owner feeling foolish that he had been taken in for buying the piece in the first place. The Lionel logo and details of models by all three manufacturers have been shown closeup throughout this book in order to

combat this problem. I am happy to state it is almost a year since I have received a forged item.

Unlike the larger O Gauge trains of the 1950s and 1960s, many of the early HO models from other manufacturers required detail to be added that included painting, decals, wire handrails, and other small parts. But the Lionel line offered was strictly ready-to-run models that required little of the above work. Those of us who have built the type of car kits that did need the extra detail should have a good eye for a Lionel item that was tampered with. Shun the anything-for-a-buck guys that think a strange decal-added road name, or a repainted roof or door, automatically produces a "rare" model worth whatever they feel like asking, with no one being the wiser. This was the sole reason that I did everything but count the number of rivets on each item in identifying each known model offered in the Lionel line of HO. I certainly am not stating that I have seen everything Lionel ever made, but with help from others across this country I have discovered some very poor jobs of painting and numbers that were changed to create a one-of-a-kind model.

Most of the models I have seen with lettering changed or the Lionel logo having been added are the Athearn rubber-stamped type of car. The silkscreen-type lettering used on the Rivarossi-made items have made it a little harder to create a supposedly rare model in that manufacturer's line. The heat-stamp method used on Lionel-made items would also present a problem for the anything-for-a-buck guys.

ODDBALLS NOT PHOTOGRAPHED

I feel many more oddball-type items exist, yet to be found. The models listed below were either in my possession at the time they were written up and/or they have been subject to close inspection.

0864-150 M.St.L. BOXCAR: Athearn production, same as (A) described in Chapter IV, but has 1/16" logo in the first panel to right of door, appearing on only one side of the car; unpainted roofwalk, door, and brakewheel, door guides painted; two-letterboard door. Geoffrey Bunza Collection.

0821 PIPE CAR: Standard car with gray pipes painted an orangish yellow; paint is very thin and chips and flakes off easily. Three of these cars have been seen by its owner in three different states. Lionel could have painted a few cars before making the switch from gray pipe to yellow in 1964. C. Sommers, K. Fairchild Collections. Value unknown.

0058 ROCK ISLAND HUSKY: Carries the white stripe on its front grille, pointing towards the rear cab on one side of the hood; factory heat stamping. Original box, like new. Gerald Potts Collection.

0647 PACIFIC: Heat-stamped 0647 with 0645W long haul tender; holes in front of boiler behind smokebox cover to accept wire handrails are not punched out; brass bell on boiler, with no sign of every being disassembled; white stripe on boiler is suspect as being non-factory; probably part of late set 14300 of 1966, when many made-up sets seem to have been put together to move the last of the inventory. Shell verification requested. Gerald Potts Collection.

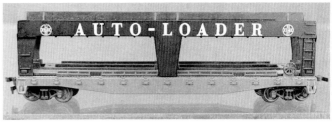

0814-200 Auto-Loader. Lionel-made 50-foot flat with Athearn-made auto rack; may very well be a transitional item of 1960. The car shown, from the Joe Otterbin Collection, has a factory-painted red body less any type of stamping or numbers. The frame carries the Lionel name and part number. Note the heavy white stamping on the black rack that is almost always

Pictured is the extremely rare desk set that was produced as gifts for top NBC executives in late 1959 or early 1960. With the help of Lt. Col. T. Turey (Ret.) of Albuquerque, New Mexico, who owns this board, and his good friend Jim Spatophore, who owns the switcher, this model appears here. When these two fellow collectors first sent the information and a snapshot of the display, Col. Turey's letter explained he had purchased the board while his friend bought the AEC a year earlier at the same flea market. It struck me as amusing that one of the rarest known Lionel items should be found in this manner. Talk about good luck! No value can be placed on such a piece, at least not by this author. But we now know there are at least two out there. Thom Shepler Collection.

The first 0-4-0 switcher I have ever seen with factory heat-stamping that includes the word "LIONEL" as shown. A true prize, it is part of the Joe Otterbin Collection. Having no way of knowing how many such exist, I cannot place a value on this; it surely is a rare item.

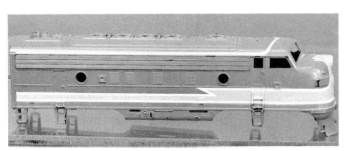

Examining the shell pictured here makes it apparent that Athearn also had some problems with its decorating. All lettering on this F-7, Athearn-produced for Lionel, is stamped twice. Joe Otterbin Collection. Value unknown.

Bottom left: 0625 Pacific. Less tender; number heat-stamped on cab but with smoke unit and light. The frame is identical to those used on the 0635 Pacifics. A very close inspection revealed no sign of filling or drill of the inner smokestack hole to make the shell fit the smoke unit-style chassis. I believe the locomotive shell to be a 0635 that was mistakenly stamped to be a 0625. The inside of the smokestack on these units, if factory, should be unpainted black with very smooth sides and no edge on the inner boiler. A second way of knowing if a 0625 boiler was drilled out to accept a thumb screw is to remove the shell. The square mold mark on all but the 0625 early or late shells is approximately 3/16 inches square where this same mold mark on the 0635 shells are 1/4 inches square. If a 0625 shell has been drilled out to manufacture a rare piece, then the newly drilled hole would overlap the 3/16-inch mold mark. I believe this 0625, from the Joe Otterbin Collection, to be a factory-mismarked locomotive. Value unknown.

Oddballs. Top shelf, left: 0811-25 Rivarossi-made Reading flatcar. Red, as described in the text, with the exception of the twelve clear plastic stakes found on this oddball car. Logo on one side only. Matt Padgett Collection. Verified by George Horan. The two lighted Lionel-made bumpers shown on the car were not part of the car but added by G. H. at the photo session. Car value unknown.

Top shelf, right: 0864-175 Timken boxcar. Found mint in Athearn original box, a yellow picture window carton. Stamped kit #2229, price $2.25. The car has the brown Lionel logo stamped on both sides but without the circle. The car also held unfinished silver door guides. Matt Padgett Collection. Value unknown.

Second shelf, left to right: 0593 Northern Pacific GP-9. Factory-misstamp: far side is properly stamped while the other side shows a single stamp of the "0" of the "0597" with the last three digits, "597", being stamped twice, slightly crooked, running up-hill on the shell. Joe Otterbin Collection. Value unknown.

Note: *The second Northern Pacific GP-9 shown on the second shelf is also a double-stamped 0593 on one side only. Matt Padgett Collection. Value unknown.*

Third shelf, left: 0535W unmarked B unit. With horn intact; purchased, along with a stamped original box, at Rosewood Hobbit in northern New Jersey just before the store closed five years ago. Value unknown.

Third shelf, right: Lionel-made hopper. Carries Alaskan road name in decal form. I must admit when I first saw the car I thought I had found another mock-up model. Closer inspection revealed the lettering was a dry transfer type never used by Lionel. All other mock-ups I have seen were lettered in decal form only. Value unknown.

Bottom shelf, left: 0864-150 M & StL boxcar. ¹/₁₆-inch Lionel logo on one side only. Original boxed piece. Matt Padgett Collection. Value unknown.

Bottom shelf, right: 0873 Rodeo Car. Mint original boxed car with an unlettered body. Value unknown.

Top, a 0593 Northern Pacific is crudely changed to "0597", modified by the owner after the item left the factory. The second is a true factory miss, with the original number of 0597 overstamped with "0593", Matt Padgett Collection; I have now seen three of these units, with two mint in the original box in the Collection of Gerald Potts.

FORGERIES SHOWN IN PHOTOGRAPHS

On the top shelf, left, of the photograph below is 0532, an Athearn-made F-7 A unit in B & O road name. The unit is a 1950s factory-made piece in every way except for the Lionel logo. Although there is only a slight difference in the gold color, the Lionel logo is a forgery and was added to the body at a later date. It appears in the proper side panel and is "almost" the ⅛-inch size used on the Athearn-made Lionel items. This is from the Fred Coppola Collection.

The 0585 Milwaukee GP-9 shown on the third shelf, left, is also a forgery. This, along with the 0865 Michigan Central gondola and the 0836 Lehigh Valley hopper, both shown on the second shelf, are of Athearn 1950s production and carry the Lionel logo slightly "larger" than the ⅛-inch size Athearn used. All three are stamped logos in "almost" the right shade of color. All are lighter than the original stamping of the road name or numbers. All are applied with paint and are stamped with a rubber stamp of some kind, and there is a slight gloss to the finish. Athearn was known to use a flat white stamping on its cars. Using a lighted magnifying glass, one can see that the edge of the logo is not as even as the other printing on these Athearn-made items. Also, most important is the vertical and horizontal legs of the letter L in the Lionel logo. They are perfectly straight vertically and horizontally instead of the banana-shaped L that was typical of Lionel's logo no matter where it appeared or what it appeared on, including their O Gauge items.

The two boxcars shown on the first and third shelves in the photograph on page 103 were purchased by me, as explained previously. The 0864-700 Santa Fe in an unmarked carton is merely a Lionel shell with Hobbyline doors and roof added. Since Lionel reworked and used

The forgeries pictured here are described in detail in the text, pages 103-105.

The two passenger cars shown on the top shelf can really be considered as oddballs. The first is lettered in red for the Santa Fe and carries the 0713 Pullman number. The same goes for the second car in Pennsylvania colors with the 0723 Pullman number. Both shells are, however, for "dome" cars, with a Pullman-style roof added. It seems Lionel did just about anything to get rid of inventory. Both are factory-stamped. The second shelf shows two of the 0864-175 Athearn-made Timken boxcars, unlike the car listed in the text. Both have blue roofs and ends and were sold in Athearn cartons. The Lionel logo appears to the right of the door on the first car while the second car has the "check mark"-type logo, without a circle. The last item is the 0860 Lionel-made derrick car. While the car is gray with a black derrick, the car itself is lettered in white and carries the "0870" number and lettering of a maintenance car. It is factory-stamped and original. These cars are part of the collections of Ken Fairchild and Seth Giem.

the Hobbyline dies on this car, the Hobbyline parts will fit with little difficulty. The car was only produced as described in the text, and there are no known variations of color or door types.

The red "Warheads" car shown on the top shelf, right, was purchased by Fred Coppola and was also in a Lionel carton. The floors and ends are from the 0847 Exploding Boxcar made by Lionel. The roof and sides, although almost exactly the same as the Lionel car, including the inside bracing that fits into the holes in the floor of the car and that lines up perfectly, are not Lionel-made. The two small cutouts at the bottom of the car sides are also present. Also, although slightly smaller, the printing on the car is also almost exactly the same. The word "EX-PLOSIVES" is replaced with the words "DANGER WARHEADS" at the top of the car side, and the line below these words does not extend across the entire car, as does the known Lionel side. The capacity and weight markings are also exactly the same, with the last three numbers used on the Lionel car missing. The large white circle is also present in the same place on the car side, with the word "DANGER" being replaced with the words "DANGER BEWARE / WARHEADS" clockwise inside the circle. Two holes are present at the right of the car door where the long cast-on ladder belongs, indicating a snap-on type of ladder of metal or plastic. The missing ladder, along with the two holes and the number 9841 on the car side, are the only differences I can see.

I believe this car is made from Lionel die work, but not produced by Lionel. A letter written to Lionel asking if this particular die work had been sold and to whom produced no results. I will state that the car should not be purchased as a Lionel product. Fred Coppola Collection. Verification requested. (The car was purchased in a Lionel carton and sold as a Lionel item, thus the need for this listing.)

The Lionel HO collector must also be aware the Matchbox models of the 1950s are being remade and now include the #4 red farm tractor and in the future will include the #8 yellow bulldozer that were used as flatcar loads in 1958-1960 by Lionel (see Chapter V, under the listings for 0807 and 0808). At this writing, the new tractor version is already on the market and is very close in appearance to the original pre-1957 model except for its unpainted silver metal wheels. (A bulldozer has yet to be produced.) I mention this only to ward off the anything-for-a-buck guys and the chance it will provide them to make up a very rare 0807 or 0808 flatcar.

The new tractor version has some differences in its construction, but a novice collector could easily be fooled. This new 1992 version has

a solid cast body as opposed to the 1957-1960 hollow body Lionel used for a load. Also, the "Lesney England" name and the number 4 are not fo found on the new model, which is finished in a medium green with gloss finish, unlike the glossy red paint used on the pre-1957 model. The new version carried "Made in China" and the "Matchbox" on the inside of the rear wheel mud guards. The number 3 is cast into the inside solid rear wheels which have painted gold centers.

The second tractor shown is a repainted 1992 issue and offered on a 0808 Lionel flatcar at $40 complete with its original box. The item was sold to me as a Lionel HO car with a "reproduction" "repainted tractor load." To sell a piece in this fashion is fine as long as the buyer is told if a reproduction part is included on the model and is reflected in the asking price.

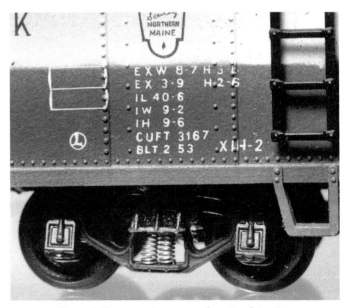

One of the surest approaches to detecting forgeries is close scrutiny of the size, placement, design, and method of applying the Lionel logo, as shown in this closeup of a Rivarossi-made car.

I must admit that at first glance I thought I had found an original 0808 car with its load, and that is the reason it is included in this chapter. I did have to look twice.

According to my friend Geoffrey Bunza, there are variations of the tractor; he has provided the following information (as well as comments on the Matchbox connection that appear in Chapter V):

There are actually three versions of the new Matchbox reproduction tractor. The first was issued in 1988 as one of five items in the "Matcbox Series 40th Anniversary Collection" made from the original dies. The tractor in this set was the pre-1957 version of the original tractor series and was *painted red as delivered* by Matchbox. The set did not provide the replica individual boxes as in the current versions. The next issue was first delivered in 1991 as part of the "Limited Edition Matchbox Originals" series — the same five items, now packaged individually with yellow replica "A MOKO LESNEY" boxes similar to the one in the original Lionel box (the original Lionel issue does not have tractor fenders on the box picture). The tractor was now painted bright *green*. In these two reissues the wheels were mounted on axles of round head pins with flat-crimped ends (the same as the original with dull gray metal wheels). The latest 1992 version

of the same green tractor in the same packaging has a new axle mount with flat axle ends on both sides, no round head, no external crimp. All three models use the solid tractor body marked "1988" on the left rear side below the driver; rear fenders are marked one "MATCHBOX" and one "MADE IN CHINA", and there are bright silver metal wheels.

DETECTING AUTHENTIC LOADS

The closeups on the next pages show original Lionel loads and include a few reproduction items as comparisons, so that you will more readily spot forgeries of the loads collectors seek to complete their HO flatcars. There is a place for reproduction replacements but sometimes they are not indicated as such by a seller.

The lower row shows both known colors of the original logs used on the 0861 log car and the 0300 operating lumber car; both were merely ½-inch wood dowels with sawdust glued to them for a rougher appearance. The last three items shown are a longer reproduction plastic pipe along with the two original colors used on the 0821 40-foot pipe car.

Listed below are the known flatcar loads now available as reproduction parts.
Most have been made for the O Gauge cars or accessories but are the same as those used on the HO cars.

Car		Reproduction Part
0806	Helicopter flat	Gray helicopter
0810	Generator flat	Orange generator, O Gauge
0813-200	Mercury capsule car	Silver capsule, O Gauge
0821	Pipe car	Yellow and gray pipe
0823, 0850	Missile flat	Solid 2½-inch wheeled missile
0842	Culvert pipe car	1⅜-inch metal pipe
0861	Log car	⅜-inch wooden logs
0875	Missile flat	5-inch red and white hollow missile; also available with solid white body
0039	Track cleaner	Gray plastic bottle
0033	Satellite launching flat	Yellow radar screen and black and silver satellite
0349	Turbo missile launch	Red and white turbo missile
0880	Maintenance flat	Metal searchlight
0865-250	Gondola	Tan crates made for Lionel's MPC line of HO, 1974–1977. They do not carry the Lionel on the side, as the original crates did.

Top: The crates used on the 0865-250 gondola, the silver airplane used on the 0800 flatcar, and the bottle of cleaning fluid found on the 0039 track cleaner. Bottom: A Cooper-Jarrett van with the name on a gold arrow, as found on the 0830 50-foot flatcar of Athearn production; a satellite from the 0333 Satellite Launching Car (the satellite has twelve ½-inch holes in its base while the reproduction does not); a metal culvert pipe from the 0842 Pipe Car is to the left of a reproduction (note that the repro culvert is slightly larger).

Top, left to right: An original capsule from the 0813 flatcar, with its skin slightly thinner than that of the reproduction below; the smooth band running around the original's base is also slightly larger than the repro, and a round mold mark is present on the repro base but not on the original. Four of the 0875 rockets found on the flatcar and missile-firing platform accessory: the first two are repros and have much smoother edges on the tailfins than do the originals. There are also two small holes present on the repros that are not found on the originals. One can see the holes on the red-tailed repro. Next is the original smooth unpainted rocket found on the 0365 Minuteman Launch Car, with two small fins molded into the upper body. No markings are used. This is followed by the original turbo missile, one of two found on the 0349 launch car. The repros of this item are extremely close to the originals, with a slightly smaller rear shaft. Two original missiles used on the 0823 50-foot flatcar and the 40-foot 0850 missile launch flatcar are shown to the right (good quality repros are also available for these items).

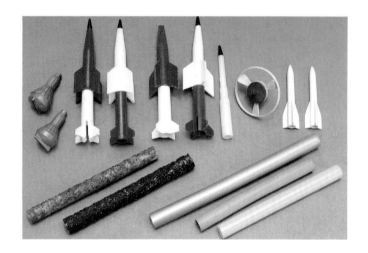

Five of the auto colors used on the Athearn-made 0814 Auto-Loader and the 0824 auto flatcar of 1958-1959. They were also used on the Lionel-made 0824-200 auto flatcar and the 0814-200 Auto-Loader of 1960-1962. The automobiles were models of Cadillac, station wagons, and sedans only.

0836 Lehigh Valley hopper of Athearn manufacture, with faked Lionel logo. It is a poor job but was nevertheless sold as Lionel to a novice collector. Note the straight legs of the letter on all items shown here. Also, most of the phony logos shown are the largest size, used on Athearn models.

This 0865 gondola falls into the same category as the Lehigh Valley hopper: it is so obviously phony. Once again, however, it was purchased as a Lionel piece by a young man with less than a year of collecting experience.

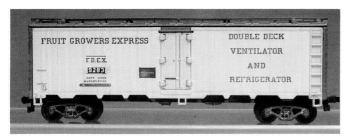

The 0872-1 shown came to me from the West Coast and clearly shows the phony logo. This one is, however, a little closer to a genuine article, with the L having the banana-shaped legs, but the circle looks like a first-grade student's artwork.

This 0585 Milwaukee Road GP-9 is another more than obvious phony, laughable to the experienced collector. This purchase was a case of a buyer becoming excited about finding something she believed her husband did not own.

Two of the 0808 Lionel flatcars. Top: The Lionel original issue. Middle: A reproduction repainted tractor and an original car purchased by George Horan. Bottom: The 1992 issue of the same tractor, marked that it was manufactured in China.

This Baltimore and Ohio 0532 power unit also carries a faked Lionel logo. It is slightly smaller than the factory-stamped ⅛-inch size found on Lionel units. Its circle is also very ragged.

CHAPTER IX
Motors, Mechanisms, Trucks, and Frames

MOTORS

Side and rear views of early motors. Left: The Athearn-made motor present on all power units offered in 1958 and 1959. Note the double shaft that had a rubber coupling and wire shaft added when used on eight-wheel drive units. Center: The single-shaft motor used on the 0642 and 0643 steam units of 1961-1963. Right: The larger motor used on the 1960 Pacific locomotives, with its fixed-sleeve bearings.

Right: The 1959 0056-207-type motor, with swivel bearing and square interpolar gap that can be seen on its top. This motor will be found in the 0056, 0057, 0058, and 0561 locomotives. Middle: Part number 0635-202 with gear drives. This motor had fixed-sleeve bearings, with skewed interpolar gap for smoother starting. It was used as shown first with gear drive in late steam locomotives. The Service Manual always carried a note of caution to its service people to use the ST-393 Magnetizer after servicing or changing a motor because the magnetic field was always weakened. The 0565-200 motor on the left was used on the two rectifiers and a number of the GP-9s.

Three of the motors used, each shown mounted in the frame of its respective steam locomotive. Left: The 1960 two-screw model mounted on the 0642 of 1962. Center: The one-screw model of the 0625 of 1959, part number 0625-121. Right: The 1960-type again, mounted in reverse and found in the Pacific locomotives.

STEAM LOCOMOTIVES

Mechanism from the 1960 0602 steam locomotive manufactured by Lionel. Note the middle driver has no flange; it is also the only locomotive to have an oil linkage in its plastic steam chest.

Mechanism from the diminutive 1959 0605 steam locomotive manufactured by Lionel. The frame itself is metal and it has a plastic steam chest and gearbox cover. Can be found with the 1959 or 1960 motor.

The mechanisms of Lionel's 2-4-2 steam switchers of 1961 and 1962 appear similar at first glance, but there are subtle differences. The 0642, shown, has both a drive rod and a connecting rod. The 0643 has a bulge in the frame, just above the space between the two drivers, that does not appear on the 0642. Note the oversized blackened drivers on both units and the cast-metal pilot with steps. The locomotive is rubber band drive.

Mechanism of the 1963 0643 steam switcher manufactured by Lionel. Note wire for front headlight. Both 2-4-2s are band-driven, with the 0643 being the Helic spring drive band.

The first Pacific (above) introduced by Lionel in 1959 is shown, with its small motor and large cast weight. In 1960 the same frame (below) was used, with the opening above the center driver being ¼ inch larger. Neither unit has smoke or sound. The gear ratio was lowered in the 1960 model.

Used on the 0637 Pacific of 1963, this is no longer the only unit known to have a pilot with cast steps. Since the original publication of this book I have seen four sets of the 0647 Pacific of 1966 with this pilot. This type of frame, less the pilot with steps, was also used on the 0635, 0636, 0645, and 0647; on the 0647 the frame will be found with and without steps. Changes were made throughout the period in the size of motor and type of drive used. Note worm drive on the 0637 frame shown.

DIESEL LOCOMOTIVES

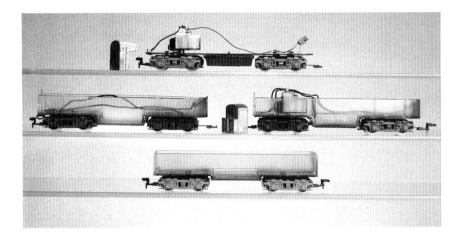

As described in Chapter III, the four frames found on Rivarossi-made FM units. Top: Early brass frame with cab-mounted weight, only found on Bakelite shells. Middle: Plastic versions of frames used on dummy A and powered A units. Bottom: Frame for dummy A.

Top: As described in Chapter IV, blackened frames, Geeps, and rectifiers. Middle: Same as top, unfinished. Bottom: Hustler drive.

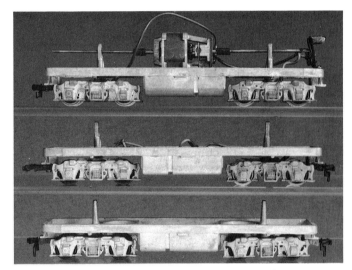

Athearn F unit frames found on A-B-A combinations. Top: Power A, lighted. Middle and bottom: Dummy B and A frames, neither lighted.

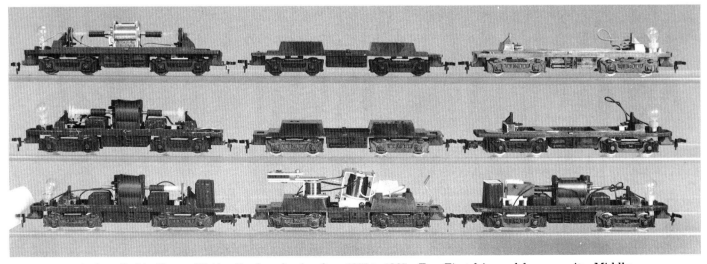

As described in Chapter V, Alco diesel mechanism from 1959 to 1965. Top: First drive and dummy units. Middle: Larger motor of 1961. Bottom: New Helic drive, 0535W B unit with horn, and first gearbox-type drive of 1964.

As described in Chapter V, Geep and rectifier mechanisms. Top: 1960 thick and 1959 thin shaft types. Middle: 1963 Helic drive belt, four-wheel drive and 1960 blackened frame with added weight and eight-wheel drive. Bottom: The only direct drive offered by Lionel and the single-truck gearbox drive of 1965.

Power frame for 0592 Santa Fe Geep of 1966. This is the only known diesel unit to have had the new direct drive motor. Note the rear truck mounting and extra large weight.

The plastic B unit frame found on many of the B unit road names, such as the 0577 Alaskan of 1959. The marking "PT. No. 0575-18" can be seen while the bottom of the frame carries "The Lionel Corporation / New York, New York / Made in / The U.S. of America". This same frame was modified and used on the horn B unit, 0535W, with one hole drilled at its center to fix the relay while a second was drilled just behind the front truck-mounting screw for the electrical power unit, while a rivet is used to hold the copper spring for the two AA batteries needed for operation. There are also four raised corners added to hold the two batteries in place.

Comparison of the first Husky-type frame used on the Athearn-manufactured models (top) and first Lionel-made model of 1959 (bottom). Note both have screwed-on couplers with Athearn drum-type axle and Lionel geared-type axle. The one insulated side can also be seen, with Lionel's covering the entire side. Neither carry a part number or name.

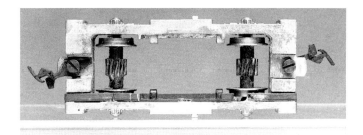

The first and second photos show the top and bottom views of the early cast-metal frame used on the Alcos FAs. The frame will be found on A units from 1959-1960 production. The part number 0565-64 is visible in the top shot, while the bottom of the frame shows "The Lionel Corporation / New York N.Y. / Made in U.S. of America". Not all frames carry a part number. Also shown, the same frame without the part number and made entirely of plastic; it was generally used on the early production of the dummy A units, such as the 0595 Santa Fe. The same information as found on the metal frame bottom is present. Note there is no rear coupler; it was part of the rear truck.

Alco FA-1 metal frames used in a variety of ways from 1960 to 1966. All carry the same information on the outer frame: "The Lionel Corporation / New York N.Y. / Made in U.S. of America". Slight changes were made to accommodate the ever-changing drive unit. First shown is the 1961-type frame built for a large motor and double drive shaft. Note the U-shaped arms at each end to cradle the shaft. Second is the same frame with factory-ground-off weights. These frames will be found on dummy A units of 1964 and 1965. The third frame is from the 1964 rear-drive truck with single shaft. It also can be found on dummy A units, as shown, of 1964-1965; rear plate shown is not present on power units. No rear coupler pocket is cast onto these frames; it is part of the rear truck.

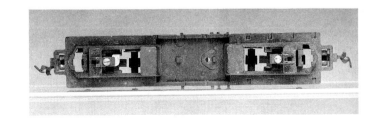

The 1960-type frame used on Geeps and electrics. It, too, carries the three lines of information found on the Alco frames. Note the two cast-on weights at the center, something not found on the 1959 Geep frames. Unlike the 1959 frame, the later one is usually found blackened.

TRUCKS

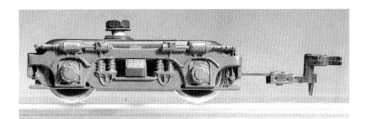

This Chicago and Northwestern dummy FM truck is of 1957 Rivarossi manufacture. It is plastic with metal wheel sets, cover, and coupler shaft. The Wabash and Illinois Central road names are the only two units not to have had painted truck side frames.

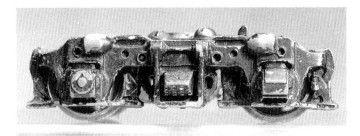

Truck used on the Athearn-made GP-9s and F units introduced in 1958, with drum-type axles.

The 1963 worm band-driven power truck that has both axles geared; the rubber O ring transmitted power from the motor shaft. Note the metal hanger that fastens to the frame with one screw. Two rubber-traction tires also present.

A Lionel-manufactured 1963 dummy truck, used on the FA-1s and GP-9s. It is the same truck as the power truck, less the worm drive shaft to drive the two geared axles. A little effort and a few plastic parts quickly transform it to a power truck.

Lionel's worm- and gear-driven rear power truck of 1965. Note the hole at the top of the housing to secure the truck to the metal collar that allows it to swivel freely. Power is transmitted by a small shaft with a rubber coupling from the motor.

Four-wheel metal talgo-type truck used on the Athearn-made passenger cars introduced in 1958. Note the pin for single screw that passes through the car's floor. The truck is quite different from Lionel's four-wheel passenger truck. G. Bunza photo.

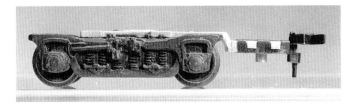

The Lionel-made passenger truck of the 1961-1966 period was of all-metal construction and had four wheels. It carries the Lionel name and part number 0712-50.

Lionel-made, six-wheel Buckeye freight truck, used on whistle tenders with the 0645, 0646, and 0647 steam engines and 0889 crane cars. G. Bunza photo.

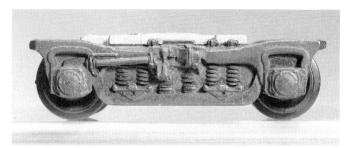

The 0715-20 truck was only used at the rear of the 0715 observation car. It is the same truck used on all the Lionel-made cars except for the missing coupler shaft and coupler.

Lionel's freight truck used on all lighted rolling stock and lighted cabooses. It is equipped with metal wheels and axles to collect power from the track for transfer to the model.

This 1959 Lionel metal sprung truck will be found on cars such as the 0847 exploding boxcar. There is no hole in the coupler cover; the pin on this coupler entered the body of the pocket itself and there was a solid cover.

The 1963 and later freight truck used on some rolling stock of Lionel manufacture, with metal body and coupler cover with plastic wheel sets and manual pivot uncoupling pin.

A metal Bettendorf-type sprung truck, found on the Athearn-made rolling stock of 1958-1959. G. Bunza photo.

Shown above is the Bettendorf-type freight truck used on Rivarossi-made rolling stock. Note the detail of the plastic side frames and the metal coupler shaft removed, below. G. Bunza photos.

A set of drive wheels used on all of the 0500 gang cars offered. The smooth black plastic axle has a raised area at its center to accept the rubber O ring that drove the axle and also held it in place.

This Rivarossi-made arch bar truck was used on the work caboose and flatcars offered as Lionel. It has the same clear detail and metal shaft as does the Bettendorf truck. G. Bunza photo.

This solid frame truck of half metal, half plastic construction was used from 1960 until 1966 on an array of rolling stock. The hole at the top of the metal coupler cover holds it firmly in place.

LIONEL HO ORDER FORM LISTING, DATED 1959

The following is copied from an order form headed
"THE LIONEL CORPORATION / 15 East 26th Street, New York 10, N.Y."

Stock No.	Description	Suggested Retail Selling Price
HO OUTFITS		
5719	3 car AEC Switcher Frt. (4)	19.95
5721	4 car Texas Special Frt. (4)	25.00
5723	4 car Steam Switcher Frt. (4)	29.95
5725	5 car New Haven Recitifer Frt. (4)	29.95
5727	5 car N.Y. Central GP-9 Frt. (4)	35.00
5717	6 car 4-6-2 Steam Frt. (4)	39.95
5729	5 car Alaskan "AB" Frt. w/Trestle Set (4)	39.95
5731	5 car 4-6-2 Steam Frt. w/Trestle Set (4)	49.95
5732	4 car Texas Spec. "ABA" 2 Motored Pass. (4)	49.95
5733	7 car S.F. "ABA" 2 Motored Fig. 8 Work Train (4)	59.95
LOCOMOTIVES & MOTORIZED UNITS		
0050	Gang Car NEW	7.95
0056	AEC Husky NEW	5.95
0560	Snow Plow	5.95
0561	Minn. & St. Louis Rotary Snowplow NEW	7.95
0565	Alco Santa Fe Powered "A" NEW	7.95
0566	Alco Texas Special Powered A NEW	7.95
0567	Alco Alaskan Powered A NEW	7.95
0570	Navy Yard Switcher	5.95
0591	New Haven Rectifier NEW	10.95
0596	N.Y. Central GP-9 NEW	10.95
0605	0-4-0 Steam Switcher NEW	10.95
0625LT	4-6-2 Steam Loco & Tender NEW	14.95
DUMMY B UNITS		
0575	Alco Santa Fe NEW	3.50
0576	Alco Texas Special NEW	3.50
0577	Alco Alaskan NEW	3.50
DUMMY A UNITS		
0586	Alco Texas Special NEW	3.95
0587	Alco Alaskan NEW	3.95
0595	Alco Santa Fe NEW	3.95
HO POWER PACKS		
0100	2½ Amp. AC-DC Power Pack	15.95
0101	1¼ Amp. AC-DC Power Pack	10.95
0102	Fixed Voltage AC-DC Power Pack	18.95
0103	800 m.a. DC Power Pack NEW	7.95
0150	1½ Amp. DC Rectifier	7.95
0181	Cab Control	6.95
1144	75 Watt AC Power Supply	12.95

Stock No.	Description	Suggested Retail Selling Price
HO CARS		
0266	HO 64 Car Assort. w/Free Display NEW	211.40
0704	Tex. Sp. Baggage Car w/Red Stripe NEW	3.95
0705	Tex. Sp. Pullman w/Red Stripe NEW	3.95
0706	Tex. Sp. Vista-Dome w/Red Stripe NEW	3.95
0707	Tex. Sp. Observation w/Red Stripe NEW	3.95
0800	Flat Car w/Airplane	2.95
0801	Flat Car w/Boat	2.95
0805	A.E.C. Car w/Blinking Light NEW	3.95
0806	Flat Car w/Helicopter NEW	2.95
0807	Flat Car w/Bulldozer NEW	2.95
0808	Flat Car w/Tractor NEW	2.95
0814	4 Auto Transport Car	3.95
0815	Chemical Car	2.50
0817-275	N.H. Caboose NEW	2.50
0819-225	S.F. Work Caboose NEW	2.50
0824	Flat Car w/2 Autos	2.95
0830	Flat Car w/2 Vans	3.95
0834	Illum. Poultry Car NEW	3.95
0836	Alaskan Hopper NEW	2.50
0860	Derrick Car	3.95
0862	Gondola	2.00
0864-175	Timken Box Car	2.50
0864-300	Alaskan Box Car NEW	2.50
0864-325	D.S.S.A. Box Car NEW	2.50
0864-350	State of Maine Box Car	2.50
0865	Gondola w/Canisters	2.50
0866-200	Circus Car NEW	2.50
0870	Maintenance Car w/Generator NEW	2.95
0872-200	R'way Exp. Reefer NEW	2.50
0875	Flat Car w/Missile NEW	2.95
0879	Wrecker Crane	4.95
0880	Maintenance Car w/Light NEW	3.95
HO ACCESSORIES		
0110	Graduated Trestle Set	3.95
0111	Elevated Trestle Set NEW	1.50
0114	Factory w/Horn	8.95
0117	Factory NEW	4.95
0118	Factory w/Whistle	10.95
0119	Landscaped Tunnel NEW	2.00
0145	Gateman NEW	5.95
0197	Radar Tower	5.95
0214	Girder Bridge	1.50
0252	Crossing Gate NEW	5.95
0310	Billboard Set NEW	1.00
0410	Suburban Ranch House Set NEW	1.00
0411	Figure Set w/Switchmans Shanty NEW	1.25
0412	Farm Set NEW	1.50
0413	Railroad Structure Set NEW	2.50

Stock No.	Description	Suggested Retail Selling Price
0414	Village Set NEW	3.00
0430	6 Tree Assortment NEW	1.00
0431	Landscape Set NEW	2.00
0494	Rotating Beacon NEW	5.95
0927	Maintenance Kit NEW	2.50

HO TRACK & SWITCHES

Stock No.	Description	Suggested Retail Selling Price
0903	3" Straight Track	.25
0905	1½" Straight Track	.25
0906	6" Straight Track	.25
0909	9" Straight Track	.25
0983	3" Curved Track 18" Rad.	.25
0984	4½" Curved Track 18" Rad.	.25
0985	9" Curved Track 15" Rad.	.25
0986	4½" Curved Track 15" Rad.	.25
0989	9" Curved Track 18" Rad.	.25
0922	R.C. Switch Right Hand	4.50
0923	R.C. Switch Left Hand	4.50
0942	Manual Switch Right Hand	2.95

Stock No.	Description	Suggested Retail Selling Price
0943	Manual Switch Left Hand	2.95
0925	Straight Terminal Sec 9"	.75
0929	Uncoupling Track Sect.	1.00
0939	Uncoupling Unit Only	.75
0950	Re-Railer Section	.60
0960	Bumper Track	.49
0975	Curved Terminal 18" Rad., 9" Long	.75
0990	90° Crossover	2.25

REPLACEMENT LAMPS

Stock No.	Description	Suggested Retail Selling Price
L191	12V. Midget Cartridge Base	.35
L0214	12V. Midget Screw Base 1957 Locos	.35

HO DISPLAYS

Stock No.	Description	
D260	Two Tier Circular Display	
D227	HO 5 Step Display	

COMMON HO PARTS

The parts listed herein are most commonly required to service Lionel HO rolling stock. Nearly all of these parts are used in many different items and are absolutely essential for basic repair work.

Notice that only four different couplers are used in the entire HO line of cars and locomotives. Each of these has its own corresponding coupler cover.

A long or a short truck pivot screw is used on the various freight cars. However, the longer 0814-209 screw can be used on all freight cars. This long screw will hold trucks more securely where the hole may be stripped. Since this screw is long, it may protrude the top surface of certain flat cars. This excess screw can be easily removed with a cutting pliers.

Coupler covers which are slightly bent or distorted will often restrict the freedom of the coupler action. Therefore, since coupler covers are inexpensive, they should be replaced and the old cover discarded.

PART NO.	PART NAME	ILLUSTRATION	PRICE	WHERE USED
0766-5	Coupler		.15	1959 Freight Trucks 1959 Locomotives 1959-60 "Husky" Locos
0766-51	Coupler		.15	1960 Freight Trucks 1961 Passenger & Freight
0565-61	Coupler		.15	1960 Locomotives 1961 Locomotives
0705-6	Coupler		.15	1959-60 Passenger Cars
0705-7	Coupler Cover		.05	With 0705-6 Couplers
0766-6	Coupler Cover		.05	1959 Freight Trucks Using 0766-5 Couplers
0766-55	Coupler Cover		.05	1960-61 Freight Trucks 1961 Passenger & Freight
0565-18	Coupler Cover		.05	1959 Locomotives Using 0766-5 Couplers
0565-65	Coupler Cover		.05	1960 Locomotives Using 0565-61 Coupler

(OVER)

LIONEL SERVICE MANUAL

COMMON HO PARTS
(CONTINUED)

PART NO.	PART NAME	ILLUSTRATION	PRICE	WHERE USED
0605-64	Coupler Cover		.05	1960 0602 & 0605 Locomotives
0605-39	Coupler Cover		.05	1959 0605 Locomotive
0056-9	Coupler Cover		.05	"Husky" Locomotives
0056-10	Coupler Mtg. Screw Machine Screw		.05	"Husky" Locomotives
0800-208	Truck Mtg. Screw (short)		.05	Most freight trucks
0814-209	Truck Mtg. Screw (long)		.05	Some flat cars with loads; also useful for stripped holes
0565-41	Drive Belt	3/4"	.20	1959-60 Diesels and Electric Locomotives
0605-21	Drive Belt	11/16"	.20	1959-60 0605 Tank Switcher
0050-34	Drive Belt	5/8"	.15	0050 Gang Car
0565-124	Motor Brushes		.25pr.	All HO Motors (Except 0050)
0565-205	Brush Springs		.10pr.	All HO Motors (Except 0050)
0050-21	Motor Brushes		.25pr.	0050 Gang Car
0050-22	Brush Spring		.10pr.	0050 Gang Car

LIONEL SERVICE MANUAL

"HUSKY" LOCOMOTIVES NOS. 0054, 0055, 0056, 0057, 0058 AND NO. 0561 ROTARY SNOW PLOW

Locomotives of the "Husky" type are typical diesel-electric industrial and switching engines made by General Electric, Vulcan, Whitcomb and other concerns in the 25-35 ton range.

The series was initiated by Lionel in 1959 with No. 0056 "A.E.C." locomotive. In 1960 the motor was redesigned and the series continued with the other locomotives listed below.

CAT. NO.	NAME	REMARKS
No. 0054	Canadian Pacific	No ornamental horn
No. 0055	Minn. & St. L.	No ornamental horn
No. 0056	A.E.C.	
No. 0057	Union Pacific	
No. 0058	Rock Island	
No. 0561	Minn. & St. L.	Rotary Snow Plow

No. 0561, a similar locomotive with "Minn. & St. L." markings, was equipped with a rotary snow plow driven by a rubber cone on the motor armature shaft and did not have either a front coupler or a headlight.

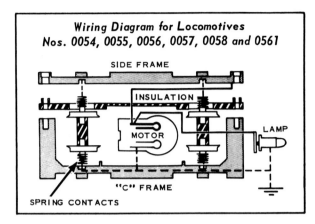

Wiring Diagram for Locomotives Nos. 0054, 0055, 0056, 0057, 0058 and 0561

SIDE FRAME
INSULATION
MOTOR
LAMP
"C" FRAME
SPRING CONTACTS

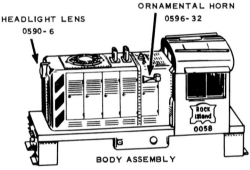

HEADLIGHT LENS 0590-6
ORNAMENTAL HORN 0596-32
ROCK ISLAND 0058

BODY ASSEMBLY

0054-2 CANADIAN PACIFIC	0057-2 UNION PACIFIC
0055-2 MINN. & ST. L.	0058-2 ROCK ISLAND
0056-2 A.E.C.	0561-2 MINN. & ST. L.

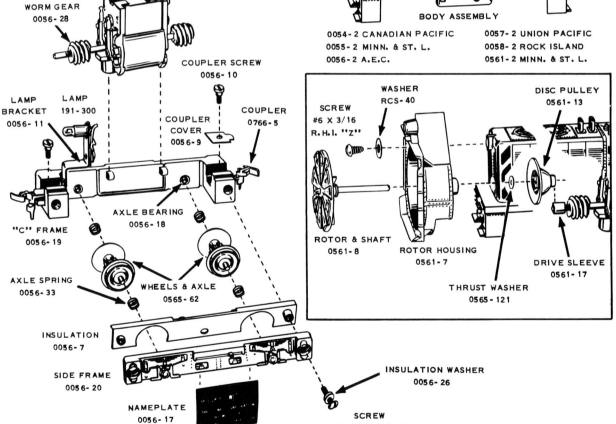

MOTOR WITH GEARS 0056-207
WORM GEAR 0056-28
COUPLER SCREW 0056-10
LAMP BRACKET 0056-11
LAMP 191-300
COUPLER COVER 0056-9
COUPLER 0766-5
AXLE BEARING 0056-18
"C" FRAME 0056-19
AXLE SPRING 0056-33
WHEELS & AXLE 0565-62
INSULATION 0056-7
SIDE FRAME 0056-20
NAMEPLATE 0056-17
INSULATION WASHER 0056-26
SCREW 2-56 X 5/16" B.H.I.

SCREW #6 X 3/16 R.H.I. "Z"
WASHER RCS-40
DISC PULLEY 0561-13
ROTOR & SHAFT 0561-8
ROTOR HOUSING 0561-7
THRUST WASHER 0565-121
DRIVE SLEEVE 0561-17

LIONEL SERVICE MANUAL

HO LOCOMOTIVES NOS. 0581, 0591, 0596, 0597 AND 0598

All of the locomotives listed in this section have identical chassis assemblies and differ only in the design and markings of the cabs. The series was initiated in 1959 with locomotives Nos. 0591 and 0596, which modeled New Haven's GE Type EL-C 3,300 horse power rectifier electric locomotive and GM's GP-9 diesel with N.Y.C. markings, respectively.

In 1960 all the operating components of these locomotives were redesigned, including new motors, (See HO-LOC Motors) new power trucks and couplers, and the series continued No. 0581 Pennsylvania electric rectifier locomotive and No. 0597 Northern Pacific GP-9 diesel. No. 0598, added to the series in 1961, is a model of GM's GP-7 diesel with New York Central markings.

Motors and trucks made in 1959 are not considered repairable, but can be replaced with later components when necessary. The redesigned motors fit all locomotives. New power trucks can be used in 1959 models if the pivot hole on the locomotive frame is enlarged with a No. 25 drill to accommodate the new larger mounting screw (No. 0565-67).

Couplers used in the later models differ from 1959 couplers in having an integral pivot shaft extending upward through a hole in the locomotive frame. Couplers and Coupler Covers are not interchangeable.

Gears and Trucks

The first few locomotives produced had a slight mis-alignment between the worm and worm-wheel. This was corrected and electrical conductivity was also perfected by chrome-plating the wheels. Therefore, diesel locomotives which have trucks with blackened wheels should be replaced with Chrome-Wheeled Truck No. 0566-10. This truck will have free gear action and good electrical conductivity.

It has been found that long periods of inactivity may result in temporary sluggish gear action. A "break-in" period for approximately 2 or 3 minutes at 12 to 15 volts should correct this situation. This can be best accomplished by running-in one truck at a time. Disengage the more active truck by removing the drive belt from the top pulley allowing the motor power to be concentrated in driving the slower truck. If the worm will not readily rotate, help it by pushing it lightly with your index finger.

The worm clips which hold the worm gear in place are also bearings. If these clips are not fully and squarely locked in place, the worm gear may not rotate freely. Observe these clips from the underside of the truck and press inward against the clip hooks making certain they are fully locked to the worm gear saddle.

Lubrication

Do not lubricate the gears. Oil or grease on these gears may result in a build-up of dust which will offer resistance. In addition, oil or grease can easily find its way to the pulleys causing the drive belt to slip. A drop of light machine oil should be placed on each of the motor bearings.

Please note that unless otherwise specified the parts listed below are for the post-1959 models.

LOCO. NO.	YEAR	TYPE	NAME
0581	1960	Rectifier Electric	Pennsylvania
0591	1959	Rectifier Electric	New Haven
0596	1959	GP-9 Diesel	New York Central
0597	1960	GP-9 Diesel	Northern Pacific
0598	1961	GP-7 Diesel	New York Central

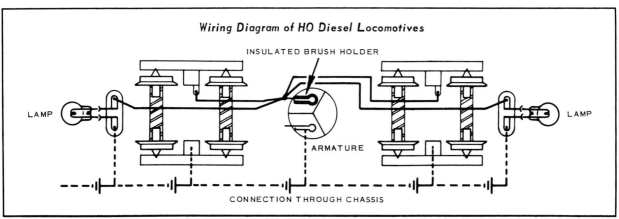

Wiring Diagram of HO Diesel Locomotives

INSULATED BRUSH HOLDER

LAMP   ARMATURE   LAMP

CONNECTION THROUGH CHASSIS

Printed in U.S. of America

(Replaces Page 1, Sec. HO-LOC-0581, dated 12-60 and Page PL, HO-LOC-0597, dated 10-60)

LIONEL SERVICE MANUAL

NOS. 0581, 0591, 0596, 0597 AND 0598 HO LOCOMOTIVES

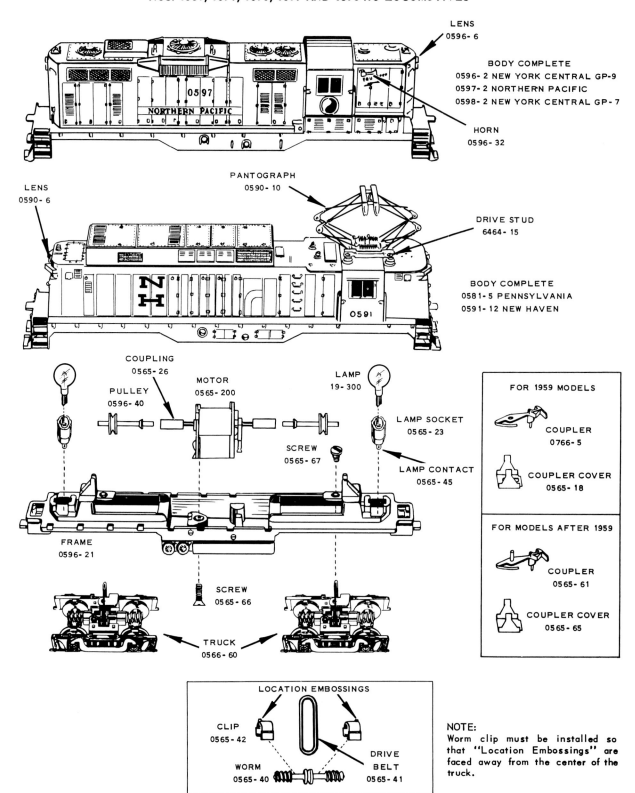

LENS
0596-6

BODY COMPLETE
0596-2 NEW YORK CENTRAL GP-9
0597-2 NORTHERN PACIFIC
0598-2 NEW YORK CENTRAL GP-7

HORN
0596-32

PANTOGRAPH
0590-10

DRIVE STUD
6464-15

LENS
0590-6

BODY COMPLETE
0581-5 PENNSYLVANIA
0591-12 NEW HAVEN

COUPLING
0565-26

PULLEY
0596-40

MOTOR
0565-200

LAMP
19-300

LAMP SOCKET
0565-23

SCREW
0565-67

LAMP CONTACT
0565-45

FRAME
0596-21

SCREW
0565-66

TRUCK
0566-60

FOR 1959 MODELS

COUPLER
0766-5

COUPLER COVER
0565-18

FOR MODELS AFTER 1959

COUPLER
0565-61

COUPLER COVER
0565-65

LOCATION EMBOSSINGS

CLIP
0565-42

WORM
0565-40

DRIVE
BELT
0565-41

NOTE:
Worm clip must be installed so that "Location Embossings" are faced away from the center of the truck.

LIONEL SERVICE MANUAL

NO. 0545 GE-44 HO SWITCHER

No. 0545 Erie Switcher is modeled on General Electric's 44-ton hp diesel-electric switching locomotive, and was first built in 1961.

It employs the motor and chassis used in "Husky" locomotives, described in Section HO-LOC-0054. The principal difference is that the couplers are not mounted on the frame. The couplers are mounted instead in coupler pockets in the body molding.

Notice that the lamp bracket differs from the bracket used on "Huskies". Although this locomotive is produced with one lamp, another lamp bracket may be added to the opposite end.

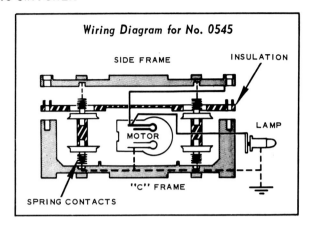

Wiring Diagram for No. 0545

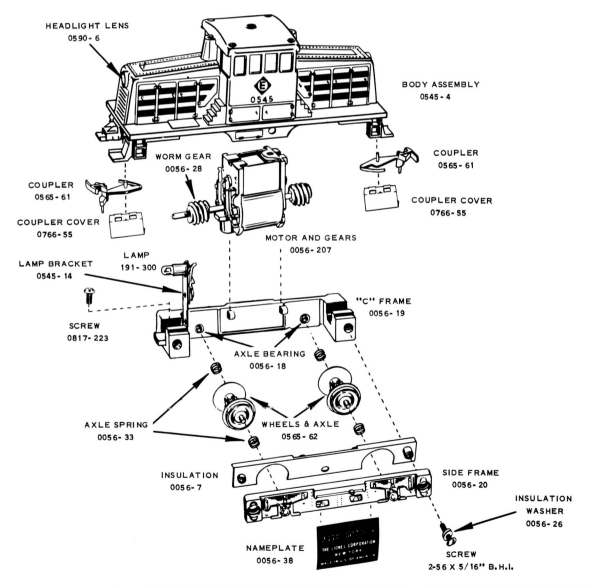

HEADLIGHT LENS
0590-6

BODY ASSEMBLY
0545-4

WORM GEAR
0056-28

COUPLER
0565-61

COUPLER
0565-61

COUPLER COVER
0766-55

COUPLER COVER
0766-55

MOTOR AND GEARS
0056-207

LAMP BRACKET
0545-14

LAMP
191-300

"C" FRAME
0056-19

SCREW
0817-223

AXLE BEARING
0056-18

AXLE SPRING
0056-33

WHEELS & AXLE
0565-62

INSULATION
0056-7

SIDE FRAME
0056-20

INSULATION WASHER
0056-26

NAMEPLATE
0056-38

SCREW
2-56 X 5/16" B.H.I.

LIONEL SERVICE MANUAL

NO. 0605 HO LOCOMOTIVE

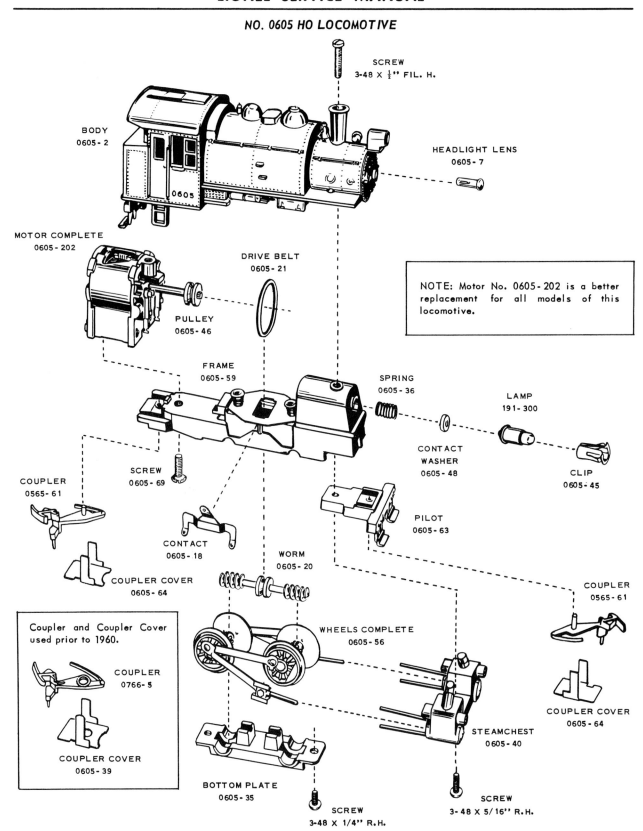

NOTE: Motor No. 0605-202 is a better replacement for all models of this locomotive.

Coupler and Coupler Cover used prior to 1960.

COUPLER 0766-5

COUPLER COVER 0605-39

LIONEL SERVICE MANUAL

NOS. 0625 1959-60 MODELS STEAM LOCOMOTIVES

The locomotives in this series are typical Pacific 4-6-2 steam engines but do not have an exact prototype. No. 0625 locomotive was first produced in 1959. Engineering improvements introduced in 1960 model made the two locomotives quite different in in several respects and many of their components are not interchangeable.

In 1960 both the motor and the method of mounting it on the frame were changed. The 1959 motor is not available but a specially-machined 1960 motor (No. 0625-121) which can be mounted on 1959 frames.

The 1959 model uses ball bearings on both ends of the drive shaft. In 1960 the rear ball bearing was replaced by a thrust plate and the chassis casting was altered to suit. The easiest way to distinguish the 1960 and 1959 models is by their motor mounting. In the 1960 model the motor is held by a screw from the underside of the chassis above the rear truck. In the 1959 model the motor is held down by the gear cover. The 1961 models of No. 0625 and the No. 0635 locomotive are described in Section HO-LOC-0635.

SERVICE NOTES

Cradle Block: Since the wheel assemblies of these locomotives are held to the chassis by the gear cover, it is advisable before removing the gear cover to cradle the locomotive chassis so that the drive wheels are raised from the work bench.

Replacing Wheels: It is not practical to replace individual wheels because they must be position in very accurate relationship to the teeth on the axle gear. For this reason wheels are sold in assembled pairs. When replacing wheel pairs care must be taken so that they are indexed properly to align with the side rods. Make sure also that the hub insulators all face the side with the wheel contact (left side of locomotive.).

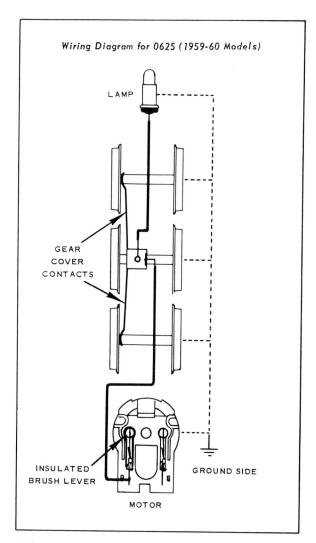

Wiring Diagram for 0625 (1959-60 Models)

LAMP

GEAR COVER CONTACTS

INSULATED BRUSH LEVER

GROUND SIDE

MOTOR

Lubrication: Light grease such as Lionel Lubricant should be applied in limited amount to all gears. One drop of light oil should be placed on each bearing point.

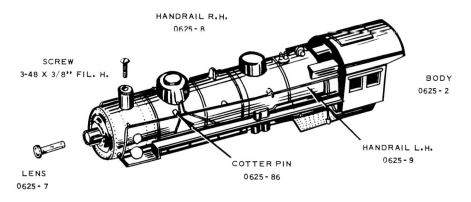

HANDRAIL R.H.
0625-8

SCREW
3-48 X 3/8" FIL. H.

BODY
0625-2

LENS
0625-7

COTTER PIN
0625-86

HANDRAIL L.H.
0625-9

LIONEL SERVICE MANUAL

NO. 0625 1960 MODEL

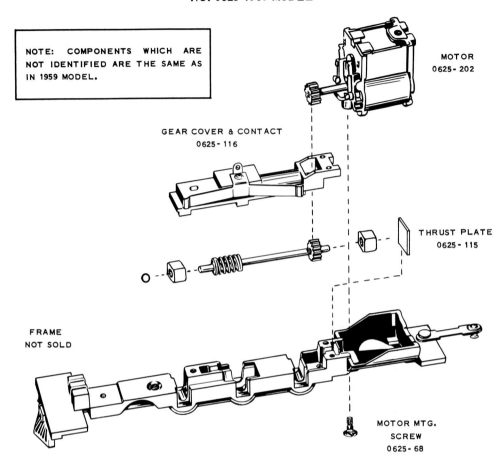

NOTE: COMPONENTS WHICH ARE NOT IDENTIFIED ARE THE SAME AS IN 1959 MODEL.

MOTOR
0625-202

GEAR COVER & CONTACT
0625-116

THRUST PLATE
0625-115

FRAME
NOT SOLD

MOTOR MTG.
SCREW
0625-68

NO. 0625T TENDER

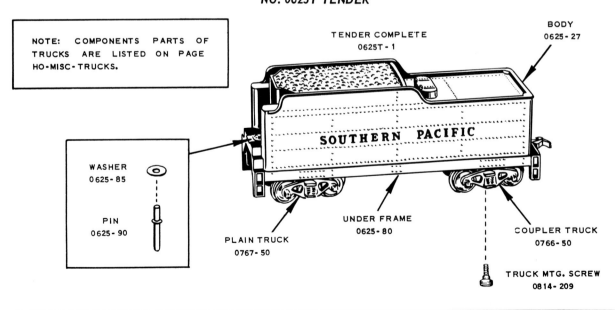

NOTE: COMPONENTS PARTS OF TRUCKS ARE LISTED ON PAGE HO-MISC-TRUCKS.

TENDER COMPLETE
0625T-1

BODY
0625-27

WASHER
0625-85

PIN
0625-90

PLAIN TRUCK
0767-50

UNDER FRAME
0625-80

COUPLER TRUCK
0766-50

TRUCK MTG. SCREW
0814-209

LIONEL SERVICE MANUAL

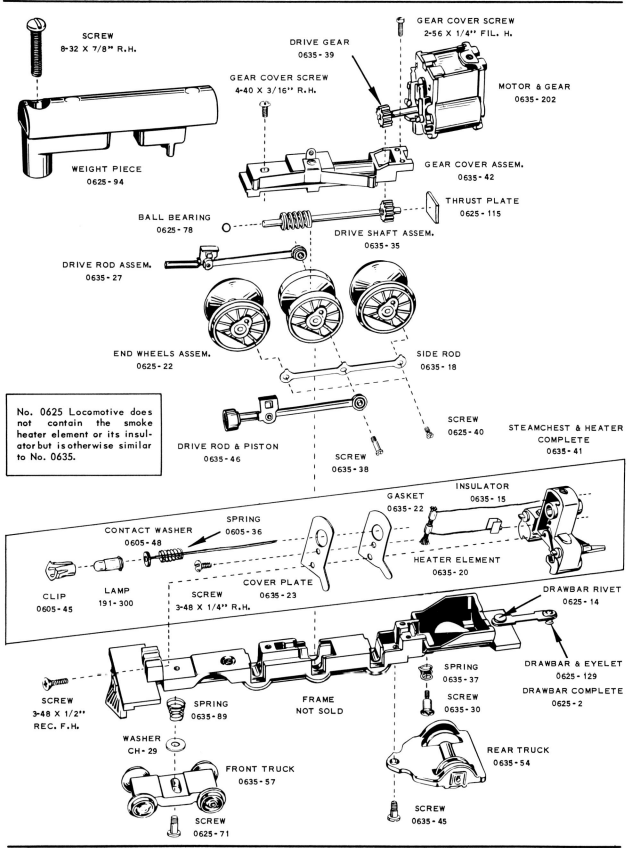

SCREW
8-32 X 7/8" R.H.

GEAR COVER SCREW
2-56 X 1/4" FIL. H.

DRIVE GEAR
0635-39

GEAR COVER SCREW
4-40 X 3/16" R.H.

MOTOR & GEAR
0635-202

WEIGHT PIECE
0625-94

GEAR COVER ASSEM.
0635-42

THRUST PLATE
0625-115

BALL BEARING
0625-78

DRIVE SHAFT ASSEM.
0635-35

DRIVE ROD ASSEM.
0635-27

END WHEELS ASSEM.
0625-22

SIDE ROD
0635-18

SCREW
0625-40

STEAMCHEST & HEATER
COMPLETE
0635-41

No. 0625 Locomotive does not contain the smoke heater element or its insulator but is otherwise similar to No. 0635.

DRIVE ROD & PISTON
0635-46

SCREW
0635-38

GASKET
0635-22

INSULATOR
0635-15

SPRING
0605-36

CONTACT WASHER
0605-48

HEATER ELEMENT
0635-20

CLIP
0605-45

LAMP
191-300

COVER PLATE
0635-23

SCREW
3-48 X 1/4" R.H.

DRAWBAR RIVET
0625-14

SCREW
3-48 X 1/2"
REC. F.H.

SPRING
0635-89

SPRING
0635-37

SCREW
0635-30

DRAWBAR & EYELET
0625-129

DRAWBAR COMPLETE
0625-2

FRAME
NOT SOLD

WASHER
CH-29

FRONT TRUCK
0635-57

REAR TRUCK
0635-54

SCREW
0625-71

SCREW
0635-45

LIONEL SERVICE MANUAL

NO. 0642 LOCOMOTIVE AND TENDER

No. 0642 was patterned after steam-switchers universally used in yard work. It is propelled by a combination of a belt and a worm gear which is purposely "geared-down" for realistically slow operation.

Service Notes. Several readily corrected reasons may result in erratic movement.

1. Flash or foreign matter in the worm gear.

2. Bent side rods or wheels rubbing the chassis sides.

3. Motor wire which runs down through the chassis to the contact on the gear cover may be interfering with the drive belt.

4. Improperly indexed wheels which may have gotten "out of quarter" when gear cover was loosened or removed.

5. Loose or too-tight side rod pins will cause rods to lock.

6. Crosshead guides may have spread and as a result are not holding the crossheads so that they slide freely.

Electrical Circuit. All wheels are completely insulated from each other and the chassis. The positive voltage is picked up from the drive wheels on the left side by a contact strip which is fastened to the gear cover. A wire connection is made from this contact strip to the insulated brush-holder.

The negative voltage is conducted, from the drive wheels on the right side, through contacts which are fastened by the front and rear truck screws to the chassis.

The lamp is grounded to the chassis and receives positive voltage by wire connection to the insulated brush-holder.

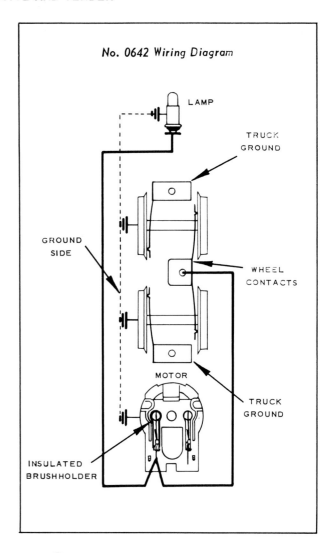

No. 0642 Wiring Diagram

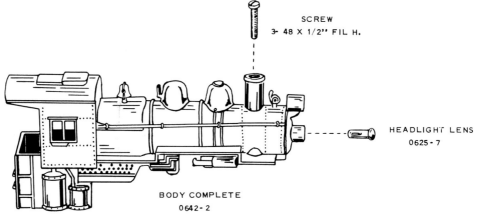

SCREW 3-48 X 1/2" FIL H.

HEADLIGHT LENS 0625-7

BODY COMPLETE 0642-2

LIONEL SERVICE MANUAL

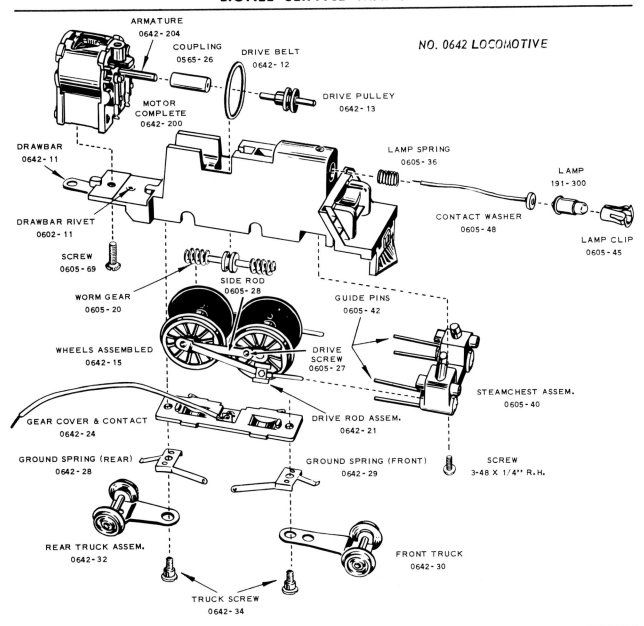

ARMATURE
0642-204

COUPLING
0565-26

DRIVE BELT
0642-12

NO. 0642 LOCOMOTIVE

MOTOR
COMPLETE
0642-200

DRIVE PULLEY
0642-13

DRAWBAR
0642-11

LAMP SPRING
0605-36

LAMP
191-300

DRAWBAR RIVET
0602-11

CONTACT WASHER
0605-48

LAMP CLIP
0605-45

SCREW
0605-69

WORM GEAR
0605-20

SIDE ROD
0605-28

GUIDE PINS
0605-42

WHEELS ASSEMBLED
0642-15

DRIVE
SCREW
0605-27

STEAMCHEST ASSEM.
0605-40

GEAR COVER & CONTACT
0642-24

DRIVE ROD ASSEM.
0642-21

GROUND SPRING (REAR)
0642-28

GROUND SPRING (FRONT)
0642-29

SCREW
3-48 X 1/4" R.H.

REAR TRUCK ASSEM.
0642-32

FRONT TRUCK
0642-30

TRUCK SCREW
0642-34

NO. 0642T TENDER

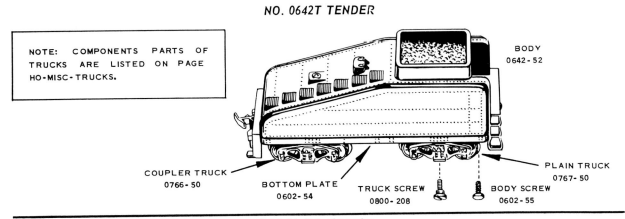

NOTE: COMPONENTS PARTS OF TRUCKS ARE LISTED ON PAGE HO-MISC-TRUCKS.

BODY
0642-52

COUPLER TRUCK
0766-50

BOTTOM PLATE
0602-54

TRUCK SCREW
0800-208

BODY SCREW
0602-55

PLAIN TRUCK
0767-50

LIONEL SERVICE MANUAL

NO. 0827 HO ILLUMINATED CABOOSE

No. 0827 HO Illuminated Caboose is equipped with special trucks which have metal wheels on one side.

These trucks must be installed so that the metal wheels of one truck contact, one track rail and metal wheels of the other truck will be on the other rail.

The lamp socket is grounded by a speednut to one truck stud. The lamp lead is soldered to the other truck stud.

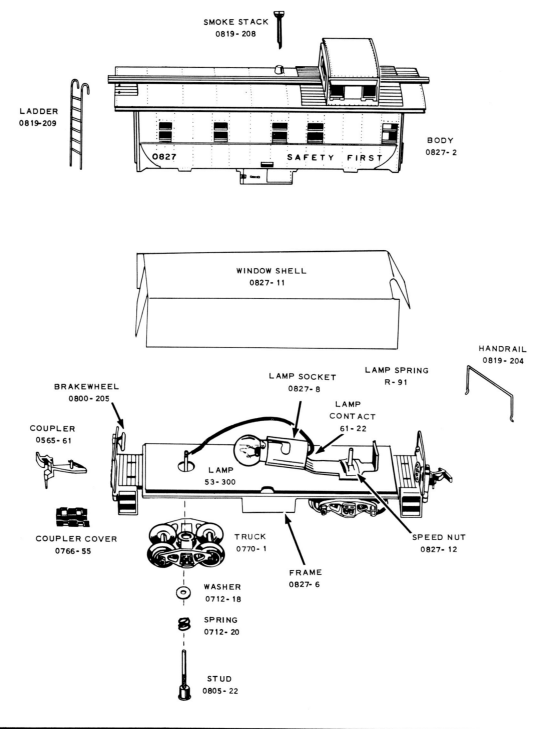

SMOKE STACK
0819-208

LADDER
0819-209

BODY
0827-2

0827   SAFETY FIRST

WINDOW SHELL
0827-11

HANDRAIL
0819-204

BRAKEWHEEL
0800-205

LAMP SOCKET
0827-8

LAMP SPRING
R-91

LAMP
CONTACT
61-22

COUPLER
0565-61

LAMP
53-300

SPEED NUT
0827-12

COUPLER COVER
0766-55

TRUCK
0770-1

FRAME
0827-6

WASHER
0712-18

SPRING
0712-20

STUD
0805-22

LIONEL SERVICE MANUAL

NO. 0039 TRACK CLEANING CAR

No. 0039 Track Cleaning Car, first made in 1961, is equipped with a pair of rotary motor-driven washing sponges and a rectangular sponge wiper. The rotary sponges are fed with track cleaning fluid through the top of the hollow wiper shaft. The motor driving the rotary sponges is stopped and started by means of a slide-type switch located in the floor of the car.

For cleaning the track the car must be towed by a locomotive so that the rotating sponges precede the sponge wiper.

Note that the rotary shaft and the rotary drive gear are assembled by means of tightly-fitting retaining rings. A convenient method to spread the retaining rings in order to fit them over the parts is to press the

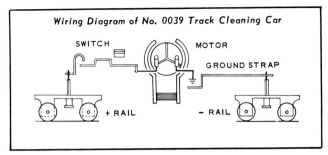

Wiring Diagram of No. 0039 Track Cleaning Car

corner of a screwdriver blade into the slot of the retaining ring and push the ring up the widening side of the blade until the ring is spread enough for assembly.

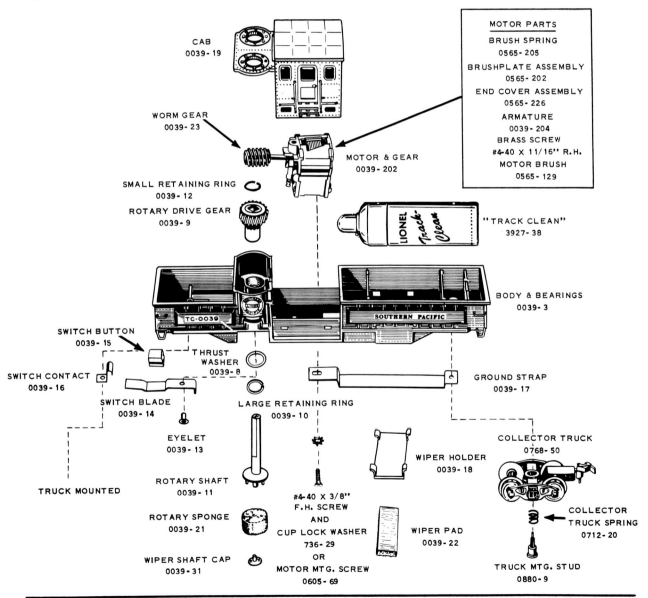

LIONEL SERVICE MANUAL

NO. 0068 EXECUTIVE CAR & NOS. 0068-50 AND 0068-100 RACE CARS

No. 0068 Executive and Race Cars are designed to operate on HO track. These cars have identical motors and chassis as used in "Husky" locomotives described in manual pages HO-LOC-0054.

Since the car body is located low on the chassis, the inner roof must be shielded from motor heat by an aluminum foil piece (Part No. 0068-8).

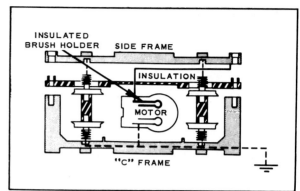

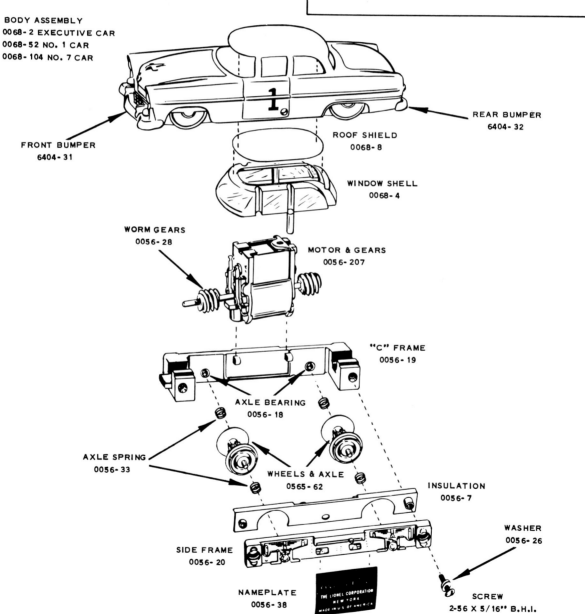

BODY ASSEMBLY
0068-2 EXECUTIVE CAR
0068-52 NO. 1 CAR
0068-104 NO. 7 CAR

FRONT BUMPER
6404-31

REAR BUMPER
6404-32

ROOF SHIELD
0068-8

WINDOW SHELL
0068-4

WORM GEARS
0056-28

MOTOR & GEARS
0056-207

"C" FRAME
0056-19

AXLE BEARING
0056-18

AXLE SPRING
0056-33

WHEELS & AXLE
0565-62

INSULATION
0056-7

WASHER
0056-26

SIDE FRAME
0056-20

NAMEPLATE
0056-38

THE LIONEL CORPORATION
NEW YORK
MADE IN US OF AMERICA

SCREW
2-56 X 5/16" B.H.I.

LIONEL SERVICE MANUAL

NOS. 0300 AND 0301 HO OPERATING CARS

No. 0300 and 0301 HO unloading type cars are entirely mechanical. Both cars are indirectly electrically operated by the No. 0900 Operating Platform. This accessory is described in Section HO-ACC-0900. Testing equipment for these cars will have to include the No. 0900. This will serve to check the lever action.

Lubrication is not required with the exception of axle bearing points at the truck sides. All other moving points on these cars should be clean and dry.

No. 0300 and No. 0301 have identical frame mechanisms.

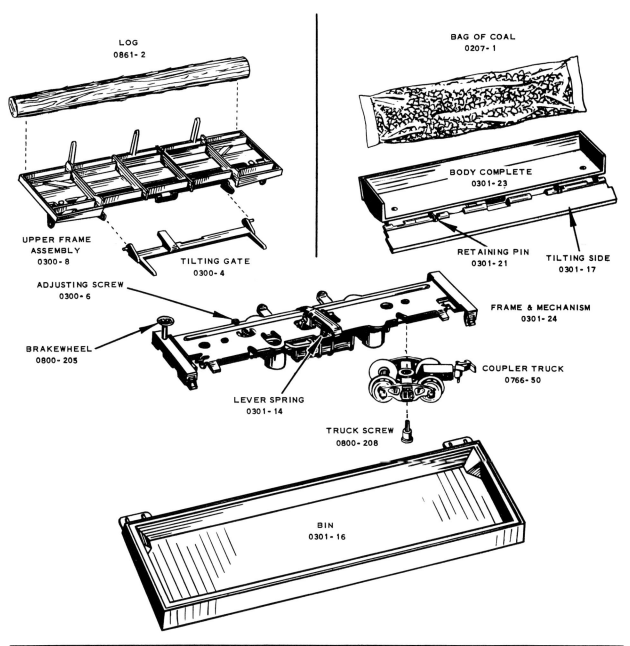

LOG
0861-2

BAG OF COAL
0207-1

BODY COMPLETE
0301-23

UPPER FRAME
ASSEMBLY
0300-8

TILTING GATE
0300-4

RETAINING PIN
0301-21

TILTING SIDE
0301-17

ADJUSTING SCREW
0300-6

FRAME & MECHANISM
0301-24

BRAKEWHEEL
0800-205

COUPLER TRUCK
0766-50

LEVER SPRING
0301-14

TRUCK SCREW
0800-208

BIN
0301-16

LIONEL SERVICE MANUAL

NO. 0319 HELICOPTER LAUNCHING CAR

No. 0319 Helicopter Launching Car made in 1960 is powered by a spring-wound mechanism which is triggered when the car is backed over a release mechanism fastened to the track.

The car is disassembled by pulling the winding spool straight up from its shaft. If tight, it can be pried up with a screwdriver.

The underframe assembly is held by two screws on the top of the car body. The mechanism cover plate is held by two hex head "stick" screws.

Because the reaction of the released spring was sometimes strong enough to derail the car; silicone grease was used to damp the action of the spring.

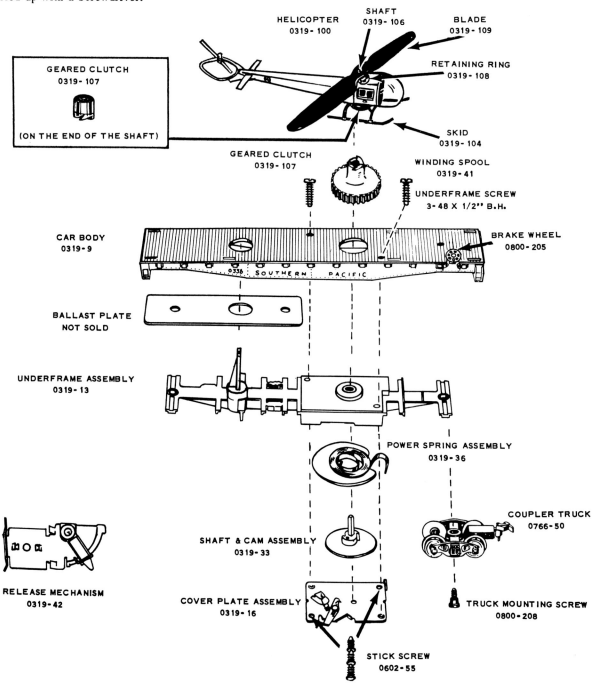

GEARED CLUTCH
0319-107

(ON THE END OF THE SHAFT)

HELICOPTER
0319-100

SHAFT
0319-106

BLADE
0319-109

RETAINING RING
0319-108

SKID
0319-104

GEARED CLUTCH
0319-107

WINDING SPOOL
0319-41

UNDERFRAME SCREW
3-48 X 1/2" B.H.

CAR BODY
0319-9

BRAKE WHEEL
0800-205

BALLAST PLATE
NOT SOLD

UNDERFRAME ASSEMBLY
0319-13

POWER SPRING ASSEMBLY
0319-36

COUPLER TRUCK
0766-50

RELEASE MECHANISM
0319-42

SHAFT & CAM ASSEMBLY
0319-33

COVER PLATE ASSEMBLY
0319-16

TRUCK MOUNTING SCREW
0800-208

STICK SCREW
0602-55

LIONEL SERVICE MANUAL

NO. 0333 SATELLITE LAUNCHING CAR

No. 0333 Satellite Launching Car, made in 1961, is similar mechanically and operationally to the No. 0319 Helicopter Car. It is powered by the same spring-wound mechanism and released by the same mechanism.

Disassembly of the Satellite Car is similar to the Helicopter Car, but the underframe cannot be re-moved without breaking off the antenna pedestal which is cemented to a part of the underframe projecting through an opening in the car body.

The two major components of the two cars which are not interchangeable are the underframes and the winding spools or cranks supporting the Helicopter and Satellite.

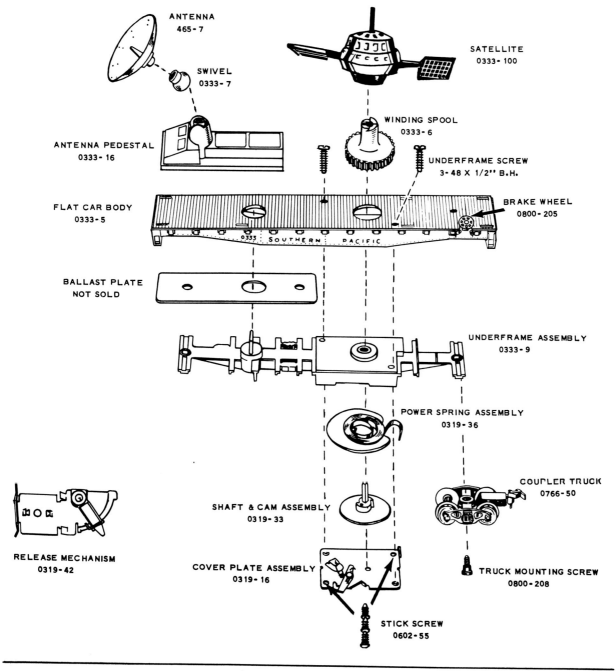

ANTENNA
465-7

SWIVEL
0333-7

SATELLITE
0333-100

ANTENNA PEDESTAL
0333-16

WINDING SPOOL
0333-6

UNDERFRAME SCREW
3-48 X 1/2'' B.H.

FLAT CAR BODY
0333-5

0333 SOUTHERN PACIFIC

BRAKE WHEEL
0800-205

BALLAST PLATE
NOT SOLD

UNDERFRAME ASSEMBLY
0333-9

POWER SPRING ASSEMBLY
0319-36

COUPLER TRUCK
0766-50

RELEASE MECHANISM
0319-42

SHAFT & CAM ASSEMBLY
0319-33

COVER PLATE ASSEMBLY
0319-16

TRUCK MOUNTING SCREW
0800-208

STICK SCREW
0602-55

LIONEL SERVICE MANUAL

NO. 0337 ANIMATED GIRAFFE CAR

No. 0337 Animated Giraffe Car contains a counterweighted giraffe head which is made to duck under a tell-tale signal. The car is actuated when a magnet fastened underneath the car is attracted to an iron strip or blade fastened to the track by means of the tell-tale mast support clip. Normal position of the head is restored by a tension spring.

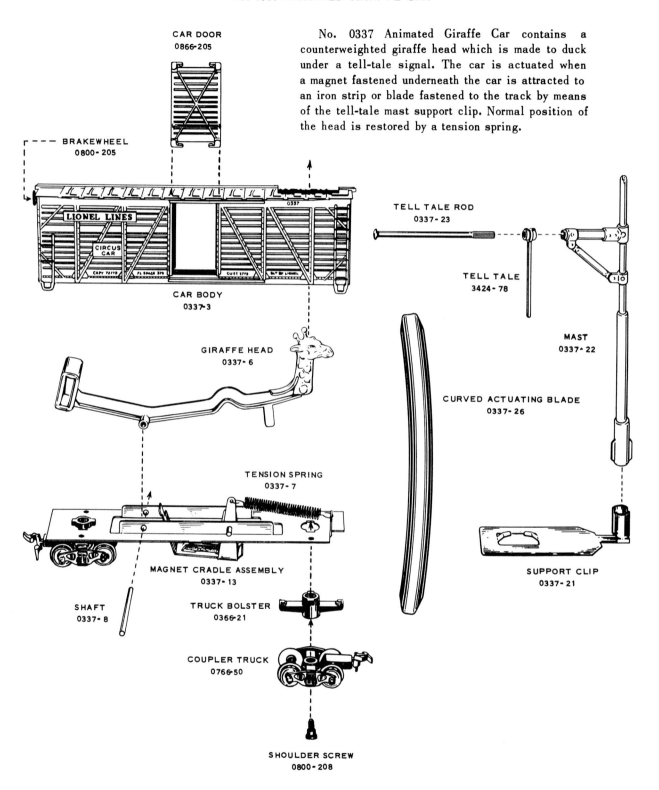

CAR DOOR
0866-205

BRAKEWHEEL
0800-205

LIONEL LINES
CIRCUS CAR

CAR BODY
0337-3

TELL TALE ROD
0337-23

TELL TALE
3424-78

MAST
0337-22

GIRAFFE HEAD
0337-6

CURVED ACTUATING BLADE
0337-26

TENSION SPRING
0337-7

MAGNET CRADLE ASSEMBLY
0337-13

SUPPORT CLIP
0337-21

SHAFT
0337-8

TRUCK BOLSTER
0366-21

COUPLER TRUCK
0766-50

SHOULDER SCREW
0800-208

LIONEL SERVICE MANUAL

NO. 0847 EXPLODING BOX CAR

No. 0847 Exploding Box Car was first produced in 1960 and was designed to "explode" when its target side was struck by a missile fired by the No. 0850 Missile Launching Car or by one of several missile launching platforms.

Initially the car ends were simply snapped in place under the metal frame work of the car but proved too loose and were eventually cemented to the plastic bottom so that they could not be removed.

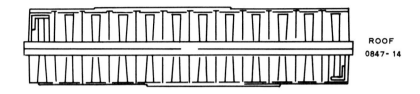

ROOF
0847- 14

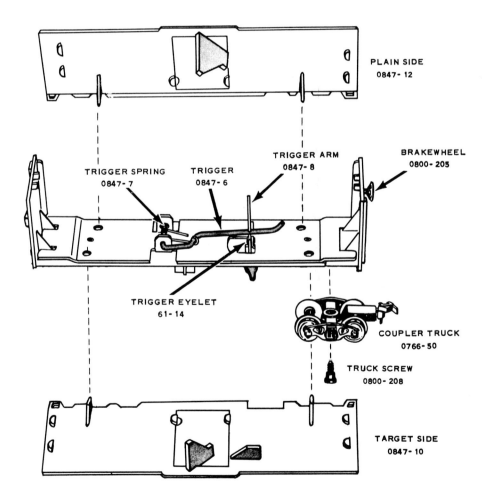

PLAIN SIDE
0847- 12

TRIGGER SPRING
0847- 7

TRIGGER
0847- 6

TRIGGER ARM
0847- 8

BRAKEWHEEL
0800- 205

TRIGGER EYELET
61- 14

COUPLER TRUCK
0766- 50

TRUCK SCREW
0800- 208

TARGET SIDE
0847- 10

LIONEL SERVICE MANUAL

NO. 0889 WRECKER CRANE CAR

No. 0889 Wrecker Crane, first built in 1961, is a model of a typical heavy-duty 200-ton diesel powered railroad crane.

The car is designed so that the hooks may be mounted on the boom either in fixed position, or suspended from strings attached to a pair of windlasses which may be wounded up by hand cranks.

The illustration on the right shows fixed assembly. The movable method is below.

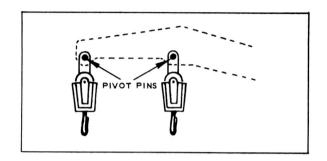

PIVOT PINS

> Do not remove rubber band from Swivel & Yoke Assembly. It is there to provide friction for positioning the boom.

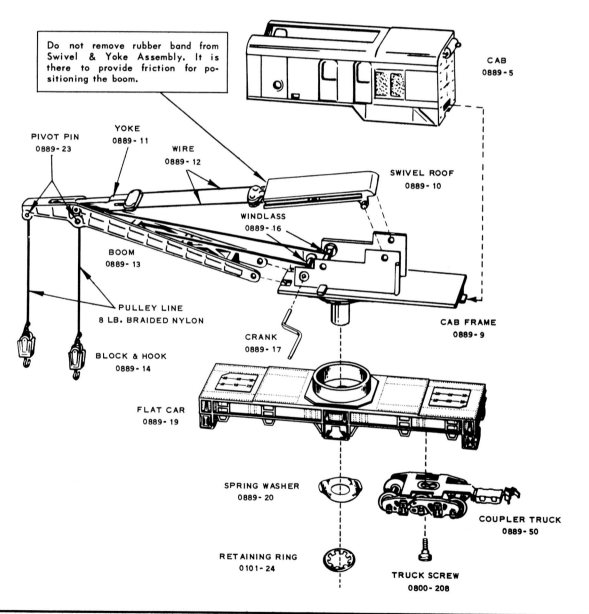

PIVOT PIN
0889-23

YOKE
0889-11

WIRE
0889-12

SWIVEL ROOF
0889-10

WINDLASS
0889-16

BOOM
0889-13

CAB
0889-5

PULLEY LINE
8 LB. BRAIDED NYLON

CRANK
0889-17

CAB FRAME
0889-9

BLOCK & HOOK
0889-14

FLAT CAR
0889-19

SPRING WASHER
0889-20

COUPLER TRUCK
0889-50

RETAINING RING
0101-24

TRUCK SCREW
0800-208

LIONEL SERVICE MANUAL

NO. 0900 HO OPERATING PLATFORM

No. 0900 HO Operating Platform first produced in 1959 is necessary to operate HO unloading-type cars such as No. 0300 Lumber Car, No. 0301 Dump Car and No. 0366 Milk Car. Equipped with a solenoid coil and a bar-lever, this platform provides the leverage to activate these cars.

Service Notes:

The bar-lever has a tendancy to be bowed inward. This bar should be straight so that it will always come in full contact with the lever under the car. Lubrication is not required and as a matter of fact it should be kept clean and dry.

Special Note for use with No. 0366 Milk Car:

The platform will require that a magnet (0366-42) and a magnet retaining clip (0366-43) be installed under the platform cover. These are not standard equipment with the No. 0900 Platform. The magnet and retaining clip are supplied with the milk car.

COVER
0900-10

COVER SCREW
#4 X 1/2" F.H. "Z"

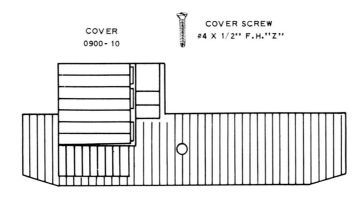

CONTROLLER
0190-25

CONTROLLER SCREW
3-48 X 3/16" B.H. BRASS

COIL & BRACKET
0900-8

EYELET
0900-12

TERMINAL CLIP
0900-15

SPRING
0900-7

PLUNGER
0900-6

LEVER BAR
0900-5

TRACK CLIP
0929-20

TRACK RAIL
0145-215

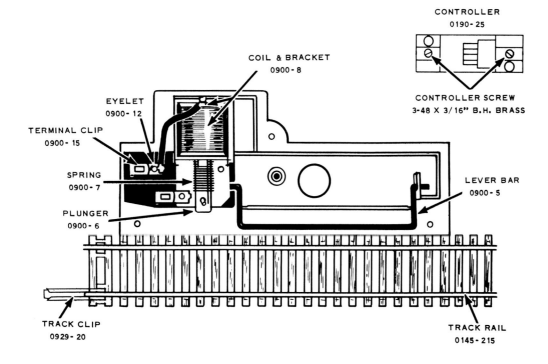

LIONEL SERVICE MANUAL

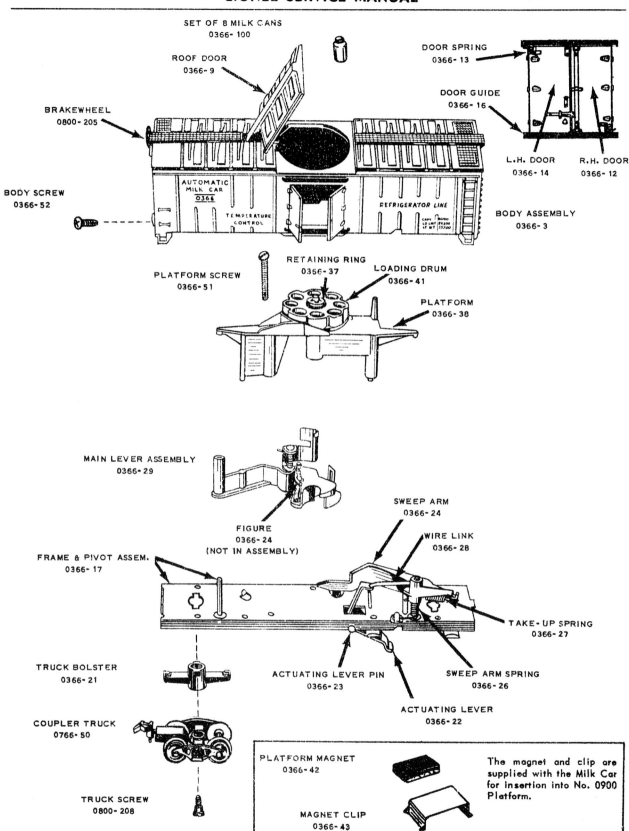

SET OF 8 MILK CANS
0366-100

ROOF DOOR
0366-9

DOOR SPRING
0366-13

DOOR GUIDE
0366-16

BRAKEWHEEL
0800-205

L.H. DOOR
0366-14

R.H. DOOR
0366-12

BODY SCREW
0366-52

AUTOMATIC
MILK CAR
0366

TEMPERATURE
CONTROL

REFRIGERATOR LINE

BODY ASSEMBLY
0366-3

RETAINING RING
0366-37

LOADING DRUM
0366-41

PLATFORM SCREW
0366-51

PLATFORM
0366-38

MAIN LEVER ASSEMBLY
0366-29

SWEEP ARM
0366-24

WIRE LINK
0366-28

FIGURE
0366-24
(NOT IN ASSEMBLY)

FRAME & PIVOT ASSEM.
0366-17

TAKE-UP SPRING
0366-27

TRUCK BOLSTER
0366-21

ACTUATING LEVER PIN
0366-23

SWEEP ARM SPRING
0366-26

COUPLER TRUCK
0766-50

ACTUATING LEVER
0366-22

TRUCK SCREW
0800-208

PLATFORM MAGNET
0366-42

MAGNET CLIP
0366-43

The magnet and clip are
supplied with the Milk Car
for insertion into No. 0900
Platform.

GLOSSARY

Advance catalogue A catalogue sent to dealers prior to release of consumer catalogue for a given year; Lionel used this tool to obtain advance reservations for new items; items which did not receive sufficient interest would be omitted from the consumer catalogue.

Alco FA-1 Type of powered locomotive (prototype) used on main line freight and passenger service.

Athearn Manufacturer of models sold as Lionel, 1958–1959.

Axle drum A large piece placed over axles on the Athearn Hi-F diesels to effect a better reduction in speed.

Bakelite A brand of **thermoplastic**.

Body-mounted couplers Couplers housed in a pocket attached to or molded on car floor; opposite of talgo type.

Cast-on detail A detail apparent on a part, such as body shell; opposite of separate detail parts, which are molded or cast individually and added to the main body.

Chemically blackened metal part A part which has been colored black by use of a chemical process rather than painting.

Decorative horn A scale model of the horn found on prototype locomotives; the decorative horn, as distinct from an electrical horn placed inside the unit to produce actual sounds, serves only to enhance the realism of the model.

Die-casting A process which makes smooth and accurate castings by forcing molten metal into a die or hollow steel block.

Direct drive A power truck with the motor being attached to and a part of the truck itself.

Dynamic brakes The fan and tank area found at the middle top of the long hood on GP-9 models.

Four-number board door A boxcar door with four flat panels on which numbers or lettering are applied.

Gang car A small railway vehicle generally used for transportation of maintenance and inspection personnel.

Gear drive A tooth gear fixed to the end of the motor shaft to transmit power to a geared axle.

Geep Slang used to identify general purpose power locomotive (GP-9).

Helic drive New in 1963, when Lionel replaced rubber drive belt in its 1959 mechanism with "Helic Spring" drive belt; belt transmits power from motor shaft to nylon worm gear in each truck; secondary shafts drive gears on axles at a 10:1 ratio.

Hi-F drive The Athearn locomotive mechanism of the late 1950s; uses rubber belts to transmit power from the drive shaft to the axles.

Hobbyline Original owner of die work used to produce most of the Lionel HO models of 1959–1966.

Horn B unit Unpowered Alco-type diesel housing a sound unit (battery powered) to reproduce the sound of a real diesel horn.

Horn hook coupler The standard coupler used by most manufacturers of HO-scale trains; designated "X2f" by the National Model Railroad Association; also called "NMRA" couplers.

Husky locomotive Lionel's term for identifying its four-wheeled diesel-type locomotive.

Hustler locomotive A term used by Athearn Corporation to identify its four-wheeled diesel-type locomotives (see Husky).

Injection molding A process which shapes plastic by using heat and pressure in molds.

Mallory magnetic coupler Variation of the X2f coupler; long lateral pin extending from shank added to enhance uncoupling characteristics; entered into production in 1962.

Neoprene belts Drive bands employed in locomotives using Athearn's Hi-F drive and Lionel's power trucks from 1959 to 1963.

Pantograph The electrical collector found atop rectifier locomotives.

Phenolic plastic Thermosetting plastics which cannot be heated and remelted once molded; Bakelite is one brand. See **Thermoplastics**.

Rectifier Electrically operated locomotive that took its power from overhead wiring by means of a metal pantograph mounted on the roof of its cab. The Lionel model received its power from the track.

Rigid frame truck A freight or passenger car truck lacking an equalization mechanism, such as a set of springs; generally, a one-piece plastic truck frame with separate wheel sets.

Silkscreened lettering Lettering applied by a painting process, in which a silk screen is employed; the screen serves as a negative to the lettering, thus paint forced through the screen forms the lettering on the model.

Smoke unit An accessory device used to generate smoke in steam locomotive models.

Sprung truck A freight or passenger car truck with springs as found on prototype cars; provides equalization for all axles.

Stamped lettering Lettering which is applied directly to item with an inked positive pad, usually rubber.

Talgo truck A freight or passenger car truck with coupler pocket attached.

Thermoplastics Plastics which can be heated and remelted and can be softened to avoid cracking. See **Phenolic plastics**.

Traction tire A rubber belt imbedded in the drive wheels of power units to improve its pulling power and lessen slippage on the track.

Worm drive Lionel's power drive used on its diesel units with a worm drive fixed to the motor shaft, transmitting power to geared axles.

INDEX

This is an index of Lionel HO cars of the period 1957–1966 (it does not include accessories offered by the Lionel Corporation, which are described in Chapter V). The index has both catalogue and side-of-car numbers. Many of the Lionel HO items, especially those produced by Rivarossi and Athearn, have a number on the side of the car that differs from the catalogue number. In these cases, the catalogue number appears in parentheses — just as it does in the listings found in this book. If the only difference is the existence of a hyphen to separate a suffix, the sequence of digits is given only once, in catalogue number order.

When Lionel moved from selling Rivarossi products to selling Athearn products and then to producing its own models, the company generally changed the catalogue numbers. However, in some cases an item such as the 0860 Pennsylvania derrick has the same catalogue number, whether produced by Rivarossi, Athearn, or Lionel. We have below provided a **bold face** indication of the producer of each item: **R**, **A**, or **L**. Index entries follow this order, which parallels the chronological development of Lionel HO.

Remember that Chapter II has guidelines by which one may determine the producer of a particular piece, as a further aid in identification, beyond this index.

Note: The page numbers in *italics* below indicate an illustration of the item. If a page number is followed by an asterisk, it indicates that the item is discussed or pictured on that page in Chapter VIII, as an "oddball" or a forgery.

ABOUT THE AUTHORS

GEORGE J. HORAN

George Horan's interest in toy trains started in or about 1946, when a lady-friend of his mother gave him a wooden locomotive. He had already started to build a train layout, but with five brothers and two sisters there was little money for toys. The buildings on George's first layout came from General Mills Cheerio cereal boxes — little did he know that General Mills would later produce the Lionel trains that he came to love. George's first job, working on a dry-cleaning truck, provided the funds to make his train table into an operating layout, and his first electric locomotive was a Hobbyline FM diesel with rubber band drive. George used his earnings to buy a sample of every item in Hobbyline's HO line. Following his graduation from high school, he joined the U.S. Marine Corps and served for four years. Finding that he still had the train bug after he finished his service, he returned to his hobby and as other companies' products caught his eye, George soon became a collector.

Before long, George realized that no reference books had been written on the subject of Lionel HO. Louis Hertz, another toy train historian, indicated that he did not have an interest in the smaller trains, but he provided George with insights into the creation of such a book. On the same day that George had this discussion with Louis Hertz, he also met Ernie Davis, president of LCCA. Earnie suggested that George's experience would be a useful guide in producing such a book. Thus, George found inspiration to undertake a project that continues to provide challenges and discoveries. His collection was also featured in *Greenberg's Guide to Athearn Trains*, and he is the author of a second volume on Lionel HO, covering the General Mills/MPC era, 1974–1977.

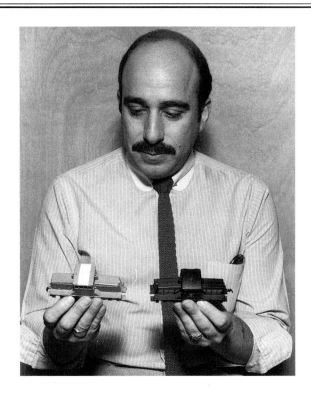

VINCENT ROSA

Vincent Rosa was born in Brooklyn, New York, and moved to Long Island where he attended Adelphi University and Adelphi-Suffolk and Dowling College, where he obtained a Bachelor's Degree in History. He holds a Master's Degree from Stony Brook University and has earned ninety credits beyond his Master's in Education and Afro-Asian Studies.

Vincent's interest in trains began when his grandmother bought him a spring-wound Marx set in 1954. Three years later his parents purchased a Lionel 646 train set for him. Although his interests in trains vary, Vincent has a large collection of Postwar Lionel trains and HO trains of all makes and varieties. His other hobbies include playing the drums and eating Italian food, but not necessarily in that order. In addition to working as a Social Studies teacher at Oakdale-Bohemia Road Junior High School, Vincent is also the proprietor of Model Cars & Trains Unlimited in Blue Point, New York, a firm that specializes in the sale of collectible trains and die-cast model cars of all varieties. *Greenberg's Guide to Lionel HO Trains* was Vincent's first train-related work, although he has published a curriculum guide for the Gifted and Talented program's Afro-Asian Studies 9 for his school district.